THE GATES OPEN SLOWLY

The Gates Open Slowly

A History of Education in Kentucky

by

FRANK L. McVEY

UNIVERSITY OF KENTUCKY PRESS
Lexington :: 1949

COPYRIGHT 1949
UNIVERSITY OF KENTUCKY PRESS

To
Frances Jewell McVey
1889 - 1945

PREFACE

MY RESIDENCE in Kentucky has now covered thirty years; during more than two-thirds of that time I was president of the University of Kentucky. As a consequence, I have become tremendously interested in the history of the state. From my reading I have gained some knowledge of the activities of the pioneer period, the peculiar laws, the educational and religious feuds that then prevailed; as a result, many questions have arisen in my mind about education and what happened to it in the century and a half of state history.

Other men have written books and reports on this subject. One of the best of these is by Professor Alvin F. Lewis who in 1899 published his *History of Higher Education in Kentucky* under the imprint of the United States Bureau of Education. Professor Lewis's book deals with the growth of colleges only. In 1914 Barksdale Hamlett, then Superintendent of Public Instruction, brought together in a considerable volume a sketch on education in the state up to 1838, followed by a summary of the administrations of the state superintendents including that of his own incumbency. A volume by Professor Moses E. Ligon, issued by the Bureau of School Service of the University of Kentucky in 1942, is devoted to the history of public education to the year 1935. The author does not discuss sectarian or higher education.

My interest in this history extends to wider fields, involving the reasons for certain legislation and why so many educational efforts failed to achieve anything of value. Cannot the study of these historical data furnish information that the citizen may understand the errors of the past and thus profit in dealing with the problems of the present? In an attempt to answer these and other inquiries I have written this book.

Fortunately, I have had the help of a number of efficient persons and obliging organizations in gathering the large amount of data bearing on the subject of education in Kentucky. Much of the spadework has been done by Mrs. Frances B. Cassidy assisted by Mrs. Myrtle Smith, of Lexington, whose services were compensated for by the Federal Emergency Relief Administration. Miss Mary H. Cooper and the director of the University of Kentucky Bureau of Source Materials in Higher Education, Professor Ezra Gillis, also were very co-operative, as was Miss Norma Cass of the University of Kentucky Library. To Mrs. Carroll Robie and Miss Dorothea Bell I am indebted for their faithfulness during the long task of typing notes and the manuscript. And to Dr. Merton England, editor of the University Press, I am obligated for suggestions and helpful comments.

The committee in charge of the Press publications have placed their approval upon this study, and I am grateful. The manuscript was read in its entirety by Professor Thomas D. Clark, the late Dr. W. D. Funkhouser, and Professor Howard Beers, and in part by President H. L. Donovan and the late Dean William S. Taylor. My thanks to them.

FRANK L. McVEY

Lexington, Kentucky
September, 1949

CONTENTS

PREFACE vii

CHAPTERS

I. THE PEOPLE OF KENTUCKY AND THEIR
EDUCATIONAL BEGINNINGS 3
II. EARLY SCHOOLS AND SCHOOLTEACHERS 17
III. LAND-GRANT ACADEMIES 33
IV. THEY WALKED IN THE DARK 47
V. TEXTBOOKS AND SCHOOL CURRICULA DRIFT ALONG 63
VI. A CENTURY OF SECTARIAN EDUCATION 79
VII. AND FINALLY A STATE UNIVERSITY 106
VIII. THE FALLS CITY EVOLVES AN URBAN UNIVERSITY 125
IX. THE COLOR LINE IN EDUCATION 141
X. THE BIRTH, DEMISE, AND RESURRECTION OF THE
STATE SCHOOL FUND 160
XI. TEACHER TRAINING BEGINS AND REACHES A
PROFESSIONAL STATUS 175
XII. A KENTUCKY EDUCATION ASSOCIATION 191
XIII. EDUCATIONAL CAMPAIGNS AND SURVEYS 206
XIV. "THE TUMULT AND THE SHOUTING DIES" 221
XV. THE PUBLIC SCHOOLS MOVE FORWARD 237
XVI. INDEPENDENT DISTRICTS IN TOWNS AND CITIES
ESTABLISH SCHOOLS 255
XVII. THE CRISES OF TODAY AND THE
CHALLENGE OF TOMORROW 271

APPENDIXES

A. State Superintendents of Public Instruction, 1836-1948..... 289
B. Colleges in Kentucky Accredited by the Southern
Association of Colleges and Secondary Schools............... 290
C. The Evolution Controversy 292
D. State Aid for Negroes 297
E. Supplementary Education in Kentucky 300

INDEX 315

THE GATES OPEN SLOWLY

CHAPTER I

THE PEOPLE OF KENTUCKY AND THEIR EDUCATIONAL BEGINNINGS

THE EARLY movement of peoples into the Kentucky country was checked until the American Revolution by the British policy governing the settlement of Indian lands and by the menace of marauding savages. These obstacles deterred any large migration over the mountains into the Kentucky area, although a considerable number of pioneers reached the Holston Valley of eastern Tennessee at an early date and remained there. When people did begin to stream into Kentucky, they came to find land and sought to set up homes where there would be greater chances for advancement and the gaining of a livelihood than were afforded them in the East.

The Kentucky migration was a continuation of a frontier process that had deep roots in the colonial history of Virginia and Pennsylvania. In contrast to this folk movement, marked by individualism, the westward march from New England was often made by groups of people from the same towns. Their ancestors' purpose in undertaking the long voyage to America had been to escape religious persecution or to establish a theocratic state, as in the instance of the Massachusetts Bay Colony. They had not been greatly interested in large tracts of land, for they had soon found that fishing in the seas and trading with the Dutch and French, as well as the mother country, were more lucrative and quicker ways of gaining wealth than grubbing stumps and raising crops on land that cost years of labor to clear. On the contrary, the pioneers who began to pour into the Virginia territory of Kentucky

County were land hungry. They wanted good land and plenty of it; and what is more, they intended to find a place in which to live and to bring up their families. Some came from the tidewater of Virginia; others, in large numbers, pushed down from western and southern Pennsylvania through the valley into the western country.

Archbishop Hugh Boulter, of Ireland, writing in March, 1728, said: "The humour of going to America still continues, and the scarcity of provisions certainly make many quit us."[1] The Presbytery of Tyrone complained that "The bad seasons for three years past, together with the high price of lands and tythes, have all contributed to the general run to America, and to the ruin of many families, who are daily leaving their houses and lands desolate."[2]

Edmund Burke wrote in his *Account of the European Settlements in America,* published in 1757: "In some years more people have transported themselves into Pennsylvania, than into all the other settlements together." Burke further said: "The number of white people in Virginia is between sixty and seventy thousand; and they are growing every day more numerous by the migration of the Irish, who, not succeeding so well in Pennsylvania as the more frugal and industrious Germans, sell their lands in that province to the latter, and take up new ground in the remote counties of Virginia, Maryland and North Carolina. These are chiefly Presbyterians from the northern part of Ireland, who in America are generally called Scotch-Irish."[3] Thus transplanted to America, thousands of these dissenters later were to take up arms against the royal government and join the Revolutionary armies. After the war, disbanded soldiers emigrated to Kentucky and formed an important element in the inhabitants of the region. The population of Kentucky came from several

---

[1] Charles A. Hanna, *The Scotch-Irish, or the Scot in North Britain, North Ireland, and North America,* 2 vols. (G. P. Putnam's Sons, New York, 1902), II, 179.

[2] Henry J. Ford, *The Scotch-Irish in America* (Princeton University Press, Princeton, N. J., 1915), 195, 198-199.   [3] Quoted, *ibid.,* 199.

strata of society; it was recruited from tenants and farmers from Ireland and England, who, after migrating from the motherland to Pennsylvania, Maryland, and Virginia colonies, traveled over the long roads into Kentucky.

At Harrod's Town and Boonesborough permanent settlements were made in 1775. From Pittsburgh, down the Ohio to Limestone creek by boat and by land to the Bluegrass, came a continuous line of pioneers with their families. Others, journeying by the trails through the Valley of Virginia to the Holston Valley, passed through the Cumberland Gap to the Crab Orchard country in Kentucky. Scotch-Irish folk from the middle section of western Pennsylvania and Virginians from the upcountry used the route of the Ohio River, while the Boone Trace was followed by the folk from the foothills and the Valley of Virginia. As early as 1773, Lord Dunmore had sent surveyors into the new country.[4] These men, among them John Floyd, Benjamin Logan, the Harrods, the Mc-Afees, the Calloways, and Daniel Boone, did the early exploring and much of the work of settlement. They had in their minds a genuine purpose to establish homes and to develop the country. A roster of the leaders of Kentucky of that day contains the names of the employers of the surveyors and explorers who soon followed their advance agents to the lands that had been prospected and claimed. They were speculators in land either on their own account or as representatives of large holders of Kentucky land who had acquired extensive acreage through congressional grants. Almost before the settlers had begun to arrive in the Bluegrass section, the lands had been taken up and titles obtained.[5] In many instances, not only one title but many brought complications into the ownership of land which made for insecurity and often created hard feelings, since a settler might be ousted as a squatter from the land he had regarded as his own. Such

[4] T. P. Abernethy, *Three Virginia Frontiers* (Louisiana State University Press, University, La., 1940), 63.
[5] *Ibid.*, 65.

a situation tended to establish class lines and thereby enlarged the opportunities for lawyers to defend their clients' rights in court. The constitution of 1792 conferred upon the Court of Appeals original jurisdiction over matters involving land titles, a provision unusual in most states, that in this instance gives point to the statement about confusion of land claims.

The pioneers who poured into this rich section of Kentucky were not unlike a stream flowing over a dam. Others were there in advance of them. Some had come with warrants in their hands only to find other persons claiming the land described in their papers. Still others with no such forehandedness thought to find free territory in this rich area that could be had for the taking. But many were unable to establish their claims and, in order to find a place to settle, turned back on the Wilderness Road to acquire lands less desirable but available for settlement. As the main outlet from Kentucky to the East through Virginia and Maryland, the Road became a busy line of communication and transport.[6] Over it passed cattle, sheep, and horses on their way to the seaboard markets. The late-comers settled upon the best land that flanked the road, and those that followed pushed into the valleys and coves that debouched upon the trail. And another group coming later still, after all the lands had been taken up, scattered to the rim of the Bluegrass to become tenants or boatmen on the rivers which were extensively used as means of transportation. Even as late as 1925, students from some of the counties bordering on the Cumberland River were excused two days early at the Christmas holidays by the dean of their college at the University of Kentucky to take the boat at Burnside, Kentucky, in order that they might reach their homes in time for the Christmas celebration.

In other parts of the state, the struggle for land never reached the same intensity as it did in the central portion.

---

[6] Virginia Clay McClure, "The Settlement of the Kentucky Appalachian Highlands" (Ph.D. thesis, University of Kentucky, 1933), 33-34.

Along the Ohio, the settlements established on the banks of that beautiful river flourished with the growth of the river trade and with the transport of goods and passengers from the landing places to the hinterland. On the tributaries of the Ohio, hamlets came into being and furnished business, which increased greatly in amount with the coming of the steamboat. Evidences of the extent of that trade can be appreciated by the traveler who has seen the rather large and pretentious houses built on the banks of the lower reaches of the Kentucky River. Captain Thomas Bullitt, in 1773, chose the Falls of the Ohio as the site of the city of Louisville. From this point on, river and trail settlers spread south and west taking up the land in the Green and Tennessee River valleys. From the state of Tennessee, settlers pushed up into the Purchase country; and from the Ohio River migration, many found homes in the "Pennyrile" and Barrens or Great Meadow territory. The population of Kentucky grew from 70,000 in 1790 to more than 200,000 inhabitants by 1800. The state had a government organized under the first constitution of 1792. The second constitution, adopted in 1799, provided for courts, militia, and the meager beginnings of a system of public education. The land difficulties, arising from the indiscriminate issue of deeds based on the "metes and bounds" system of survey and record, had been straightened out in some measure, but the sores caused by many a legal contest remained unhealed, resulting in the harassment of courts and legislative assemblies for many years.

In his essay on "The Significance of the Frontier in American History," Professor Frederick J. Turner points out that the waves of migration pushed on to new lands and there re-established the customs, laws, and habits of the older section from which the pioneers came.[7] But the customs, attitudes, manners, laws, and even the languages of the older settlements were modified by the new environment to which

[7] Frederick Jackson Turner, *The Frontier in American History* (N.Y., 1921), 19-21.

they were brought. In time the new frontier took on a more conservative tinge, and in turn it made a contribution to another frontier until the continent had been covered by these recurring waves of population, and the country settled down to consolidate the gains made during the pioneer period. The more ardent followers of Turner maintain that his theory of the frontier explains the American development as one of succeeding waves of population. He assumed that the aquisition of land was not hampered by the inadequacy of titles, and that the social levels existing in the older settlements were lost in the wilds of the new country. However, the frontier development in Kentucky did not follow the pattern set out so convincingly by Turner—at least not in some respects, for from the beginning of settlement, there were divisions of ownership and social position. Comparatively few people were secure in the titles to their lands; and owing to the speculative tendencies of the leaders in the new territory, the common man lacked confidence in them.

Thomas Perkins Abernethy, in his *Three Virginia Frontiers,* writes: "The peculiarities of this frontier [Kentucky] were due, therefore, not to simplicity and equality, to free land and opportunity, but to a marked stratification in which no stratum was securely established. Each group was striving for advancement and each was suspicious of the other. But rugged individualism, that famous frontier development which has been so widely advertised by the modern masters of capital, was there in large measure. The early population of Kentucky was restless and aggressive, assertive and self-confident. But if by individualism we mean intellectual independence, we do not find it conspicuous on the frontier. We find, on the contrary, that no man must differ too much from his neighbor in any obvious way."[8]

Thus the Kentucky frontier country varied in its development from the settlements to the north of it. There was a

---

[8] Abernethy, *Three Virginia Frontiers,* 68.

distinct class antagonism in Kentucky not seen on the surface in frontiers elsewhere. Class conflicts and group opposition were not a part of an agricultural regime even where slavery accompanied it. The causes of the difficulties in Kentucky were the extensive land speculation and insecure titles to the land. Men would fight to retain what they regarded as their own; not necessarily by armed force, but through political organization, the use of the courts, and by legislative action. In Kentucky, the first and second constitutions show something of this conflict; yet in the second constitution, the leaders among the speculative landowners were able by their shrewdness and larger knowledge of political procedure to check the tendency toward a radicalism that might control by majority power, regardless of the rights of any minority. An example of this procedure was to be found in the opposition of the majority of the people to a bill of rights as a part of the early constitutions. Without such bills of rights, the constitutions in other states could not have mustered enough support for adoption. In fact, it may be said, in view of the very small margin by which the Federal constitution was adopted in some states, that the failure to frame a bill of rights would have forced the supporters of the constitutional document to find some other means of organizing a central government. In Kentucky, the radicals proposed and strongly urged that no bill of rights be adopted as a part of the constitution or given a place in the law. The objections to the bill were based upon the guarantee of property rights and the maintenance of suffrage on a freehold basis. Property rights, of course, included slaves; and as the radicals were opposed to slavery in any form, they saw no reason to guarantee its protection. The constitution went further than those of other states by establishing manhood suffrage as the basis of voting instead of ownership of a freehold. The uncertainty of titles and the fact that many men did not own land, but were tenants or squatters, explain the provision for a majority rule which the broad basis of male suffrage would give.

The Kentucky constitution, however, did provide for a guarantee of property, manhood suffrage, vote by ballot, and a senate chosen by an electoral college which also selected the governor. The upper class was able to entrench itself in the management and direction of the state government. Almost from the start, opposition manifested itself against the government inaugurated by the constitution of 1792. The radicals wanted a one-chamber legislature, election of officers by ballot, the payment of taxes in kind, prohibition of the use of British law decisions in the courts of the state, and representation in the legislature on the basis of population. The fight over the second constitution was won handily by the conservatives. The institution of slavery was strongly entrenched by making it difficult to amend the constitution; the vote by ballot, won in the first contest over a constitution, was lost and viva-voce voting restored. The electoral college was dropped and the election of governor and senate by popular vote provided for. The radicals had, in reality, gained very little; for control of government in Kentucky remained in the hands of the conservatives.

Areas south of the Green River were settled by people who had obtained their lands from the state on the promise to pay at a future time. Most of the settlers were in arrears, so the attempt of the state to collect the payments raised questions that soon got into politics. This situation resulted in the abolition of the district and quarter-sessions courts and the establishment of county courts over which a judge devoid of legal training should preside. Kentucky was disturbed socially and economically by the difficulties arising from the confused and chaotic records of land titles. The controversy crept into every form of activity and divided the people on all the issues that came to a political decision. Thus the radicals were those who were dispossessed or who tried to cultivate reluctant soil. The conservatives were in possession of good lands, held the important offices, controlled the political machinery, and from time to time proposed and secured the enactment of legislation beneficial to themselves. The Bluegrass was the center of their empire, and Lexington was its metropolis.

The large landless element which existed in the earlier period of Kentucky's history had clashed with the politicians of the land speculator group. There was, in consequence, much rivalry, suspicion, and jealousy between the rank and file as well as among the leaders of the groups. The conservative leaders were fairly enlightened men and ready to help the progress of the state if that did not place too heavy a burden upon them. A public educational system required taxes; in addition, the ideas about such a system were in many respects vague, and the enthusiasm necessary to carry through a great social enterprise was not there to support it. The radicals were interested only in the titles to their own property, in the opening up of new lands, and in getting on from scratch. Education might be all right for the hoity-toity folk, but not for them. They believed that children in the wilderness could learn more from the everyday tasks of getting food, clothes, and shelter than from books. There was some effort made to educate the children in fort and village as soon as pioneers began to arrive in the state, but even for those days much of the schooling was inadequate. The main stream of the people's lives was untouched by any plan of education.

When Kentucky, having attained a population of 70,000, was admitted to the Union, it was a unique commonwealth in that no other such large population existed north, south, or west of it. This state was an island in a vast wilderness from which the culture and customs of older states were to be carried on to the south and the west. The people had no helping hand from the Federal government in the tremendous tasks of establishing their own government, building roads, and creating an orderly system of land surveys and title descriptions. Many mistakes were made that served to increase the difficulties of a pioneer and frontier society which are to be seen in the cleavage created by the excessive speculation in land and the uncertainties of land titles. Such conditions in building up family, rather than community, support turned the minds of men away from the important question of popular education. It is not to be denied that many of the settlers had ideas about education, but too often the educational efforts were denominational in their aspect and direction, which may explain the controversies and hard feelings developed later on by those who did not agree with such teachings or who believed not at all in the orthodoxy of the teachers. School facilities for the masses were not in the institutional pattern inherited by America from England.

It has been noted that Kentucky in the first two constitutions made little or no provision for a system of public education. Prior to the adoption of the first constitution, the university and academy system was proposed, and provision in the form of land grants was made to support it. The states of North Carolina and Georgia had done something for the cause of public education by incorporating a plan in their constitutions before Kentucky had entered the Federal Union. No attention was paid to the intellectual growth of the people which could be fostered by a public system of education in Kentucky. Individuals urged the establishment of a university; but the cleavage between the enlightened and virtuous who might take advantage of its opportunities and those who felt themselves beyond the pale was too great to permit cooperation toward an elementary educational system so direly needed by the children of the tenant and landless man.

What would the new state do about education? The leaders offered the idea of small academies here and there to prepare students for a larger institution or university. The plan was a comprehensive one which the formulators implemented and set going in the first decade of the state's constitutional history, but it was one-sided in that it did not deal with the problems basic in the history and structure of the state and left the common people without adequate schooling for their children. A university and a group of academies were the principal and important factors in this system of education.

The plan thus projected is traceable to the initiative of John Todd and Caleb Wallace, and is their contribution to Kentucky's educational system. The academies, however, were in a state of decay by 1820, and Transylvania University which advanced until 1827 under the leadership of its distinguished president, Horace Holley, fell upon evil days. This scheme for higher education and secondary schools, founded on land grants without other public money support, which had offered so much promise, dwindled and finally was absorbed by a public system of education. While these efforts to maintain a kind of educational system came to little, Kentucky had turned its attention to plans for a state bank and internal improvements, leaving public education to shift for itself. People engrossed in the making of a living under pioneer conditions were not to be bothered by tax collectors for educational purposes. And, too, the heritage they had received from the mother state, Virginia, did not include a public system of education other than the meager maintenance of the most elementary schools for the children of those who could not afford to send their sons and daughters to private schools or employ tutors in their homes. Nevertheless, at the time Kentucky was admitted to the Union there was more than a little talk about the need of an educational plan in the new commonwealth. Humphrey Marshall, in his *History of Kentucky,* remarks: "There were many well educated: and more means to be applied in that way, than most other countries could afford. While a general propensity for giving, and receiving literary instruction was obviously a prevailing sentiment throughout the country."[9]

In discussing the university system advocated by Judge Caleb Wallace, the Rev. W. H. Whitsitt, in his biography of Wallace, says, while referring to the combined acts of

---

[9] Humphrey Marshall, *History of Kentucky,* 2 vols. (Frankfort, 1824), I, 443.

February 10, 1798, and December 22, 1798, "They established the most enlightened, practical, and complete system of education that could at that period be witnessed in America, or perhaps anywhere else in the civilized world."[10] No doubt, limited knowledge of what had been done in the field of education led many men of that time and their biographers to overestimate not only the value of a central university and supplementary academies, but the stability of such a plan largely based as it was upon grants of wild land in a pioneer country. The elementary schools so much needed in a democracy were to come later; the only need at the beginning, William Littell declared, was that "those persons whom nature hath endowed with genius and virtue should be rendered by liberal education worthy to receive and able to guard the sacred deposit of the rights and liberties of their fellow citizens; and that to aid and accelerate this most desirable purpose must be one of the duties of every wise government."[11]

The selective process of segregating genius and virtue by which the rest of the people were to be guided was confined to those who had the means of attending the new university and of securing the elementary education before going on to college. It has been said that the frontier state needed secondary and college educational facilities because of the presence of many young men and boys who were of the age to profit by an education beyond the elementary school level. The idea was that elementary schools could be set up later; or that, here and there, young pupils could be taught at home the requirements of a limited education. Thus the system so enthusiastically enunciated and persistently started on its way was not essentially democratic; and, in consequence, it never received the support of the people. The educated men who came into Kentucky, and they were many, thought of education as something desirable for the elite and the gifted, but

---

[10] W. H. Whitsitt, *Life and Times of Judge Caleb Wallace* (Louisville, 1888), 135.
[11] William Littell, *The Statute Law of Kentucky*, 5 vols. (Frankfort, 1809-1819), II, 108-109.

not for the common man. The traditions brought from Virginia supported such a view, and so generally accepted was this concept of education that it pervaded the history of Kentucky for nearly seventy-five years, causing delays in the development of a real system of public education and injecting into it political considerations that were concerned with the values of land and the material business of getting on in the world.

The first two constitutions, 1792 and 1799, did not provide for public education. The third constitution, of 1850, recognized and protected the Literary Fund which provided for a public school system, from which meager grants were made to schools on a per capita pupil basis. The grand schemes for a public university, with a supplementing system of academies and (ultimately) elementary schools, were based on the idea that the sale of public lands would furnish the endowment, buildings, and operating expenses of such an educational system. On paper, the plan in all of its parts was impressive, filling with gratification those who developed and later fostered it. Here, they thought, was a scheme for public education without the need of taxation that would provide the commonwealth with schools and colleges turning out statesmen, lawyers, teachers, and professional men as well as, in time, giving the children of the common man that training for democracy so necessary to the growth of a free people.

In 1816 Governor Gabriel Slaughter spoke briefly on the lack of educational plans and the dire need for a real effort in behalf of education. He was the first governor of Kentucky to comment at any length on educational needs. Due perhaps to the questions of defense, the building of roads, and organization of local governments, his message to the legislature bore no fruit. Ever alert against any increase of taxes, the legislature of 1821 failed to vote money for the state's public school system, and contented itself with appointing a committee to investigate the Federal procedure by which northern states received public land grants for education. The governor, while urging that something more should be done for public education, was compelled to accept the appointment of a committee to study educational systems and to formulate a plan for the establishment of common schools in Kentucky.

After the passage of nearly thirty years from the adoption of the first constitution, the state yet had no system of common schools. There were the University, Transylvania, and many academies at the top of a semiprivate and semipublic system of higher education, but these institutions found it hard to get on.

The real beginning of public education in Kentucky can be dated from 1870, when an act was passed by the legislature implementing the paper system set up by the legislature of 1838. In the interim, the years from 1838 to 1870, appropriations had been made to support Transylvania University; and land grants were used to endow the University and to found the county academies. Efforts were made to establish a school fund. However, no general taxes were levied by legislative act compelling the support and the establishment of public schools until 1904.[12]

---

[12] This is an unusual statement that will be questioned by many readers, but in support of it attention is called to the comment of the Kentucky Educational Commission on completion of a survey of public education in Kentucky, published in 1921:

"The constitution of 1850 declared the principal of the common school fund to be inviolate, but laid upon the general assembly no mandate to establish schools. The general assembly therefore consistently declined to levy taxes for school purposes. Nevertheless, on four different occasions—in 1849, 1855, 1869, and 1882—the people by large majorities approved successive propositions to levy state taxes for school purposes. Thus, the income of the common schools was increased by *popularly imposed levies*, amounting in the aggregate to twenty-two cents on each $100 of taxable property.

"The mandate requiring the general assembly to 'provide for an efficient system of common schools throughout the state' and to appropriate to the common schools the income from the common school fund and any sum which may be produced for purposes of common school education by taxation or otherwise, *first appeared in the constitution of 1891*. Even so, the general assembly on its own initiative and without a direct mandate from the people *did not levy a dollar of public taxes in support of public schools until 1904—thirteen years after being empowered to do so*. Not until 1893 did the statute books contain a single line of legislation *actually requiring* the establishment of schools and the levying of local taxes in support thereof, *and not until 1908* was this mandatory legislation made general for all local units.

"This legislation of 1893 and 1908 transformed *a voluntary into a compulsory system*, and thus registered an entirely new conception of the state's relation to public education." (Italics added.) Kentucky Educational Commission, *Public Education in Kentucky* (New York, 1921), 7-9.

CHAPTER II

EARLY SCHOOLS AND SCHOOLTEACHERS

JOHN FILSON, one of the early schoolmasters in Fayette County, Kentucky, projected a school at Lexington in 1782. It is not, however, for this entrance into the rank of pedagogues that the name of Filson appears in the pages of history, but rather for his book, containing a famous map, published in 1784 at Wilmington, Delaware. Filson's purpose, so his preface said, was "to inform the world of the happy climate and plentiful soil of this favored region." Under the title *The Discovery, Settlement and Present State of Kentucke,* he has given the historians a book that has been of the highest use to them, and a map accurate for that period.

A striking feature of Filson's map is the location of forts scattered throughout the Kentucky land area. The very number of stations reveals the circumscribed and hampered life led by the pioneers shut up in their stockades. A line drawn from the Falls of the Ohio to the great bend of the Licking, southward through Boonesborough to the Old English Station toward the head of Dick's River, and thence through Bardstown and back to Louisville, would have encompassed a territory in which there were more than fifty fortifications. In these forts thousands of men, women, and children were shut up, unable to venture out unless "Indian season" was over. Only within a limited range from the fort could the crops be cultivated while vigilant guards watched for the wily enemy.[1]

[1] Reuben T. Durrett, *John Filson, the First Historian of Kentucky* (Louisville, 1884).

The conditions in the forts must have been insanitary to say the least, with a pest of flies attracted by various unwelcome odors. Here the people were crowded in, undergoing, without doubt, a considerable discipline. The numerous children who needed schooling presented a constant problem. Under such stress it was natural that some effort should have been made to establish schools in the forts. Thus a little school was started as early as 1775 or 1776 in Harrod's Town by Mrs. William Coomes; and at McAfee's Station nearby, John May began another school in 1777. Young Joseph Doniphan of Stafford County, Virginia, taught a school in Boonesborough two years later with an enrollment of seventeen pupils.[2] As forts and stations multiplied, instruction of some kind was undertaken in them. The number of these outpost schools increased to more than two hundred by 1790.

The children of the poorer whites, like their ancestors before them, were unlettered. The yeomen received their only education from the experiences of everyday life, and many of them could neither read nor write, as shown by the preponderance of crosses on the legal papers of that day. In fact, illiteracy among a large part of the white population was high indeed. The children in the forts and stations were greatly outnumbered by the adults; thus the attitude of the older folk determined the pressure for instruction in the individual fort. Any effort toward elementary education depended upon the initiative of a few individuals, often only two or three, and upon the reliability of the teacher.[3] In many cases, one of the women of the fort would act as the teacher, using the cabin of an obliging member of the community as a schoolhouse. Sometimes the pupils were furnished with a paddle, on the smooth surface of which were cut the letters of the alphabet and the numerals up to ten. Now and then, a textbook would appear, such as Dilworth's Speller,

---

[2] William E. Connelley and E. Merton Coulter, *History of Kentucky*, edited by Charles Kerr, 2 vols. (Chicago, 1922), I, 304.
[3] N. S. Shaler, *Kentucky, A Pioneer Commonwealth* (Boston, 1885), 16, 17.

EARLY SCHOOLS AND SCHOOLTEACHERS 19

and sometimes an arithmetic by the same worthy pedagogue.[4] In other schools the manuscript textbook was used. This book, compiled by some ardent soul, would be written in neat script, setting forth on pages as large as those of a ledger the intricacies of arithmetic. Manuscript textbooks, often more than a hundred pages in extent, were treasured and carefully guarded from harm. Only one was used in a school, and from it the teacher guided his pupils in the mysteries of mathematical calculation.

Regardless of the fact that the Indian menace continued until General "Mad Anthony" Wayne had overwhelmingly defeated the Indian forces at the battle of Fallen Timbers in 1794, the dwellers in the forts, tired of their confinement within the stockades, began as early as 1780 to build their houses outside the walls. Lexington, Boonesborough, and Harrod's Town had ambitions much beyond a station's existence; and their energetic citizens extended trade and even manufacture beyond the confines of the military posts. Boonesborough was incorporated in 1779; Louisville, Washington, and Limestone (Maysville) obtained legal governments by 1780; and Lexington began its career as an incorporated town in 1781.[5]

George W. Ranck, in his history of Lexington, has John Filson teaching school there in 1783.[6] He was followed by "Wildcat" John McKinney, whose fame rests largely upon his encounter with a wildcat in his schoolhouse one morning. For the next twenty years, the *Kentucky Gazette* carried numerous advertisements of schools that offered instruction in a considerable list of subjects at a tuition cost that we would now consider low.

In 1788 or 1789 Joshua Fry came from Virginia and settled in Mercer County. He had inherited a large estate,

---

[4] Z. F. Smith, *School History of Kentucky* (Louisville, 1889), 174.
[5] Thomas D. Clark, *A History of Kentucky* (New York, 1937), 94.
[6] George W. Ranck, *History of Lexington, Kentucky* (Cincinnati, 1872), 74, 97.

possessed many Negroes, and was a man of means. His removal to the "Kentucke" territory was for the purpose of finding new lands and a good return from the cultivation of his acres. He soon discovered that the facilities of education were limited, not only for his own family and dependents, but for those around him. He therefore opened a school at his house for the children of the neighborhood. Those who could pay did so; those who did not have the means, he taught with equal zeal and purpose.[7]

The *Kentucke Gazette* of January 5, 1788, carried a notice indicating that Messrs. Jones and Worley at the Royal Spring, in Lebanon Town, Fayette County, would open a school. The house in which the school was to be conducted was sufficiently large to accommodate fifty or sixty scholars. Jones and Worley would teach Latin and Greek (at twenty-five shillings a quarter) together with such branches of the sciences as were usually available in public seminaries. For diet, washing, and house room for a year, each scholar was to pay three pounds in cash or five hundredweight of pork on entrance, and three pounds in cash on the beginning of the third quarter. A postscript admonished each boy to have his sheets, shirts, and stockings marked to prevent mistakes.

A few days later, January 12, the *Gazette* printed a statement that the Lexington Grammar School was again to be opened, where Latin, Greek, and the different branches of science would be carefully taught by Isaac Wilson, formerly professor in a Philadelphia college. The tuition was to be four pounds, payable in cash or produce. On November 22, 1788, an item in the Lexington paper announced that James Priestly would superintend and conduct the education of students in a seminary of learning at Bardstown. An attached note said that the price of tuition would be five pounds a year, twenty shillings in money and the remainder in cattle and country produce at money prices. About the same date, James

---

[7] Richard H. Collins, *History of Kentucky*, 2 vols. (Louisville, 1924), II, 625.

Graham announced that a Seminary for Education would be opened immediately in Lexington. The school, though called a seminary, proposed to instruct in reading, writing, arithmetic, grammar, speech, composition, and geography. There would be two classes, one of which was to be taught in part; the other group would be enrolled for the whole of the program of studies. Graham, anxious to supplement his income— eight or ten shillings per quarter for each pupil in his school— offered to do deeds, bonds, and other writings with accuracy at a moderate rate.[8] James McConnell, a minister, informed the public that he designed shortly to open a school in Georgetown, Scott County, teaching the following "branches of Literature": the Latin, Greek, and Hebrew languages; likewise geography, and the "Mathematicks" in their various branches. Due care would be taken of the pupils, not only for their instruction, but also in regard to their moral character. The school was to be under the direction of trustees chosen by the promoters of the school. In this advertisement appeared two items generally missing in the early announcements of schools: the care of moral character and the appointment of trustees to direct the school.[9]

The conduct of scholars and the advantages of town as against country in the location of a school must have been gossiped about a good deal, for John Filson, returning to Lexington after his journey to the East, where he found a publisher for his book, made special mention of the discipline his northern teachers would maintain to suppress every species of vice and immorality. Historian Filson wrote a long dissertation about the fruits and practice of virtue, the exploding of party spirit, and the need of instruction in the general system of Christianity. He continued more specifically:

> The ideas of mankind with respect to the seats of education are various, some prefer a town or city, others the country; the latter, viewing the many

[8] Lexington *Kentucke Gazette*, October 4, 1788. The title changed to *Kentucky Gazette* on March 14, 1789.
[9] *Ibid.*, April 12, 1794.

temptations youths are exposed to in towns, and supposing they are fewer in the country, think that the most eligible: however probable this may appear, yet experience proves, that a being, determined on folly, will find as many opportunities in the country, as in town, with the addition of a greater secrecy in accomplishing his designs: many mean and vicious practices can be effected, which in a public situation the unavoidable idea of detection would effectually prevent; this is obvious from a view of a country student walking out of school, he carelessly hulks his body along in clownish gestures, pays no respect to a genteel movement, from a consciousness that no eye beholds him, fears not the contempt or ridicule which must be consequent upon such a conduct in a respectable town, or if in a public situation indecorum should pass unnoticed by all, but the teachers, then is the most pertinent season for admonitions, when the culprit must be sensible upon the smallest observations of the ruinous consequences to all character and future reputation, which he must unavoidably sustain. I conceive the voice of thunder could not make more serious impressions. Experience beyond doubt will confirm these observations.

The advantage of knowing mankind also, which those in a recluse situation cannot, and after a series of time except their studies are mere infants and frequently upon their first approach into public life, by awkwardness, blast all their future fame; the contrary is evident with the young gentleman educated in public life, by frequently viewing the deformity of vice, he naturally abhors it, especially where it is treated with contempt; with the knowledge of science, he becomes acquainted with human nature, has a proper idea of the world, and by the time his studies are compleated, is the gentleman as well as the scholar.[10]

This learned article, spread over nearly a column of the *Gazette,* attracted the eyes of a citizen who in his comment on Professor Filson's philosophy of education waxed wroth and sarcastic, pouring forth his opinions in a lengthy letter:

For the KENTUCKE Gazette.
To Mr. FILSON
Sir,

As I am a citizen of Kentucke and have a number of children to educate, it gives me a great deal of pleasure to see schools raising so thick in various parts of the district. How happy for this infant country that we have so many gentlemen of learning and abilities, who are ready to take our youth by the hand and lead them through the whole circle of arts and science, at so

[10] *Ibid.,* January 19, 1788.

modest an expence. Only a few months ago I was puzzled to find a proper school for my sons: now the scene is changed, and I seem equally embarrased to know which seminary to prefer.

At one time I had concluded to suffer my boys to drink at the *Royal Spring,* and try the efficacy of that wondrous font: but, being a very stanch whig, I hate even the name of *royal,* though applied to the waters of Parnassus. I then turned my attention to Lexington school, and was about putting my sons under the tuition of the former professor of Philadelphia colledge. But before this could be accomplished an ingenious production from some of the promising youths of Jessamine seemed to pre[vail upon?] me to send them to that celebrated seat of the Muses.

However Sir, upon a careful revisal of your late publication and seriously weighing the matter in my own mind, I have at length come to a fixed resolution to keep my boys at home till your academy is opened. For of all plans of education hitherto offered to the public yours certainly bears the palm, and promises the most extensive utility. Your design is great and important. To unite the scholar, the gentleman and the christian all in one, is the supreme, the ultimate end of science. Indeed, a design like this will stamp divinity on your institution, sanctify philosophy, and raise humanity to a consummation which every good man must devoutly wish. And in this view of it, I have the pleasure to inform you, that all my acquaintance are charmed, are delighted with the institution, and determined to give it every encouragement. And as we feel so deeply interested in this institution, we wish to know more of it, and fully to understand every sylable that has droped from your learned pen concerning it.

But, here, Sir, we labour under an unhappy disadvantage. In my neighbourhood all are illitterate and unaccustomed to high flowery language or abstruse reasonings. Your sentiments are, many of them so new; your style is so lofty; your periods are so lengthy, and crowded with such a variety of matter, your conclusions are often so remote from their premises, and relatives quite out of sight of their antecedents, that we are totally lost in the maze, and the longest line of our understandings are not able to fathom the depths of such erudition. I have, therefore: by the desire of my neighbours, flung those parts of your advertisement that we could not understand into a few plain questions. As

1. what is meant by the word *popular,* as applied to the situation of your intended academy?

2. Is it necessary that your scholars should travel a mile every day, in all weather, in order to find boarding at eight or nine pounds a year?

3. Are youth who receive their education in populous cities generally more virtuous than such as have a private education?

4. what peculiar charm have *northern* teachers to inspire virtue, suppress vice, and explode all party spirit that southern teachers do not possess?

5. What is the meaning of the verb *hulk?*

6. Are young ladies, educated in the country, guilty of this sin—of hulking?

This question comes from the fair sex themselves, who have taken the alarm. They fully believe that the crime of hulking, which you have indiscriminately charged upon their brothers, is a rude stroke of satire, indirectly aimed at them. Take heed, good sir; tis death to provoke the Fair.

Lastly, for the benefit of such as cannot give their children a public education, be pleased to point out that peculiar moment, that particular nick of time when admonition, like a thunderbolt, shall knock a hulking boy out of his "awkward gestures" into a "genteel movement."

By giving a plain, easy solution to these questions, you will, sir, much oblige many of your well wishers, and, with the rest, your most obedient and humble servant.

AGRICOLA.[11]

To these aspersions upon his school and in particular to those addressed against his philosophy, the pedagogue replied in a brief letter which was printed in the *Gazette* on April 19, 1788:

To Agricola.
You have taken the liberty to animadvert upon the publication of the intended Seminary, proposing a few silly and impertinent questions, which I shall take no notice of: Your officious performance Reflects no reputation, indicating a Spirit of altercation, which in every attitude I View with contempt. As you have been so personal with me, you will please to leave your proper name with the Printer and oblige

JOHN FILSON.

"Agricola" did not leave his name with the printer but closed the controversy with a reply a month later.[12] Both gentlemen having expressed the strength of their feelings, this exchange of viewpoints came to an end. Nevertheless, "Agricola" had put his finger upon much of the overstatement and exaggerated promises of the one-teacher schools. Though

[11] *Ibid.*, March 8, 1788.
[12] *Ibid.*, May 17, 1788.

referred to as public, such schools required a tuition payment and had no supervision by public trustees.

The grammar school established by the trustees of Transylvania Seminary was an exception to the above statement. This school was opened at the Public School building adjacent to the Presbyterian Meeting House in Lexington in 1789.[13] Again, in the county of Woodford, at the Pisgah Meeting House, a grammar school was established under the care of the Transylvania Presbytery. "Particular attention will be paid to the education and morals of youth, who may be sent to said School by the Teacher and Superintendent," the announcement declared.[14] On Tate's Creek Road, eleven miles from Lexington, John Price started a school in 1795. The grammar school at Pisgah evidently changed teachers when Ance Steele, using the ever-patient *Gazette,* stated that he would receive pupils in April, 1796. John Hargy opened an English school at the Lexington Academy under the inspection of the Rev. Adam Rankin, John McCord, and Archibald McIlvain. Hargy offered instruction in surveying, navigation, dialing, and gauging, in addition to the usual subjects.[15] In the same year, Joseph Helm opened a school in Lincoln County, six miles from Danville. He added philosophy, rational and moral, and criticism, in order to attract the parents of the youths, at five pounds a year. Kentucky Academy advertised at this time that it was now open for the reception of students.[16]

Two new notes appear in the files of the *Gazette* at the close of the century. One of these is the announcement of an evening school, on High Street, Lexington, to be conducted by Jacob E. Lehre, who agreed to teach reading and writing, bookkeeping and merchant's accounts (in double entry), mensuration, and the German language.[17] The second note sounded at this period was the opening of a Young Ladies'

[13] *Ibid.,* July 19, 1789.
[14] *Ibid.,* June 14, 1794.
[15] *Ibid.,* March 11, 1797.
[16] *Ibid.,* January 10, 1798.
[17] *Ibid.,* August 8, 1799.

and Gentlemen's Academy for English Education. John Hargy himself signed this advertisement, the same Hargy who had headed the Lexington Academy three years before. From 1793 until 1800, a Mrs. Walsh advertised persistently in the *Gazette* her school for misses, offering spelling, reading, and needlework. The only variation in her announcement was the change in the appellation from "misses" to "young ladies"; and in the last three years, parents were invited to send little misses to her school in Lexington. Mrs. Walsh had a competitor in Mrs. Lucy Gray, whose school was situated four miles from Lexington, at the home of James Gray. The education of girls at that time was completely summed up in Mrs. Gray's announcement in the *Gazette*:

> Having some time since been solicited by many of her friends to open a SCHOOL for the instruction of young ladies in the knowledge of Reading, Writing, and the various branches of Needle-Work, also the art of Drawing sprigs, flowers, &c. for the use of the needle, [Lucy Gray] takes the liberty of informing the public through the channel of the Kentucky Gazette, that if she can get between six and twelve genteel scholars, she will open school on the 1st day of May next, at the house of James Gray, about four miles from Lexington, where she will provide good board, washing and lodging. Her price for tuition, boarding, &c. will be four pounds per quarter for such ladies as please to favor her with their custom. . . .
>
> Mrs. Gray would also inform the ladies of Kentucky, that she writes the Italian hand in the neatest manner, and if required, will teach the most useful rules of Arithmetic.[18]

It is evident that Lexington had grown by this time into a considerable city, for an advertisement telling all and sundry that Captain Thomas Young would commence a dancing class on Thursday, April 3, 1788, would not have appeared in the press of an Indian-menaced town. The famous Professor Moriarty taught a dancing school the following year, according to the *Kentucky Gazette*. Similar classes were conducted by B. Holrich in 1798, by Charles V. Lorumer in 1799, and

[18] *Ibid.*, March 29, 1797.

by Waldemar Mentelle who added the French language as an inducement to those who sought refinement. A man by the name of R. Gilbert, advertising in the *Gazette* of June 13, 1798, called attention to his school of fencing in the upper brick house on Main Street, Lexington.

During the early part of the nineteenth century, many "Select Schools for Young Ladies" were established in Kentucky. Some were incorporated and others operated without any charter or legal status. These schools were located in or near the larger towns, especially Lexington and Louisville. The subjects offered were the three R's, geography, composition, and the refinements of drawing, music, and needlework. Instruction in the classics was generally limited to boys, while female education was designated as "those useful and ornamental branches designed to insure the polite accomplishments." It was quite evident that those responsible for the education of girls regarded woman's place as in the home. Those schools ran into the hundreds, including both incorporated and unincorporated. From 1850 to 1860, forty-eight such institutions were chartered; and in the following decade, thirty-four more were incorporated. The Civil War brought a serious break in the continuance of these schools. With the development of public education, the instruction of girls in small private schools declined rapidly; nevertheless, a number of the girls' institutions attained considerable reputation.[19]

In the newspapers published in 1808, an advertisement appeared stating that Mrs. Keats had opened the Ladies Domestic Academy in Washington, Mason County. This school had been in operation a year before the advertisement was published in Lexington and Frankfort.[20] The first seminary for girls in the state was conducted by the Rev. John Lyle in Paris. For four years, from 1806 to 1810, this school continued, closing in the latter year upon Lyle's withdrawal

---

[19] Jo Della Alband, "A History of the Education of Women in Kentucky" (M. A. thesis, University of Kentucky, 1934), 154-157.

[20] Lexington *Kentucky Gazette and General Advertiser*, March 1, 1808.

from its direction. Mrs. Keats' school attained considerable fame. Her English birth and the fact that her brother was Sir George Fitzherbert of London were no mean assets in attracting the socially ambitious. In addition, Mrs. Keats' husband claimed relationship to the English poet, John Keats. The Becks, too, had a school in Lexington at this time which was highly regarded. The Science Hill School at Shelbyville had the longest history of any of the schools for girls started in Kentucky before the Civil War. Founded in 1825, it continued for more than a hundred years, maintaining high-grade instruction, particularly in the last thirty years of its history.

In his *Lincoln and His Wife's Home Town,* W. H. Townsend writes of the education of Mary Todd. Miss Todd first attended the school of Dr. John Ward in Lexington. Dr. Ward was rector of Christ Church and combined the duties of teacher and pastor in his coeducational school. Six years later, when she was fourteen years of age, Mary Todd attended the school of Madame Victorie Charlotte LeClerc Mentelle, who had fled with her husband to America from the French Revolution in 1792 and had reached Lexington by 1798. The young French couple made their way in the new country by giving lessons in French and dancing. As time went on, they extended the curriculum until they had a school of considerable merit, offering, Madame Mentelle said, "a truly useful & 'Solid' English Education in all its branches." Board, washing, and tuition came to $120 a year, paid quarterly in advance.[21]

In contrast to the refinements described above, another historian writes that "early Kentucky was as distinguished for its lack of schools as for its disregard of religion." He continues:

There were, of course, no public schools in Kentucky and such private ones as there were could boast of little but the name. The teachers were generally

[21] William H. Townsend, *Lincoln and His Wife's Home Town* (Indianapolis, 1929), 57, 60-62.

Irish, and their principal qualification seemed to be a capacity for consuming "moonshine" in indefinite quantities. The alphabet was commonly learned from characters painted on a shingle and other knowledge was acquired in similar ways. Books were scarce, and, as a consequence, there was much studying together—a state of things resulting in much confusion, inasmuch as everyone studied aloud. The good students were often rewarded by the teacher passing around a bottle of whiskey or a "plug" of tobacco. Unremitting application of the rod was relied upon to remedy all defects physical, mental or moral. These schools were designated as Old Field Schools for the reason that the school building was erected on ground that had been exhausted and thrown out."

One cannot doubt that there were teachers whose ability was limited and who depended upon the strong arm to keep school in the early pioneer days. Some of them consulted the bottle to stimulate the Muse as well as to relieve the boredom of their duties. Among those who sought places to teach were adventurers, temporarily out of funds, who welcomed the opportunity of teaching school for a time. There were others, mostly young men of promise, who regarded teaching as a means of advancing their interests in a calling or profession. The trustees were often hard put to find a suitable candidate. In the *Kentucky Gazette* of May 21, 1791, the board of the Lexington school advertised: "a person who can come well recommended for his abilities as an English teacher, and for his sobriety, and who is willing to take charge of a school, will meet with encouragement by applying." The teacher elected had served but one year when the trustees announced: "As the time for which the present teacher of the Lexington school is employed expires on the last day of May next; and as he has informed the trustees that his health is so far declined that he cannot continue any longer, therefore, wanted a Teacher, etc."[23]

Contracts were made with teachers which set forth their duties and obligations and bound the trustees to pay salaries

---

[22] R. S. Cotterill, *History of Pioneer Kentucky* (Cincinnati, 1917), 248-249.
[23] Lexington *Kentucky Gazette*, April 7, 21, 1792.

in money or produce or both. "An Article" bearing the date of November 7, 1800, is interesting as it points to the nature of the contract and what was expected of a teacher; because of its content, it may well be reproduced here. "To whom it may concern," begins the article:

David Barrow of Montgomery Co., and State of Kentucky proposes to teach an English School in the following year, in a house to be erected on a corner of Maj. J. Paines land on a branch Lullebegrud to begin the first of January next. Reserving to himself a court day in each month, five days at what is called Easter, Whitesuntide, and Christmas, and ten days at harvest which reduced the Number of Schooldays to 224, the year, but in every case he shall have the liberty of teaching on the aforementioned times and days if he chooses and have his vacation at any time he thinks best; except the ten days at harvest, and shall make up no lost time on Saturdays. He engages to give attention and use the utmost impartiality, have special regard to Morals and Behavior of the Pupils and to the best of his skill & Judgement forward them in the Arts of Spelling, reading, writing &c. For and in Consideration of which he shall receive from the subscribers for each Scholar entered the sum of 40/ one Fourth to be paid in Cash the Remainder in Property. Corn at 7/6 Pork at 18/ Wheat 4/6 Sugar at 11/ Six hundrede Linen at 3/ Dressed Flax at 1/ Dressed Hemp 1/ and other property as may be agreed on. To be paid and delivered at the Sd. Barrow's House on or before the last day of December 1801. And if thro sickness or by any other means the Sd. Barrow, should fail in the course of the year to regularly attend the sd. School 24 Days, a Proportional Deduction shall be made in the Sum to be paid each Scholar and to prevent and settle any vexatious disputes that may arise the Employers, concerning the sd. Barrow's Conduct management of the sd. School, they shall nominate and appoint from among themselves those of the most discreet and fit persons in their Judgment as Trustees to whom all such matters and things as respects the Sd. Barrow's conduct and management in sd. School shall be referred and their Determination in such case shall be final.

RULES FOR SCHOOL

Rules to be observed and strictly attended to in the Lullebegrud Reading School.

1st. The Teacher and Scholars to appear at the Schoolhouse each Morning if possible, by half an hour by sun; with Hands and faces cleanly washed and Hair neatly combed.

2. Fires to be raised by the male Scholars in Rotation, according to arrangement, the House to be cleanly swept twice a day by the females in the same manner.

3. Scholars to be particular careful not to dirty or tear their Books and Clothes.

4. The Pupils are to be Kind and civil to each other and by no means to call one another out of the proper Names.

5. In School Time, each one is to keep his or her Seat [unless] necessary Reasons or orders require the contrary. Two are not to be absent at one time without Leave obtained or order given, nor even one without he or she bears the token of Absence.

6. Each one is to mind his or her Business during Book Time and there is to be no teasing, Laughing, Hunching, Whispering or making Mouths to provoke others during the hours of exercise.

7. If any Scholar is at a loss and wants Instruction in any Word or part of his lesson they shall apply to the Master.

8. When the Scholars, whether in or out of school, have an occasion to speak to or of the Master it shall be with the Title of Mr. Barrow, and in like manner to or of all married Persons and grown unmarried persons ... Master or Miss with only their given names and when in Conversation with all such the Term Sir & Madam are to be used.

9. The hours of Play diversion are from half past 11 till one in the Winter, and so in proportion as the Days lengthen.

10. Diversion at Play-Time are Running, Jumping, Prison-base, but wrestling, Climing and such as endanger the Clothing or Limbs will not be admitted.

11. Quarreling, Swearing or Cursing, Lieing, using obscene Conversation, giving one another the Lie, and Fighting will deme the severest kind of Punishment.

12. The girls are to exercise innocent diversions to themselves.

13. The Punishment for Transgression are three: Viz. the Laugh block, Imprisonment and the Rod.

14. If after necessary Means have been used and there should be any Scholar that cannot be broken of Quarreling, Swearing, Curseing &C. he shall with the advise of the Trustees be expelled from the School.

15. Additions to be made to the Rules, as Occasion require.

16. No Scholar to be admitted or allowed to continue in School who has the Itch.

17. The Scholars are not at Playtime or coming to or going from School Unecessarily to be Halloing, Shouting, Noising or making fearful Outcries.

18. The Scholars are not to pillage one anothers School Baskets, Snatch Food from each others hands or take from each other or any one else, anything which is not their own.

19. If it appears necessary, a Monitor will be appointed from Time to Time to give information of Disorder that be committed out of School."

These nineteen items relating to conduct and study now appear old-fashioned and many of them quite unnecessary. The requirement that pupils use proper names in addressing their playmates was undoubtedly intended to eliminate such nicknames as "Skinny" and "Fatso." The rule that students take turns in building fires might have some vocational value today, but is set aside by central heating. Punishments by laugh block, imprisonment, and the rod are no longer used. The little item of the itch is now taken care of by school physicians. In textbooks, organization, preparation of teachers, buildings, equipment, and regulation of pupils' conduct the historian can say there has been progress.

[24] In the possession of A. C. Barrow, Mt. Sterling, Kentucky.

CHAPTER III

LAND-GRANT ACADEMIES

THE ESTABLISHMENT of a university system in a pioneer country where the menace of savage raids continued for fifteen years after the first settlement is regarded as a remarkable performance. However, unfortunate results followed in its wake which really retarded the cause of higher education in Kentucky for three-quarters of a century.

The planned system referred to above failed because it was inadequately financed in endowment, in buildings, and in equipment. No central agency existed to keep the different types and kinds of institutions in harmony and in purpose with each other. The law establishing the university and the academies emphasized the need of freedom from religious controversies and political administration; nevertheless, the university and the seminaries fell into sectarian hands that were quite willing to designate the institutions as belonging to this or that denomination. Soon controversies arose over religious interpretations, and men lost their places as teachers because here and there suspicions were created concerning their theological beliefs. As the years passed, most of the seminaries dropped by the wayside, though a small number moved on into the level of denominational colleges and found a substantial basis of support and patronage. Many of the seminaries were no longer in existence by 1850; nothing but forlorn buildings marked their former place in the state's plan to build a system of higher education.

In 1780, five years after the first settlement in Kentucky, the legislature of Virginia vested in trust eight thousand acres of escheated lands in the County of Kentucky for the purpose of establishing a public school or seminary of learning. Three years later the trustees were incorporated; and at the same time twelve thousand acres more of escheated lands were granted for the endowment of a new institution to be known as the Transylvania Seminary. The persons most active in furthering this educational enterprise were three members of the Presbyterian Church: the Rev. John Todd of Hanover Presbytery in Virginia, his nephew, Colonel John Todd, and Caleb Wallace. The last two were members of the Virginia legislature from Fayette and Lincoln counties. A board of trustees was appointed and met November 10, 1783, in Lincoln County, near Danville. The Rev. David Rice was elected chairman. Two years passed before the institution was opened to begin its work under James Mitchell, in Rice's house at Danville. Income was meager indeed, and Rice alone could be employed at a small salary to carry the instruction which was limited to a common grammar course; later in the institution's history, 1788, the school with the impressive name of Seminary was removed to Lexington, a large and prosperous town.[1] Dr. Robert Davidson in commenting on the move writes: "Whatever advantages may have been anticipated from this measure, a very serious evil resulted in a few years. The tone of sentiment among the leading men of that place had become deeply tinctured with the spirit of French infidelity."[2]

The answer to this decline in religion and the change in the control of the seminary was to set up another institution, a policy which was followed, before and after, by contending political or religious bodies where there was a divergence in viewpoint. After taking care that the new seminary would be conducted by God-fearing men, the trustees petitioned the legislature for a charter. Father Rice, now referred to in

[1] Robert Davidson, *History of the Presbyterian Church in the State of Kentucky* (New York, 1847), 288-289.   [2] *Ibid.*, 289-290.

the chronicles of the times as "venerable," though he was only in his fifties, appeared in behalf of the project and succeeded in procuring a charter for the seminary under the title of Kentucky Academy. This occurred on November 12, 1794. Along with the grant of a charter, the legislature endowed the institution with six thousand acres of land. The sponsors now pushed their enterprise with vigor, sending James Blythe and Rice on a tour in 1795 to raise funds for the new seminary. The financial agents were successful in securing money and pledges to the amount of ten thousand dollars.

After this seminary had been moved from Danville, the new college was opened in the fall of 1797, at Pisgah, where a grammar school had been established in 1794. The Presbyterians now concentrated their patronage upon their own college and grammar school.[3] The trustees of Transylvania Seminary, viewing with some alarm the prospects of the new institution, made overtures by resolving on September 23, 1796, that a union with Kentucky Academy was desirable. On the following day, a petition to the General Assembly proposing for the first time the title of Transylvania University for the combined institutions was voted upon. It was then and there resolved "that the Transylvania Seminary and the Kentucky Academy, together with their respective trusts and funds, shall be united and compose 'one general institution for the promotion of learning,' to be styled and known by the name of Transylvania University."[4] The charter was granted December 22, 1798, to take effect on January 1, 1799. Thus the two seminaries, before they had proved the value or the wisdom of the law establishing them, were gathered into the larger organization and became a university in name.

As indicated by the comments of Dr. Davidson, the Virginia legislature authorized the creation of a seminary in the

[3] *Ibid.,* 294.
[4] Robert and Johanna Peter, *Transylvania University, Its Origin, Rise, Decline and Fall* (Louisville, 1896), 70.

County of Kentucky in 1780; and the legislature of Kentucky, two years after the creation of the state itself, passed an act to establish the Kentucky Academy, incorporating the trustees thereof in 1794.[5] With this act and the legislation that followed, the state entered upon a system of financing and assisting seminaries and academies until 1837 when it discontinued the practice of granting such aid to institutions of the academy type operated and controlled privately. Nevertheless, the process of making appropriations and grants of one kind or another to private institutions continued until the state's partnership with Kentucky University was dissolved by the withdrawal of state support in 1878. The long story of public aid to private institutions in Kentucky then came to an end.

Although the General Assembly had authorized the creation of the Kentucky Academy, the Transylvania Seminary, and the Franklin Academy, by acts of 1794 and 1795, the real beginning of the academy system in Kentucky rests upon an act of 1798 "for the endowment of certain seminaries of learning and for other purposes."[6] In this act, the trustees of the four seminaries known as Bethel, Salem, Franklin, and Kentucky were granted six thousand acres of public land for each of the new schools; but to obtain these lands, the trustees were required to make a survey of any unappropriated lands on the south side of Green River within ten months after the passage of the act. The plot in rectangular form was ordered filed in the office of the Register of Lands. So long as the lands belonged to the seminaries, no taxes were to be levied upon them. The same act extended the benefits of land donations to Lexington and Jefferson seminaries. Trustees were permitted to sell one-third of the land they held for the seminaries; beyond that amount, legislative authority must be secured before further sales could be made. For the endowment of other schools, the lands south of the Cumberland River, below Obey's River, and south of Green River were forever re-

[5] Littell, *Statute Law of Kentucky*, I, 228.   [6] *Ibid.*, II, 108-109.

served for seminaries and academies. Additional land areas were opened for land grants through the error made by Dr. Thomas Walker when he surveyed the boundary line between Kentucky and Tennessee. The compromise was not made until 1825, when the legislature gave six thousand acres each to Simpson Seminary, Hardin Academy, Southern College, and Augusta College.[7] When the Purchase area west of the Tennessee River was acquired in 1834, six thousand acres each were granted to the counties in the western part of the state for the endowment of seminaries of learning before further sales could be made.[8]

The liberality of the legislative assembly in making these extensive grants for education raised some criticism, for the next meeting of the General Assembly, in 1798, prefaced the further grant of lands by a formal declaration of purpose and reason. The language and philosophy are the same as in earlier acts, emphasizing that "for promoting the public happiness, . . . those persons whom nature hath endowed with genius and virtue, should be rendered by liberal education, worthy to receive and able to guard the sacred deposit of the rights and liberties of their fellow citizens; and that to aid and accelerate this most desirable purpose, must be one of the first duties of every wise government." The act of 1798 was the legal beginning of the academy system, not only by announcing a philosophy and a purpose but by authorizing the creation of twenty-one schools, showing that the communities in the older section of the state were glad to accept the assistance handed out by the legislature. That body, unwilling to face any suspicion of playing favorites, authorized the county courts to establish academies and directed the courts that purposed to establish schools to make surveys within eighteen months from the passage of the act. The conditions under which an academy could be established under this act

[7] Kentucky, General Assembly, *Acts, 1825-26*, 97-98.
[8] *Ibid., 1833-34*, 182, 733.

undoubtedly constituted one of the main reasons for the legal organization of so many counties.

During the entire history of the state, 120 counties have been established in Kentucky. Of this number, 100 had been organized before 1850; and of these 100 counties, 81 had one or more academies located within their borders. By the time the academy expansion neared its end, there were 82 counties with 88 academies; but the system was practically complete by 1825, for only 16 such schools were chartered after that date.[9] The small receipts from the land endowments brought real concern to the founders of the academies, for most of the grants realized only a thousand dollars, and only three of all the academy grants brought as much as five thousand dollars. The academy system had its good points, but it was a source of considerable disappointment since it did not meet the needs of the day.

The first governor of the state to speak with any understanding of the need of a common school system was Gabriel Slaughter, who, in his message of December 12, 1816, addressed to the legislature, said: "I presume you will agree with me that nothing in this government . . . is more worthy of your attention than the promotion of education, not only by endowing colleges and universities upon a liberal plan, but by diffusing through the county seminaries and schools for the education of all classes of the community; making them free to all poor children, and the children of poor persons."[10] It was upon this last point that the criticism of the academies and schools rested most heavily, for not one of them admitted scholars without the payment of a tuition that was considerable even in those days. The concept of real public education was new and little understood; and in those groups where it was understood, there was strong opposition. After the governor's message and the part on education had been re-

---

[9] Luther M. Ambrose, "The County Academy System in Kentucky" (Ph.D. thesis, University of Kentucky, 1939), 662-664.

[10] Kentucky, General Assembly, *Senate Journal, 1816-17,* 18.

ferred to appropriate committees, nothing more was heard of a public educational system for a decade.

The termination of the seminary system has been said to have been brought about by the act of the legislature creating a Literary Fund for public education in 1821. The fact is that the seminaries and academies not only continued beyond that date, but the legislature created and incorporated seminaries, academies, and other institutions of learning and gave them the right to allocate to themselves the traditional six thousand acres not already assigned to other institutions or sold to individuals. Even when the supply of lands had been exhausted, the law was used to incorporate additional institutions because of the liberality of its provisions. After the adoption of the third constitution in 1850, the legislature continued to grant charters, but under more restricted conditions, with the result that the seminary movement, which had elements of public education in it, became a movement for the development of private institutions of learning.

It was not the need for higher education that caused the better and older established institutions to expand upward, but rather the ambitions of towns, aided by the hopes of denominational organizations for institutions devoted not alone to the higher education of youth, but to the interests of the denominations as well. Of the academies chartered before 1800, L. M. Ambrose says that nine made the transition from academy to college. Among these were Transylvania Seminary and the Kentucky Academy which united to form Transylvania University. Augusta College, now defunct, came into existence through the efforts of the Bracken Academy trustees to persuade the Methodist Church to take their funds and organize a college. In 1829 Rittenhouse Academy became the basis for the establishment of a Baptist college at Georgetown. The Shelbyville Academy, chartered in 1798, entered the college field when the site belonging to the Academy was turned over to Shelby College, and then to St. James College; finally, the property of the latter was deeded to the trustees of the common schools. Out of the Stanford Academy, chartered in 1798, the Stanford Female College was organized in 1869, the successor of Stanford Female Seminary. Over the door of the present high school building in Hartford, Kentucky, is the inscription "Hartford College," indicative of the educational round from seminary to college and then to high school. The Newton Academy, 1798, has a legislative relationship to Bethel College, established in 1889.[11]

In the two decades from 1800 to 1820, thirty academies were chartered; of the thirty, six became colleges. Centre College, in its one hundred and twenty-first year of operation, is the only one of that group now carrying on college work. Columbia College, the successor of Robertson Academy in Adair County, maintained college instruction from 1837 to 1854. Glasgow Academy took on the name of Urania College from 1819 to 1833, when the authorities returned the institution to an academy status. Then hopes for a collegiate career caused the name Urania College to be revived and held until 1874.

One more instance of these transitions may be cited by referring to the case of Warren Seminary. This institution, ambitious for a larger career, became Southern College in 1819. Under the stress of church controversy over slavery, the college transferred the property owned by the institution to Warren College in 1859; and in time, Warren College sold the property to Ogden College, using the proceeds to assist ministerial students at Vanderbilt University.[12] The academy plan steadily lost prestige through these years, owing to causes inherent in the plan: bad management, poor instruction, and lack of support. A promising idea came to naught, strewing the path of education with old buildings, discarded courses of instruction, dissatisfied patrons, considerable indebtedness, and many untrained children who grew up indifferent to educational advantages.

[11] Ambrose, "The County Academy System in Kentucky," 48-50.
[12] Ibid., 294-295.

To the north of Kentucky, under the provisions of the Land Ordinance of 1785, a section of land in each township was specifically designated for the maintenance of public schools; and seventy-two sections in each of the states formed from the Northwest Territory were retained for the establishment of an institution of higher learning. The states, as they were admitted to the Union, could not depart from the plan established in the territorial act, and thus came into the possession of definite amounts of land which were sold, and the proceeds of the sale were used as state funds for a public system of education. The Kentucky system of land titles and holdings on the contrary made it impossible to designate specific plats of land for public purposes. The legislatures, from time to time, granted charters and a title of acres to various academies, but each board of trustees made a survey of the lands and filed the plat with the Register of Lands.

Often there were conflicting claims, as in the case of Cumberland County. In other instances no charters were issued, but the lands designated for the county were turned over to the common school commissioners. Now and then the county received the land but no school building was erected. In Morgan County, the county court appointed one Peter, a surveyor, to locate the seminary lands.[13] Peter agreed to do this for as much as the land would allow. The trustees did not think much of the land; certainly they were not of the opinion that the proceeds would erect a seminary building. So they applied to the legislature for relief, and that body showed its attitude by declaring in the act "that the said lands are mostly of an inferior quality, worth but little and greatly inadequate to the purpose of erecting a suitable building as a Seminary; and that if said lands are permitted to be sold by said trustees, and the proceeds vested in the completion of the court-house of said county, the result will prove more beneficial to the inhabitants of said county, and the benevolent

---

[13] Morgan County Court, Order Book No. 1, April Court, 1823.

intentions of the law in relation thereto, more completely carried into effect."[14]

The act permitted the school to use the courthouse when court was not in session. This transaction was typical of the time and belongs to the cake department of local government—to have your cake and eat it too. Other instances appear in the records and laws where counties were permitted to use the lands for purposes other than that of education. In Perry County, the commissioners entered on the public records a total of 5,350 acres between the years 1820 and 1841. In the middle of this twenty-year period, the county court was permitted to sell as much of the seminary lands as was necessary to complete the public buildings of the county.[15] The land record of the county seminary in Perry was closed in 1831, when all the resources and lands of the seminary were used to build a road from the Estill County line to the Virginia state boundary.

In a careful gathering of facts about the seminary lands, Ambrose calls attention to the failure of some of the counties to operate academies after the charters were granted. Other counties, in the latter part of the seminary period, made no pretense to charter or to organize a seminary; but the county treasurer was authorized to sell the lands granted to the county and turn the proceeds over to the common school commissioners.[16] Graves and Wayne counties are examples of such action in disposing of the county lands. Some of the counties received no lands. The Meade County authorities reported that their surveyors could find no land to fill the grant of six thousand acres, so the state appropriated one thousand dollars to make up for the failure to find lands. Anderson Seminary, having received no lands, was given six hundred dollars by the state and escheated property valued at three hundred dollars. In Oldham County, Funk Seminary, possessed of

[14] Kentucky *Acts, 1827-28*, 47.
[15] *Ibid., 1829-30*, 199.
[16] Ambrose, "The County Academy System in Kentucky," 672, 679.

some endowment of its own when taken over by the Masons to form the nucleus of the Masonic University, was better provided for than many of the academies; so Oldham County did not ask for the six thousand acre grant.

In the latter part of the academy period, the counties which refused to create academies were able, in a number of instances, to establish small endowments that have continued as permanent educational funds. Outside of the sale of some land, property usually in the form of town lots, there was little left of the 402,022 acres that had been appropriated by the legislature as land grants to establish the academy system. Ambrose cites some cases of seminary property held in 1938 by banks, courts, and church organizations. This property was all that was left of the seminary system, and, under the statutes adopted since 1890, could be turned over to the public school boards in the counties where the property was held.[17] This authority on the academy system finds that the data for twenty-two academies are insufficient to reach a judgment about the disposal of the property, but the lands, buildings, and other resources of more than a third of the seminaries were absorbed in the public school system; seven academies became colleges; the possessions of four were lost to public education; and in four other instances the property was used for purposes other than educational. In ten additional cases, the county school boards retained control; and in nine more, the county rights were recognized by the independent districts.[18] These adjustments came in the main after the constitutional convention of 1890 had adopted Section 120.

Legislative enactments of 1894 and 1896 made the transfer of property dependent on the consent of the trustees of the county seminary.[19] In 1904 the color line in the property settlement was drawn when it was specified that seminary properties and funds should be used for white children. The justification for this legislation was founded upon the creation

[17] *Ibid.*, 46-47. [18] *Ibid.*, 679.
[19] Kentucky *Acts, 1891-93*, 1471-72; *ibid., 1894*, 22; *ibid., 1896*, 19.

of the seminary system long before the adoption of the Thirteenth Amendment in 1865; and the sense of a responsibility in the minds of the members of the Assembly to return the property to the descendants of the early settlers further justified their action. Again in 1910, recognizing the fact that the transfer of seminary property was not compulsory, the legislature passed an act providing that "whenever the number of the trustees of any county academy or seminary ... has been reduced by death, resignation, or otherwise, to less than a quorum, the County Court of the county for which such academy or seminary was created, shall have authority, and it shall be its duty, to fill said vacancies by appointing trustees for such academy or seminary. The trustees so appointed shall have the authority heretofore conferred, or that may be hereafter conferred, upon trustees of such academy or seminary."[20] The final scene in the county academy plan was enacted when the revised school code of 1934 stated that funds held in trust for purposes of education may be turned over to school boards of districts in whose interest they may be held.

What were the reasons for the failure of the county academy plan as it was organized and developed in Kentucky? It is apparent from the very outset that the support of the schools was insufficient because the directors of the schools were compelled to rely upon the returns from land endowments and the payment of tuition by those who attended the schools. The first source of revenue was inadequate for the erection of the buildings, and the tuition fees were sufficient in the most successful of the schools to pay only small salaries to the one or two teachers employed. How important this part of the school income was is pretty well indicated by the fact that the more successful academies were located in the most populous districts of the state. Now and then the schools received small gifts from interested persons; but in the main

[20] *Ibid., 1910*, 162.

the teachers who taught and managed the institutions were expected to get on as best they could, while the trustees furnished a public background for the enterprise.

The almost immediate failure of some of the schools was due to the poor locations selected for the buildings. What would be an excellent location today for an academy, on the cliffs overlooking the Kentucky River, was inaccessible in those early days. Bishop Francis Asbury, who was responsible for the location of Bethel Academy on the Kentucky River, admits in his journal that it was a mistake to establish the school in a place so out of the way.[21] The principal of Bethel, after a few years' experience in the remote location, resigned and moved to Nicholasville where he erected a good log schoolhouse in 1803. Similar stories are told of other schools that were badly placed due to the failure to understand the problem involved in the location of a school, or because the zeal of the promoters to add something of value to the community led them to place self-interest first, either in the sale of the lands for the location or in the hope that a crossroads settlement might grow to some proportions on account of the school.

No specific plan prevailed for the selection of the trustees. Many of the charters, especially in the early days of the academy system, provided for self-perpetuating boards of trustees. Some of these boards performed their duties quite in accord with honest and helpful procedure, but in others they were neglectful and even dishonest. As the system grew older, a larger public control appeared; and the law required the trustees to report to the county court. In some instances the patrons of the school elected the trustees, as in the case of the Christian, Logan, and Woodford County academies. A number of the towns and counties where the institutions were located voted for the trustees to conduct the affairs of the

---

[21] Francis Asbury, *The Journal of the Rev. Francis Asbury*, 3 vols. (New York, 1821), II, 473.

academies; and in other counties the county courts appointed the trustees. No particular method of government was required by law, a fact which could be either a weakness or a strength.

The truth is that the academies went their way in all matters pertaining to their careers as seemed best to each one. Some central control should have held them to uniform standards of instruction and established a goal for the schools and pupils to meet, for they varied greatly as they fell into the hands of able teachers and honest and careful trustees or were the victims of poor teaching and inadequate management of such funds as they had. By 1820 the academies, with a few exceptions, came into disrepute, a situation which decidedly affected the public interest. "So far as there was any interest [in education], it centered about the academies, but even they did not prosper, and their lands and funds were not infrequently mismanaged or squandered."[22]

[22] E. P. C[ubberley], "State of Kentucky," in *A Cyclopedia of Education*, edited by Paul Monroe, 5 vols. (New York, 1911-1914), 592.

CHAPTER IV

THEY WALKED IN THE DARK

THE CITIZEN of today who takes the public school system for granted is astonished to find how recently that system was established in Kentucky. He is grieved to read that the state ranks fortieth or even lower when an examination is made of the status of Kentucky's public education.[1] What is the explanation?

Some historians refer to the year 1838 as the beginning of public schools in the state, but the law of that year was only a recognition of a proposed school fund arising from the distribution of the Federal surplus of 1837, and that law compelled neither the support nor the supervision of public education. The constitution of 1850 had a section declaring the principal of the school fund to be inviolate, but there was no mandate in that document requiring the legislature to levy a tax for school purposes. The people voted by large majorities approving proposals to levy state taxes for school purposes in 1849, 1855, 1869, and 1882; but the legislatures of those times failed to take seriously the vote of the people, and hence did not enact legislation to carry out the wishes of the majorities. In the present constitution, that of 1891, the instrument provides for an efficient system of common schools throughout the state and the appropriation of the income of the school fund for the support of the schools and, in addition, such sums as may be levied by taxation for such purposes. Thirteen years after the people had adopted this, the fourth, constitution and after more than a century of statehood, the legislature

---

[1] Raymond M. Hughes and William H. Lancelot, *Education, America's Magic* (Iowa State College Press, Ames, Iowa, 1946), 22.

levied a mandatory tax in support of the schools. Prior to that time, schools could be set up and supported voluntarily by a community; but in 1908 the establishment, support, and supervision of public schools were made obligatory in the state of Kentucky.[2] Thus an excellent Anglo-Saxon stock lost, as far as public education was concerned, the first century of its history in this state.[3]

The public school system in Kentucky, viewed as a going concern with full powers to carry on, is not yet fifty years old. In contrast with that statement, Kentucky was the fifteenth state to be admitted into the Union. Between the two dates 1792 and 1908, there is a period of more than a hundred years filled with the struggle for a living and a place in the wilderness, with political conflict, and religious controversy. The indifference to the needs of public education arose where denominationalism sought its own ends. From this distance, the contest for religious liberty seems feeble indeed, but not so at the end of the eighteenth century and the beginning of the nineteenth. Men had become concerned about their religious liberties quite as much as their political rights. Some there were who went so far as to insist upon religious belief as a qualification for public office.[4] Such views kept the waters of controversy stirred to their depths. The importance of these controversies, as far as the purpose of this chapter is concerned, lies in their effect upon an educational plan for all the people.

The frontier, because of its difficulties and problems of living, transporting, and trading, did not encourage religion in the lives of the settlers. After the Great Revival of 1798 to 1803, however, there grew up many schisms dividing the Christian community into new sects. The Baptists and the Methodists, endeavoring to create new bodies of Christians, delivered their message to the poor and uncultivated who comprised the majority of the dwellers in Kentucky. It was the

---

[2] Kentucky Educational Commission, *Public Education in Kentucky*, 7-9.
[3] *Ibid.*, 5.   [4] Frankfort *Kentucky Palladium*, July 17, 1800.

purpose of the two sects to overcome the religious indifference and the low conventional morality then prevailing on the frontier. Unlike the Presbyterians, the Baptists and Methodists did not want a learned clergy. The Baptists drew their leaders from the gifted among their members, while the Methodists employed circuit riders distinguished by zeal and devotion. The Baptists, because of their experience in Virginia, were strong advocates of the separation of church and state. The Methodists were devoted to the spiritual needs of their people. Neither sect was intent upon the control of education. The Presbyterians, on the other hand, were anxious to educate their laity to become Christian politicians; but their church was not interested in carrying its religious mores to the lowly. The Presbyterians were ambitious to educate political and commercial leaders who would dominate the government policy and social life of the state. They placed education in the hands of the clergy so that sound doctrine would be the basis of sound morality. To them education was not complete without doctrinal instruction. It was such views that kept Kentucky disturbed for several decades and thus raised questions of sectarian control of education. The storm centered around the early history of Transylvania University and was important because of the controversy over the control of that institution. The whole state became involved and carried the issue into politics and church polity.[5]

In his book from which much of the material in the previous paragraph was taken, Niels Henry Sonne quotes from a letter to the editor of the *Kentucke Gazette,* dated November 10, 1787, in which "A Transylvanian" says he was not against all religion in the Seminary, but believed that there should be a distinction between church and school. Teachers should be selected from all the denominations and the board should restrain narrow-minded views. An opposite view appeared

[5] Niels Henry Sonne, *Liberal Kentucky, 1780-1828* (Columbia University Press, New York, 1939), chap. 1.

in the same paper on December 22, 1787, signed by "A Sectarian," in which the writer "disparaged liberalism and wished sectarian control, as this alone could teach the truth and produce virtue."[6] These sentiments grew in intensity through the years, leaving an indelible mark on the educational purposes of the state.

In earlier chapters there have been occasional references made to the positions taken by some of the governors of the state on the need for common schools. These official comments have shown a limited sympathy for public education; but because of opposition existing among the leading citizens of the state, even the most purposeful of the earlier gubernatorial officers were unable to accomplish anything of importance.

Governor Slaughter, in 1816, was free to say that the landgrant seminaries and the funds to endow them from the sale of lands were inadequate to meet the enlightened views of the legislature, and it was essential that schools be more diffused to suit the convenience of the people. The funds, he said, were within reach to establish throughout the state a system of education which would be attended by incalculable advantages. Quite in advance of his time, the governor declared that every child born within the state should be considered a child of the republic and educated at the public expense when the parents were unable to do it. To effect these objects so valuable and desirable, the governor recommended an inquiry into the titles of lands forfeited and escheated to the state on the supposition that the state would gain funds by the repossession of such lands. Banks and corporations were to be taxed, and these taxes, with part of the dividends on the bank stock of the state, would comprise a fund to be used for the purpose of establishing an extensive and convenient system of education. The public schools included in his proposal were to be free only to the indigent; no general or local taxes were to be levied for their support. However, the governor's estimate

[6] *Ibid.*, 50.

of income from the above sources was entirely out of line; he had but little conception of the cost of such a public school system. Nevertheless, his was a call in the dark that guided the way out.[7]

Another stirring of the waters occurred when the legislature passed an act in 1821 to establish a Literary Fund to be made up from one-half the clear profits "from the operations of the Bank of the Commonwealth of Kentucky . . . for the establishment and support of a system of general education, to be distributed in just proportions to all the counties of this state." This act provided for the appointment of David R. Murray, John Pope, John R. Witherspoon, William T. Barry, David White, Jr., and William P. Roper to collect the information necessary to enable them to organize a plan for schools of common education to be submitted to the next legislature.[8]

The select committee suggested by the governor in his message to the General Assembly in 1821 made a report on the "Common Schools." The report stated that the commissioners doubted the practicability of maturing and adopting an appropriate system at that time. If immature and unsystematic, such an attempt would prove not only unsuccessful but inauspicious. They reported that the Literary Fund was insufficient for the accomplishment of its object. The committee was neither prepared nor inclined to submit any plan for adoption; nevertheless, it did make a number of suggestions, among which was a school tax. This tax the committee was willing to push to the point of making it voluntary for any community to vote such a tax for the support of schools.

Aware of their lack of information on the subject, the committeemen made a plan for a school census. They referred to the Literary Fund, and held out hopes that there might be means for creating a school fund of almost any assignable magnitude. The committee recommended the adop-

[7] Kentucky, General Assembly, *Senate Journal, 1816-17*, 18.
[8] Kentucky *Acts, 1821*, 351-352.

tion of a system of Common Free Schools. In this scheme, the county officers were to act as treasurers and inspectors; the county court was to pass on the districts; the sheriffs were to receive the money from the Literary Fund and pay it over to the district treasurers, and the district collector was to collect all taxes levied at district meetings. Inspectors were to be appointed to examine persons proposing to teach school, and they were to visit the schools in the county at least twice each session. To guard against an educational deficiency, any county district that refused to tax itself in an amount sufficient to support a school for three months would find its part of the public fund held in reserve until it was sufficient to support a school. The Secretary of State was to act as Superintendent of Public Schools.[9]

Five years after the passage of the act creating the Literary Fund (1821), the legislature enacted a law encouraging the establishment of private schools. Five or more persons could associate to form a school in their own neighborhood; they could acquire land, not exceeding two acres, build a house, and employ a teacher. The county court was authorized to appoint seven trustees who were to be responsible to that body. It was the purpose of the previous act to grant a sum of money to support the school.[10] In an act of 1828, the parents and guardians were given the power to select the trustees of their school in an election. The act also authorized the circulation of subscription papers to provide money for the cost of erecting the building.[11]

"This state has done much for a university and for county seminaries, but nothing for common schools ... ," said Governor Joseph Desha in his message to the legislature of 1826. "Our University, though still respectable, has ceased to unite the confidence and affections of the people; and a great portion of the funds bestowed on our county semi-

---

[9] Kentucky, General Assembly, *House Journal, 1822*, 226-227, 245-248.
[10] Kentucky *Acts, 1825*, 118.
[11] *Ibid., 1827-28*, 57, 58.

naries, neglected by their Trustees, have become the prey of speculators." These are severe words, but undoubtedly justified, as shown in Chapter III. The governor called the attention of the legislature to the use of the Literary Fund, set up with high-sounding phrases in 1821. "Indeed the Legislature has been induced, by the exigencies of the Treasury, to devote the whole profits of the Bank of the Commonwealth, and even the interest of the school fund, to the support of government; so that they [the schools] have rather retrograded, than advanced, in relation to this essential concern." The governor was not averse to using the principal of the fund for internal improvements. The school fund then in the Bank of the Commonwealth, the proceeds of the sales of vacant lands, the stock in the two banks belonging to the state, and all other money which could be raised by other means than taxes, in the governor's opinion, should be invested in turnpike roads, and the net profits arising from the tolls on those roads should forever be devoted to the interest of education.[12] So the idea of no taxes and the paramount interest of roads and canals to be built from the inviolable and sacred funds resulted in the dissipation of those funds that had been set aside for education.

The diatribe about the inadequacy of public education was continued by Governor Thomas Metcalfe in his message of 1828. "The people of Kentucky have all the means necessary for their general education, and in this respect are signally favored. Nothing is wanting but the countenance and patronage of the government. But with moral and political advantages equal to those of most other States; and physical resources, superior in some particulars, to those of any other community, Kentucky is in the rear of a majority of her sister states, and even of Scotland and Sweden, on the great and vital subject of common education. Is not this a reproach? Does it not rebuke us for our unprofitable and wasteful party strifes and struggles? The literary fund has

---

[12] Kentucky, General Assembly, *Senate Journal, 1826-27*, 13.

been encroached on and very much diminished...." "Kentucky," he continued, "has been liberal to institutions for collegiate education. But what has she yet done for the poor? Nothing, but to report to the people, to convince them how desirable and practicable a diffusive education would be." Governor Metcalfe called attention to the fact that public lands could be sold, that the Federal government should be asked to appropriate money for Kentucky, since the state had not fared as well as the states north of her in provisions for education. He raised the interesting question: "Are our daughters less entitled to the parental care, and beneficence of the government?... Surely, her mind should be cultivated and adorned by the instructions and the grace of a systematic education.... Let us 'BEGIN,' and the *people* will carry on 'the good work.' "[13]

Again and again, governor after governor called the attention of the legislature to the needs of education; but the members of the legislature, no doubt uncertain of the need and of the best procedure for the financial support of a school system, failed to comply with these urgent demands.

The legislative meeting of 1828-1829 showed a renewed interest in education when a request was presented to the Rev. Alva Woods and Professor B. O. Peers, both of Transylvania University, to communicate to the next General Assembly any information which they might possess upon the subject of common schools. Peers made an extended tour of the New England area and some of the middle states and incorporated his findings in an excellent report that is a landmark in Kentucky educational history.[14] This report emphasized three things that needed to be brought emphatically to the attention of the people of the state: One was the creation of a system of education supported by the state and free to all the children of all the people; the second suggestion was the need for

[13] *Ibid., 1828-29*, 17-19.
[14] M. E. Ligon (comp.), *Report on the Status of Education in Kentucky to the Legislature and Governor Metcalfe, 1850-1851, by Benjamin O. Peers.*

accurate information about existing schools, as, for instance, the number of children of school age in school. The third recommendation dealt with the supervision of schools and the establishment of a State Board of Education. Peers went to great lengths in acquiring that information, using figures collected by the Federal census. He showed in the tabulation that there were 1,121 schools attended by 31,892 children from 136,952 of school age. By this report, it was estimated that there were nearly four times as many children out of school as in school. The population of the state at the time was 686,093, and the sum spent on education by the people of the counties was $277,706. The tuition per pupil varied from $6.74 in Pulaski County to $12.91 in Logan County. "The melancholy picture which this table exhibits of the condition of Education in our State makes it an important inquiry," said Professor Peers.[15]

The Peers report was an important inquiry, but it took the legislature seven years to get around to the passage of an act that declared for its purpose the establishment of a system of common schools in Kentucky. The incentive to pass the act was to be found in part in the receipt of the state's proportion of the surplus Federal revenue distributed to the states in 1837. The commissioners of the Sinking Fund had set aside $850,000 for schools; and if there were to be any further distribution, the fund was to receive $150,000 in addition. The act provided for a Superintendent of Public Instruction at a salary of $1,000. His bond was fixed at $25,000. The salary was to be paid from the interest on the school fund. The act was much concerned about the distribution of the interest of the school funds in those counties where the taxpayers had voted to support schools. The schools were placed under the direction of five trustees who were required to administer the funds, report on school attendance, select teachers, and appoint collectors of taxes. To increase the funds, the trustees had

[15] *Ibid.*, 12.

power to levy a poll tax not exceeding fifty cents. The act did not apply to the cities of Louisville, Lexington, and Maysville, where there were independent districts operating schools on a tax and tuition basis.[16] In 1849, the people of the state voted by 74,628 against 37,746, to instruct the legislature "to impose an additional tax of two cents on each hundred dollars of property in the State, subject to taxation, 'for the purpose of establishing, more permanently, a Common School System in the State.'" The tax increase so collected was added to the school fund and distributed, in proportion to the number of children, to those counties where the people had voted to establish schools and to tax themselves for their support.[17] Seven years later another additional tax of three cents was imposed; and in 1870 the levy was increased to fifteen cents, to be collected only from whites and to be expended exclusively for the benefit of white children.[18] In the fifty years since the act of 1821 the people had advanced considerably in their concern for public education.

Ever since the state had received its part of the surplus revenue in 1837, envious eyes had looked upon it and political hands had reached out to grab at least a part of it. The Superintendents of Public Instruction were vigorous in their reports on the declining school fund and the inadequacy of the interest necessary to aid materially the schools supported by voluntary taxation. The first Superintendent of Public Instruction was Joseph J. Bullock, who called himself President of the Board of Education. He found that public sentiment must be aroused if he wished support for the public schools. From his observations, Superintendent Bullock concluded that at least one-third of the children of school age in the state were unable to read and had no opportunity for a common school education. He carried his analysis further and declared that one-third of the white population were entirely uneducated. Bullock also complained about the small

---

[16] Kentucky *Acts, 1837-38,* 274-283.   [17] *Ibid., 1848-49,* 26.
[18] *Ibid., 1855-56,* I, 11; *ibid., 1869-70,* I, 28.

income derived from the school fund, $64,973.02, and recommended a one-third mill tax. He felt that the reporting on the school census had been inadequate, and that teachers were quite untrained, necessitating the establishment of one or more normal schools. He closed his report with an appeal for adequate support of free education and quoted Thomas Jefferson: "Give it to us in any shape, and receive for the inestimable boon, the thanks of the young, and the blessing of the old."[19]

In 1840 H. H. Kavanaugh, then Superintendent of Public Instruction following J. J. Bullock, reported on the income of the school fund, which he said was $50,415.05; but his main point was the necessity of a school system to be supported by the people. Only two reasons were given by opponents for its impracticability, the sparseness of population and the fact that Kentucky was a slave state. Instead of slavery working against school attendance, it should work for it, Kavanaugh argued, since the white children did not have to do field work and could attend school. All that was needed in Kentucky was *system* in the instruction of her children."[20]

Following the example of these first two superintendents, their successors, with missionary zeal, toured the state, made speeches, wrote hundreds of letters by hand, and interviewed scores of persons each week in their endeavor to advance the cause of education in Kentucky. They reported with solid satisfaction any gains that were made and denounced the meagerness of the general school fund. Superintendent Benjamin B. Smith told of his efforts to arouse the people and brought a new note into his report by saying that he had created a decided public sentiment in favor of the system by appealing to the clergy of the different denominations to use their influence in its behalf. Letters were addressed to the Synod of the Presbyterian Church and to the Conference of the Methodist Episcopal Church. The Methodists replied by

---

[19] Kentucky, General Assembly, *Senate Journal, 1838-39*, Appendix, 225-229, 231-232, 235-236.
[20] *Ibid., 1839-40*, Appendix, 129-144.

sending copies of the resolution adopted, in which the system was approved and the ministers and people were urged to extend to it their countenance and encouragement. The United Baptists met Smith's personal appeal with a kind and ardent response, but the Presbyterians did not reply. Then the Superintendent returned to the Sinking Fund and its relation to the school fund income. His report, although on the whole optimistic, was reduced to a satiric document when he was compelled to say that "Since the preparation of the above report, the astounding fact has been announced in the message of his Excellency, the Governor, to your honorable body, that the Commissioners of the Sinking Fund have failed of being able to make arrangements for meeting the semi-annual payment of the interest accruing upon the State bonds held by the Board of Education, leaving this department entirely without the means for meeting their engagement to pay any drafts upon them for Common School purposes, on the 10th of January, 1841."[21]

A change in the method of electing the Superintendent of Public Instruction was inaugurated in the eleventh article of the constitution of 1850, by which the officer entrusted his candidacy to the people. Robert J. Breckinridge was the first elected Superintendent of Public Instruction. He had held that office from 1847 as an appointee. During this period, he spent his time gathering information about schools and school attendance, enforcing the law, and making the people acquainted with the deficiencies of the Sinking Fund. In the legislative session of 1851 the issue was closely drawn, for the governor declared that the state could owe the state bond a debt; hence, the interest could be paid out of the proceeds of the state tax. The Superintendent declared that the fund was a sacred obligation and could not be used for any other purpose by the legislature or the Sinking Fund Commissioners, a view that was sustained in the House by a vote of 76 to 16, and in

[21] *Annual Report of Superintendent of Public Instruction* (1840), 215-218.

the Senate by a vote of 32 to 4. Thus the shadowy and uncertain claim to a school fund in 1847, amounting to $991,-000.00, had been made certain and increased to $1,400,270.01 by 1853, making it possible to advance the per capita expenditure from thirty cents in 1847 to seventy cents in 1853. The schools, however, had not become free; they were not real public schools.

This condition of the schools was much in the public mind, but Superintendent Breckinridge in his last report, written after he had resigned in 1853, felt that the state could not adequately meet the whole cost of education, and he argued that it was just as well, since the local communities should be encouraged to do something for themselves. This the communities did by voting a small tax and levying a tuition on all children except those of indigent persons. "It may be well doubted," said the redoubtable doctor in this report of 1851, "whether taking the question in its simplest and widest sense, a system of common schools in which the State only aids the community, is not really better, for every condition of human society, than one in which the State bears the whole expense, and does the whole work."[22] The Superintendent missed the real point in the arguments of the lay citizen, who recognized the value of appropriations for all children, and he also overemphasized the accomplishments of the common schools. He had the happiness, Dr. Breckinridge declared in his report for 1850, to demonstrate the complete success of the common schools. "Three years ago, I reported to the legislature, about one-tenth part of the children of the state, as being provided with district schools. Now I submit in detail, the proofs, that not much short of nine-tenths of those children are thus provided. The state may at least be satisfied with a result, that has no parallel, as to the relative amount accomplished, on so large a scale, in so short a time, and with resources, nearly all of which, substantially, have been created, within these same

---

[22] William H. Vaughn, *Robert J. Breckinridge as an Educational Administrator* (Nashville, 1937), 81-83.

three years. If it be considered further, that hitherto nothing approaching a general system of popular education, has ever before been carried into practical operation in any state where slavery was tolerated—the triumphant success which has attended the efforts of Kentucky, is no less important as an example to others, than it is honorable to herself, and beneficent to her people. . . . The common school system of Kentucky is established; and the legislature and the country may well congratulate themselves on an event so full of blessings."[23]

In the constitutional convention of 1849 there was a heated discussion over the adoption of the eleventh article, which guaranteed the inviolability of the school fund. The uncertainties and disappointments of the Sinking Fund for schools weighed heavily upon the members. Some there were who opposed a system of state common schools, and others were ardent advocates of such a system. Among the opponents was Ben Hardin, from Nelson County, who was the representative of a Catholic electorate. "On the three cents proposed to be levied," he stated, "we would pay perhaps $1,500 or $2,000; and yet we have never had a free school, nor will we ever have one in Nelson County. . . . I have no opinion of free schools any how—none in the world. They are generally under the management of a miserable set of humbug teachers at best. . . . The worst taught child in the world, is he who is taught by a miserable country school master; and I will appeal to the experience of every man here who ever went to those schools, to say how hard it is, to get clear of the habits of incorrect reading and pronouncing, they have contracted, at these country schools. For myself, I will say, it cost me nearly as much labor as the study of the legal profession itself, to get clear of this miserable mode of pronouncing, contracted before I went to a collegiate school—at the age of seventeen—your would, and could, and should, and all of that. . . . But as to

[23] "Report of the Superintendent of Public Instruction to the General Assembly of Kentucky" (1850), in *Kentucky Documents, 1850-51,* 603.

how the teachers of these free schools in these towns and cities, take care of the morals of the scholars male and female, I would like my friend from Louisville, (Mr. Rudd,) to give his experience. According to what he told me it would be a most melancholy tale that he would relate. Now, Kentucky embraces 40,500 square miles, and free schools cannot educate scholars, upon a larger theatre than nine square miles; and if we scatter them all over the state fairly, it would require a number of schools beyond what the means of the state, after paying the expenses of government, could provide. Not less than 4,500 free schools would be required; or if we do not do that, the result will be, that the poor and thinly peopled counties, although taxed for, would not have the benefit of these free schools; that will be the result. I would not send a child to a free school, and would rather pay for his education myself. At this day I send some half dozen children to the Methodist, or Catholic colleges, and would far rather do that, than see the poor children thrown into these miserable free schools; and every body who knows me knows that besides my own children, I am at all times educating not less than five or six others."[24]

Hardin was answered by Larkin J. Proctor, of Lewis County, who insisted that the permanent security of the school fund was demanded by the people. Charles A. Wickliffe, governor of Kentucky in 1836 and then a member of the convention, said he was opposed to adopting as a part of the constitution this common school system, a system opposed to the individual or private school.[25] From these remarks in the constitutional convention, it was certain that while Kentucky was on the way toward a public school system, it would be a long time before the goal could be reached.

Writing in 1867, the Superintendent of Public Instruction, Zachary F. Smith, complained as his predecessors had

---

[24] *Report of the Debates and Proceedings of the Convention for the Revision of the Constitution of the State of Kentucky, 1849* (Frankfort, 1849), 881-883.
[25] *Ibid.*, 885-895.

of the backwardness of the school system. He said: "Our Common School System was inaugurated under act of the Legislature nearly thirty years ago. It was established with the object and hope, on the part of its projectors and friends, of becoming able, in a few years, to supply the means and opportunities of elementary education to every child within the State. But, under the inauspicious legislative policies which have succeeded to the present time, it remains, to-day, incompetent and disabled for this great mission; and, indeed, but little advanced, comparatively, in the adequacy of its means or the excellence of its organization, from its first condition of a mere experiment. This incomplete and inefficient condition seems the less defensible in contrast with the evident progress and improvement made in the systems of popular free education of some of the neighboring States, and by some of the Nations of Europe, within the last thirty years."[26] It was a constantly repeated story of the neglect of public education and the need for funds. Superintendent Smith proposed an additional tax of fifteen cents which, with the proceeds of the Sinking Fund, would make it possible for Kentucky to have a five months' term for every school. But as that fund was going, the distribution would drop down to sixty or seventy cents by 1870. The answer to this eloquent plea was not to be found for many years to come.

[26] *Kentucky Documents, 1867*, Doc. No. 31, p. 5.

CHAPTER V

TEXTBOOKS AND SCHOOL CURRICULA DRIFT ALONG

MILLARD FILLMORE KENNEDY in his *Schoolmaster of Yesterday* says: "In the county towns little academies and 'elegant' female seminaries were springing up for those who could pay tuition fees, but poor folk and countryfolk had to acquire education by their own devices, if they got any at all, for there was as yet no state school system."[1]

Without doubt people in the rural communities around 1830 were concerned over the lack of schooling for their children; and after an extended discussion in a community that lasted sometimes as long as two or three years, they would reach a decision to provide a house and a teacher. A small plot of undesirable land having been donated to the cause, a crude house of logs was then erected for a primitive seat of learning. The house itself was equipped with a large, log-burning fireplace at the end opposite the door; the openings in the walls, in lieu of framed windows, were covered with greased paper; the floors in the more effective buildings consisted of split logs, and the benches and desks, of boards hewn out of logs. Without backs and often covered with splinters, seats provided for the children must have been very uncomfortable, to say the least.

The school in that early day had no public fund of its own, so the support of the educational venture depended upon subscriptions from those parents who sent children to the school. These amounted at most to a dollar a month per pupil,

---

[1] Millard F. Kennedy and Alvin F. Harlow, *Schoolmaster of Yesterday* (New York, 1940), 9.

although generally no more than fifty cents was paid. Low as such a fee was, there were many children left out because their parents could not afford to pay for the three-months term. In the effort to adjust the family budget, sometimes only the brightest children in the family were sent to school, and in other instances children would take their turn at learning. That the opportunities for education were indeed meager from the birth of the state until the middle of the century is revealed by the high percentage of illiteracy existing in Kentucky. The census of 1850 revealed illiteracy at 20 per cent for whites and free colored over twenty years of age.

Kennedy, author of the book quoted at the beginning of this chapter, says that when his grandfather left Kentucky to go to Indiana, because there were fewer distilleries in that state, the country schools in Kentucky had not improved greatly during the sixteen years his grandfather had been a teacher (1820-1836). The schoolhouse, it is true, had attained the luxury of a floor and sometimes a real table for the teacher; a few texts in grammar and arithmetic were in use, and an occasional geography or history book was to be found in the more favored schools; but the children still sat on backless benches, and the room continued to be heated in the wintertime by logs burning in a huge fireplace. Stoves did not come into use until after 1850. Under the windows in the schoolhouses were a few writing tables, and on these the pupils wrote with quill pens dipped in ink made from pokeberry juice, oak galls, and iron rust. The maple tree ooze and other saps taken from the inner lining of the bark of trees gave the color. As paper was scarce, learning to write with a quill pen on real paper was something of a privilege in the early days. As there were no blackboards and few slates in the rural schools, the teaching of arithmetic and writing was a difficult task. Perhaps because spelling could be taught by word of mouth, much emphasis was placed upon the mastery of words; indeed the ability to spell was accepted as evidence of scholarship. The spelling bee for many years was highly regarded both as a social occasion and as a means of testing the educational progress of individuals and the community where champions met in contests. It was natural enough that the spelling book should be one of the first of the school texts.

The earliest date on which schoolbooks were advertised for sale in the *Kentucky Gazette,* Lexington, was January 3, 1798.[2] In that issue, *The Kentucky English Grammar,* just published by Samuel Wilson, was offered for sale at the office of the *Gazette.* Professor Wilson was also the author of *The New American Rational Spelling-Book* which was published at a later period.[3] The spelling book was a new undertaking based on a grading of the material. In commenting on his book, Professor Wilson said that most spelling books were printed on poor paper, in small, ill-formed type, with one part of the word frequently printed in roman letters and the other in italic. The professor had compiled his speller for the instruction of his own children. "No other consideration," he says in an article in the Lexington *Reporter,* "could have overcome the reluctance he felt in descending from the higher and more inviting walks of literature, and science, to the humble, laborious, and repulsive employment of the abecedarian." Sensible that the performance was not exempt from imperfections, the author wished that his book might have been more elaborate and that he could have examined all of the proof sheets before publication. This he had found to be impracticable, due, we may suppose, to distance from his printer; nevertheless, he thought his speller comparable to any of the kind then published in America.[4]

Manuscript textbooks were used in the early Kentucky schools, and copies of them are still to be found here and there in the attic of some old family residence or in a few public library collections. An authority on the subject says that these manuscripts were, as a rule, the work of students, rarely

[2] Lexington *Kentucky Gazette,* January 3, 1798.
[3] Lexington *Reporter,* December 15, 1810, September 7, 1811.
[4] *Ibid.,* December 15, 1810.

of teachers. Those found in Kentucky were evidently designed to serve as textbooks and were probably copied from printed texts and exercises or notebooks into which the student had transcribed the solution of problems he had worked out elsewhere. Such books came into the possession of the schoolmasters of the time and were carried by them as a part of their professional equipment. "The manuscript school-books invariably follow the plan of first stating the rule, then the problem, or problems, to which there is added the solution of one or more problems exactly according to the rule as stated.... The rough work necessary in solving the problems was not performed in the pages of the manuscript book. It was performed elsewhere, and the solution was then transcribed into the book in finished form." The typical arithmetic book of the eighteenth and early nineteenth century was a complete manuscript text in which arithmetical terms were defined, rules stated, and problems solved according to the rules.[5]

The following schoolbooks were to be had at the office of the *Reporter: American Orator, Guthrie's Arithmetic, Geography and Children, Murray and Harrison Grammar,* and *The Prompter.* In September, 1809, the same paper advertised the *Webster Speller, Harrison Grammar, Wilson Grammar, The New England Primer,* and the *Kentucky Preceptor.*[6] Advertisements of this kind continued to appear in the newspapers for nearly a quarter of a century. Worsley & Smith, local publishers, set up a bookstore in Lexington and advertised schoolbooks for sale. *Cummings's Geography* was mentioned as a valuable book just received. Marshall's *History of Kentucky,* in two volumes, was ready for delivery at the author's residence or could be had at the Book Bindery of William Wood in Frankfort and at W. W. Worsley's Book Store in Lexington. The history, by H. Marshall, included

---

[5] James Malhern, "Manuscript Text Books," in *Papers* of the Bibliographical Society of America, XXXII (1938), 17-32.

[6] Lexington *Reporter*, September 26, 1809.

in the story of the state the "Ancient Annals of Kentucky, by C. S. Rafinesque, A.M., Ph.D." The advertisement said that Marshall's volumes were "now ready for delivery, at the price of 4 dollars in silver, or 8 dollars in paper."[7] The same newspaper advertised a new line of texts not appearing in earlier announcements. They were a *Primer,* a *Spelling Book,* and a *Moral Instructor, and Guide to Virtue,* all by Torrey. Professor Smiley had compiled an arithmetic and a geography and atlas which were offered for sale in Lexington.[8] *An Easy Introduction to the Study of Arithmetick,* suitable for young beginners, by Martin Ruter, A.M., President of Augusta College, was offered for sale at 18¾ cents. A larger arithmetic, adapted to the Pestalozzian method of instruction, by the same author, could be had for 37½ cents.[9] How widely used were these new books then coming from the press is not known; but, no doubt, in the larger and more prosperous towns there was a considerable sale and some use of these texts. In the rural sections much of the instruction was by word of mouth, for books were scarce and hard to come by.

Each pupil would bring from his home whatever book or books could be pressed into use, including the Bible, which served as a reader in some of the schools. In many families, the difficulty of transportation across the mountains made it necessary to reduce the goods carried by pack animal to the minimum, and few books could be brought along. It should be remembered, too, that books and periodicals were not owned in any considerable numbers in colonial and early national times. The men who had libraries of even a thousand volumes were outstanding in the communities where they lived and were regarded as learned men. Franklin and his comrades of the Junto started the idea of a common library by collecting the books of the members in one place. At a meeting of the Junto in 1731, Franklin made a suggestion regard-

[7] *Ibid.,* May 30, 1825. [8] *Ibid.,* June 10, 1827.
[9] *Ibid.,* January 10, 1830.

68   THE GATES OPEN SLOWLY

ing the organization of a subscription library. This was carried out and a fund of two hundred shillings was subscribed to be used to start a circulating library.[10] Books were scarce even in the most advanced cities of colonial America, and still more scarce in other parts of the colonies; in the hinterland they were rarely to be found. The expense of getting books for use in school was prohibitive; and in addition, those for teaching purposes were few indeed. So teaching by voice, rote, and memory was the accepted method. As a consequence, the number of textbooks to be placed in the hands of the pupils, as well as the subjects to be taught, rested with the parents.

Although the year 1838 is used by many educational writers as the date of the founding of the common school system in Kentucky, it was not until 1851 that the new State Board of Education was authorized to recommend the textbooks needed in a minimum course of study.[11] Only six years earlier than the law of 1851, the legislature had reaffirmed the earlier practice by declaring that "parents or guardians of all children sent to the Common Schools shall have the right to select, furnish, and direct what school books shall be used by their own children and wards, provided the same are not immoral."[12]

A marked improvement in the texts developed as the schools of the nation settled down to better methods and more effective instruction. In the list of books available in Kentucky, the Goodrich series appeared in 1843, although not many of the works of the gifted Samuel Griswold Goodrich were used for some time after that date. The Goodrich *First Reader* was published in 1857, under the imprint of John P. Morton and Company of Louisville; the editor was Noble Butler. Goodrich, who wrote numerous stories under the nom de plume of Peter Parley, began the preparation of a series of history books as early as 1843. A pictorial history

---

[10] Carl Van Doren, *Benjamin Franklin* (New York, 1938), 104-105.
[11] Kentucky *Acts, 1851,* 162.   [12] *Ibid., 1844,* 54.

of the United States by this author was used in the Lexington schools at an early date. Morton and Griswold, of Louisville, sold the Goodrich *Ancient History from the Creation to the Fall of Rome* for use in the Louisville schools in 1847. In a volume called *North America, or The United States and the Adjacent Countries,* published in 1847, there appeared an advertisement stating that Morton and Griswold were publishing a series of readers by S. G. Goodrich, author of the *Peter Parley Tales.* The list included a *New Primer, The Common School Primer,* and *Readers* from the first to the fifth. Two series of history class books by Goodrich are listed in the advertisement. The First, or Primary Series, included books on the United States, South America, Africa, Europe, and Asia. The Advanced Series covered Ancient and Modern History.

No series of textbooks ever held a higher place in the minds of the men and women who used them seventy-five years ago than William Holmes McGuffey's *Eclectic Readers* and other school books bearing his name. McGuffey was a professor in Miami University, president of Cincinnati College, president of Ohio University, and later a professor at the University of Virginia, from 1862 to 1873, the year of his death. McGuffey was acclaimed as a great apostle of better methods of instruction. His eclectic method combined the essential elements of several methods. Word, sentence, and phonetics were combined so that the best of each was selected and appropriated. The McGuffey *Readers* were used broadly and for many years, until more modern books were introduced into the schools by farsighted publishers. Each lesson in the McGuffey *Readers* contained a moral that was supposed to impress the pupil and give him a set of precepts which would develop his character. Relying heavily upon classical fables and folklore tales, the McGuffey *Readers* were still remembered long after the death of their author and the complete disappearance of the readers from the school lists as late as the gay nineties.

There were other popular texts, such as *Ray's Arithmetic, Venable's History of the United States, Harvey's Grammar,* with its diagrammatic system by which the pupil was expected to show the grammatical use of every word in a sentence, and Steele's *Fourteen Weeks in Science.* The teachers were called upon to buy *The Kentucky School-Lawyer, or a Commentary on the Kentucky School Laws, and the Rules and Regulations of the State Board of Education.* This Justinian Code of the pedagogue was compiled by Howard A. M. Henderson, D.D., LL.D., and printed at the Yeoman Office, Frankfort, Kentucky. Another book for the edification of the teacher was the *Encyclopedia of Education,* published by E. Staier.[13]

From the middle of the nineteenth century to the present time, the status of the textbook has gone through many stages. The authority to select the books passed from parents to district trustees, then to the county boards, and finally to the state. In going through this long-drawn-out process, the uniformity of the texts was considered to be the first essential; then came the selection and purchase of books by book commissions; and as a final crowning act came the establishment of free textbooks in the schools. The law of 1851, while giving the State Board of Education the power to recommend textbooks for a specified minimum course of study, nevertheless allowed local trustees to substitute any textbooks they preferred. This power was thus taken from the parents and given to trustees whose knowledge of books was fully as limited as that of the former, yet the change resulted in a greater degree of uniformity in the choice of texts. Superintendent H. H. Kavanaugh, in his report of 1840, had urged strongly that something should be done to give uniformity to the books used in the schools. "It seems," he said, "that in many of the schools of the country, . . . the children carry almost any kind of a book to school that may happen to be-

---

[13] Frankfort *Yeoman,* May 14, 1878.

long to the family. Hence, there is no uniformity in the books used in the schools, and it often happens, that a book is placed in the hands of a child ill adapted to the progress it has made in learning, and what is worse, sometimes containing sentiments injurious to the morals of the child. To remedy this evil, would not now be a very difficult task, since the book stores abound with regular class books, of a suitable kind."[14] The Superintendent must have known that uniformity in texts depended in many of the districts where the schools were located upon the ability of parents to pay for the books. But the situation created by the money question was not the only problem, for uniformity of textbooks rested squarely upon the grading of schools. The instruction was free for three months, and an extended term was open to the children of parents who could pay tuition. Thus uniformity of instruction was well-nigh impossible until the grading of the schools had been accomplished, a task which was not to be well finished for a half century or more.[15]

The State Board of Education created by the act of 1851 consisted of the Attorney General, Secretary of State, and the Superintendent of Public Instruction. The legislatures, for more than seventy-five years, evidently regarded these elective officers as peculiarly qualified to act as curriculum makers and textbook selectors. The weakness of this method of selection for the members of the Board was commented upon as early as 1869 by the Superintendent in his report of that year. "Now, while the Attorney General and Secretary of State are able and accomplished gentlemen, and distinguished in the spheres in which they move and act, officially and professionally; yet, if they were seated in session of the Board, protracted through a fortnight or two, to carefully and critically examine some fifteen or twenty series of

---

[14] "Annual Report of Superintendent of Public Instruction, January 3, 1840," in Kentucky, General Assembly, *Senate Journal, 1839-40*, Appendix, 142.

[15] Rolfe L. Hunt, *A Study of Factors Influencing the Public School Curriculum of Kentucky* (Nashville, 1939), chap. 2.

spelling-books, readers, arithmetics, geographies, grammars, histories, etc., and to prescribe a course of instruction, they would be the first to vote the service a burlesque or a bore. There is no more fitness or propriety in assigning such duties to unprofessional educators than there would be in assigning to a merchant or teacher the duty of drawing up a bill in chancery."[16] The result of this method of administration was to place upon the Superintendent the whole burden of selecting texts and of preparing courses of study. In the early days he had no help in carrying on so great a task; slowly through the years, however, the Department of Public Instruction has built up a professional staff that has furnished educational leadership for the schools. With this assistance from a lay board, the ex officio board has finally passed into the limbo of forgotten things.

While the legislature of 1851 created a Board of Education to direct and foster the common schools, nevertheless the lawmakers have from time to time prescribed the curriculum and even the texts to be used. In 1871 the author and publisher of Collins' *History of Kentucky* secured the passage of an act providing for the purchase of that book for each of the schools of the state, the cost to be paid out of the school fund. This the Superintendent refused to do, but the legislature consented to allow Collins to sue the state, and a judgment was obtained in the courts which was ultimately paid from the general fund of the state.

The first law on the curriculum provided that the parents or guardians of all children should have the right to select, furnish, and direct what schoolbooks could be used. This freedom of choice, which resulted in an anomaly of instruction, was taken away from parents and guardians in 1852, when the State Board was authorized to provide instruction in English, grammar, arithmetic, and geography, "a plain

---

[16] "Annual Report of Superintendent of Public Instruction, 1869," in *Kentucky Documents, 1869*, II, Doc. No. 18, p. 42.

education," so the act stated. The Friends of Education in Kentucky, an association of teachers and officers created by Dr. Robert J. Breckinridge, regarded the limited course of study as inadequate, and resolved in their meeting "that a course of good common school instruction should contemplate a thorough knowledge of spelling, reading, writing, geography, with maps, arithmetic, the history of the United States, English grammar, in its elementary principles, including composition, and the elements of general history."[17] The Board, however, steered a balanced policy, following literally the prescription of the legislature, refusing to throw out any books that were in use in the schools but attempting to mollify the enthusiasms of the Friends of Education by adding some books to the list. The Friends of Education also resolved that the Bible should be introduced and used in the schools— but with discretion in order not to arouse dissensions over theological questions. As late as 1905 the courts were called upon to rule on the reading of the Bible in schools, when a suit was brought, *Hackett* v. *Brooksville School*. In this case, the Court of Appeals ruled that the King James version of the Bible was not a sectarian book and might be read, and prayer be said if unsectarian.

When the act of 1838 was passed, the sole purpose was to encourage communities to do something on their own accord about a school. There was no compulsion, and no curriculum requirements were laid down in this law. In the law passed by the legislature in 1852, however, as a result of the eleventh article of the constitution adopted in 1850, there was a clause demanding a curriculum which would include the elements of a plain education in English. The widest interpretation that the Board of Education then gave to this mandate was to provide the teaching of the three R's with

---

[17] "Proceedings of the First Annual Convention of the Friends of Education in Kentucky," quoted in "Annual Report of Superintendent of Public Instruction," in *Kentucky Documents, 1851-52,* 201.

the refinements of grammar and geography. The legislature declared in 1864 that history must be added; but the Board interpreted this requirement as one that could be met by instruction in United States history only. This curriculum standard remained stationary until 1884, when the legislature required the teaching of the laws of health; as a result, physiology and hygiene found their way into the curriculum of the common schools. Civil government was added in 1888 and the history of Kentucky in 1893. Under the pressure of the advocates of temperance, the action and effects of alcoholic drinks and narcotics appeared in the list of required subjects the same year. Perhaps this line of instruction was the first to be forced upon the schools by pressure groups; but the legislature, responding to outside demands, required by law the teaching of fire prevention in 1918, and thrift and industry, physical education, and humane education in 1920. After a long wait of many decades, music finally was given an official place in the educational setup of 1922. Some effects of the First World War are observable in the prescriptions of 1924, when provision was required for the teaching of the United States Constitution and the reading of the Bible. Four years later, public speaking, discussion and debating, and parliamentary law were added to the list. The passage of the Smith-Hughes Act in 1917 brought the study of agriculture into the high schools of the state, with the exception of those located in cities of the first four classes.

The author of *The Kentucky School-Lawyer* was H. A. M. Henderson, Superintendent of Public Instruction from 1871 to 1879. He has much to say about textbook legislation. The last appointed and the first elected Superintendent, R. J. Breckinridge, was opposed to a uniformity of textbooks brought about by state law. He thought that the Kentucky system, the recommendation of texts by parents and guardians, was better than central control of selection. Centralization of selection in a state board was "an immense change" and a "most disastrous" one.[18] In the past, the selection of texts had been left almost entirely to the teachers in the schools who were in turn advised by those around them in their choice of the schoolbooks. Also parents or guardians reserved the power to substitute other books, if they disapproved those being used. Such was the Breckinridge view, and he would not allow himself for one moment to believe that the legislature should enact such a resolution as the one proposed. Nevertheless, when the legislature met the next year, the selection of textbooks was placed in the control of the State Board of Education. The Friends of Education met at the call of Dr. Breckinridge, hoping to recommend both a course of study and the books to be adopted by the State Board. Superintendent Henderson remarked in his report of 1874 that "Nothing, perhaps, has created more excitement during the year than the question of text-books." Uniformity of textbooks was "impolitic for Kentucky at this stage of the development of the school system," he argued, because there would be "an active canvass upon the part of rival publishing houses, which would distract counties, and array prejudices." The Superintendent was opposed to book monopolies which could be checked if the State Board of Education would select several good textbooks in a subject and then allow each district to choose from the list. Uniformity in each district should exist as a matter of course, but neither the County Board nor the State Board should have compulsory authority to prescribe a series of textbooks. In fact, he went on to say, "The action in each district should be free alike from the interference of public officers, from the conflicting interests of publishers, and the entreaties of their agents."[19] The argument for uniformity made some headway as the years went on; but the period of adoption, the makeup of the boards, and the need for state-wide uniformity created a legislative

[18] *Ibid.,* 94.
[19] "Annual Report of the Superintendent of Public Instruction" (1874), in *Kentucky Documents, 1874,* Doc. No. 1, pp. 44-45, 49.

contest that concerned the administrators of schools and made them fearful of the outcome of much of the proposed legislation.

The former president of the Agricultural and Mechanical College of Kentucky University, Joseph D. Pickett, was Superintendent of Public Instruction from 1879 to 1887. In his report of 1881 he considered the selection of textbooks to be the most important problem in the school situation. Superintendent Pickett believed that "The legal period of two years, without change, should be extended to not less than four years, for the purpose of continuing the consistent influence of a series which is adapted to the proper progress of the human mind, and the interests of those parents whose means are so limited that their children must necessarily use one after the other, the same books." In compliance with such a view, the legislature of 1884 decided that the State Board of Education should recommend a suitable list of books for the schools, and from such a list the trustees of districts should adopt the books for five years.[20] The district trustees evidently did not function to the satisfaction of all concerned, for the legislature in 1888 took away the authority from the local trustees and gave it to the county boards of education. Modifications of the law were made from time to time, permitting county boards and city boards to select the books from the list recommended by the State Board of Education. In 1904 the lawmakers set the legislative hopper on a different mesh and created a State Book Commission, composed of the governor, auditor, the clerk of the Court of Appeals, and three members of the State Board. A county board, consisting of the county attorney and the county superintendent of schools, was created; and from the lists made up by the County Textbook Commissioners, the State Board was to select the books recommended by a majority of the county boards. In all this may be found political manipulation in-

[20] Kentucky *Acts, 1884-85,* II, 116.

tended to widen the opportunities of textbook publishers for a larger field of sale. When the legislative assembly met in 1910, **a new type of county** board was created so that the educational interests might have a larger representation. The members were the county superintendent, a high school principal, two members of the County Board of Examiners, and one member of the County Board of Education. Not meeting the requirements of a law satisfactory to publishers, agents, politicians, and educators, another State Book Commission was created by the legislature of 1914. The governor and the Superintendent of Public Instruction were returned to ex officio membership; others included a representation from the faculties of the state normal schools at Richmond and Bowling Green, one educator from each of the appellate court districts, and a member of the faculty of the State University.[21] Slight changes were made in the law in 1918; but in 1926 a Textbook Commission of twelve members was created, consisting of the governor and Superintendent of Public Instruction as ex officio members and ten others to be appointed by the governor. The texts were chosen for the whole state, including the cities; the length of adoption was reduced to two years, and not more than 20 per cent of the texts could be changed at any one time.[22] Again in 1930 the textbook commission law was modified. This time, a commission of nine members was to be appointed by the State Board of Education; the ex officio members were left out, and the book adoption was extended to five years. Not more than one-third of the list could be changed at one time,[23] and here the textbook controversy rested.

On the whole the fight over the selection of textbooks in Kentucky is a sad tale. Six different schemes have been tried; but with all these attempts, no satisfactory method has as yet been devised for the selection of books for rural schools. The city districts have fared better; and because of their

[21] *Ibid., 1914,* 34-36.   [22] *Ibid., 1926,* 248-266.   [23] *Ibid., 1930,* 88-97.

political power, they have been able to protect the interests of the city schools. The report of the Educational Commission of 1921 said: "This zig-zag experience, capricious changing from one kind of machinery to another without genuine improvement, is fairly typical of the state's educational history." "The results point to the absence of clear cut understanding of principles of ethics and educational procedure, due in part, to the absence of a permanent and able leadership. The selection of textbooks is not a difficult task that could not be met by a small committee of men who know textbooks and the purpose as well as the principles used in their making. Principles and leadership would then be substituted for tinkering and political manipulation."[24]

It is a far cry from the day when children brought their own textbooks, and parents determined what books their children were to use, to the selection and purchase of textbooks by the state. The first time the issue of free textbooks came before a legislature in Kentucky was in 1928. The governor, Flem D. Sampson, stumped the state on the free textbook issue. The lawmakers passed an act to provide free textbooks for all children in the elementary grades and appropriated the funds necessary to buy the books, but made no specific provision for the collection of the money, so the legislature adjourned with no appropriation for the purchase of the books. The Court of Appeals ruled, when the case came to that tribunal, that the act was inoperative because the revenues had been appropriated for other purposes and there was no money left for the purchase of books. However, funds were provided by the legislative act of 1934 to the amount of $500,000[25]; and at long last Kentucky had reached the place in her educational progress where she could offer uniformity of textbooks throughout the state, and free books for the elementary schools.

[24] Kentucky Educational Commission, *Public Education in Kentucky*, 15, 17.
[25] Kentucky *Acts, Extraordinary Session, May 2 to July 2, 1934*, 102-103.

CHAPTER VI

A CENTURY OF SECTARIAN EDUCATION

DURING the whole of the nineteenth century there was great activity in Kentucky in the organization of colleges and schools on a sectarian or church-related basis. Dr. Nathaniel Stevenson, the president of Union College at Barbourville, while enthusiastically and zealously engaged in soliciting funds for that institution, encouraged himself and his fellow Methodists by remarking that "education as a function of the Church is second only to the preaching of the gospel." To prepare young men for the ministry and to teach the children of the church under its guidance were responsibilities enough to stimulate the zeal of the religious denominations. In his *Kentucky Sketches,* the historian Lewis Collins writes that in 1847 there were more colleges in Kentucky than in any other state of the Union.[1] These institutions were scattered from one end of the state to the other, as far east as Barbourville, as far west as Clinton, in the north at Augusta, and in the south at Bowling Green, Glasgow, and Hopkinsville. The greater number were located in the central area of the state. All told, there were fifty such institutions, not including the numerous land-grant academies that were established in the state within a hundred years. Of this number, seven had passed out of existence before the end of the century. In the next thirty years of the new century, the state started four institutions for teacher training; and many of the colleges existing in the nineteenth century in Kentucky were amalgamated, abandoned, or merged into the school

[1] Lewis Collins. *Historical Sketches of Kentucky* (Cincinnati, 1847), 272.

system as public high schools. Thus the number was finally reduced to sixteen senior colleges and fourteen junior colleges.

The minimum expenditures, collection of endowments, and construction of buildings in these educational efforts amounted to a considerable sum, at least five million dollars; yet it could have been said in 1900 that there was not a single Kentucky college, public or private, that was adequately supported or housed. Such a material test is not the only one to be applied to the results of a century of education in Kentucky; for from the schoolrooms of these colleges came a large number of men and women who rendered distinguished service to the state and nation, fully justifying the educational efforts of the century, even though the present generation was left with problems of refinancing, reorganizing, and reappraising the real objectives of education. The mistakes of the past, made by well-meaning persons and organizations whose zeal had been greater than their judgment, must then be corrected in the building of a modern type of higher education.

In the century and a half of the state's existence, there have been five attempts to establish universities as conceived and understood by the founders of those institutions. Looking back over the organizations and programs of study as they appeared in the catalogues of the time, it may be said that the incorporators had a fairly modern idea of what is meant by a university, with the exception of the departments of research which today are regarded as the most important function of a university. Able men, it was hoped, might be induced to join the faculties, who were not regarded as seekers of new truth but were thought of as reservoirs of wisdom. The universities were considered as conservators of church doctrine, and, as such, any departure from the views of the majority or the concepts of a powerful minority resulted in a split leading to the forming of two or more universities. It is an interesting story that fills many pages in the history of higher education in Kentucky. The story in many ways is a sad one, a record of foolish controversies and misunderstandings that required years to clear up.

The five institutions that have had university aspirations are: Transylvania University, Kentucky University, Central University, the University of Louisville, and the University of Kentucky. The first, Transylvania, may be called the mother of these institutions, for from this college stemmed all the others. Centre College was the result of a split of the Presbyterians from the group in control of Transylvania. The difficulties arising over the question of slavery resulted in the award of the property and the control of Centre College to the northern branch of the Presbyterian Church. The feeling among the members of that sect who sympathized with the South brought into existence Central University at Richmond, which was returned to the fold and consolidated with Centre College in 1901. The quarrels over the medical schools associated with Transylvania finally resulted in their removal and their absorption into the University of Louisville. To save the remains of three different institutions, Transylvania University, Bacon College, and the Morrill Act Agricultural and Mechanical College, the Kentucky University was organized in 1865; and from that promising attempt at a centralized and enlarged university, the University of Kentucky emerged. This was a return to the concept of a state university by which higher public education began in Kentucky at the opening of the nineteenth century. To trace this story in all of its details would require the patience and industry of the proverbial Philadelphia lawyer and a large volume of several hundred pages to record it. Much of this history has been presented in pamphlets, articles, biographies, and manuscripts written by students while fulfilling thesis requirements for graduate degrees. That part of the material which bears on the main drifts and tendencies in the field of higher education will be used here to give the reader a fair account of what happened during the establishment of colleges in Kentucky.

Transylvania received its title of university in 1799 from the union of the seminary of that name and Kentucky Academy. The institution is referred to as a public university many times throughout its early history, but in no wide sense did it ever conform to the idea of a state university since it was under denominational control. Some public lands were given and state appropriations made toward the establishment and support of the institution during the period ending in 1865. Dr. Robert Peter prepared a table covering the years 1790-1870 in which it appears that Transylvania University received 32,000 acres of land and $24,000 in appropriations, surveyors' and auction fees, lottery privileges, and bonuses from the operations of the Bank of Kentucky and from the Farmers and Mechanics' Bank in the form of commercial paper. Citizens of Lexington gave $125,000 in addition to the gifts of Colonel James Morrison, which amounted to $55,000. Individuals from other states added $14,000 to these sums. The city of Lexington itself gave $70,000 in 1839 to endow the several colleges of Transylvania University. These gifts and granted funds were spread over a considerable period, but show the interest of individuals, the state government, and the city of Lexington in the growth of this university, which went on to greater things, rivaling older institutions in the East in the quality of the courses offered and the ability and reputation of its faculty.[2] Transylvania had been under the control of a board made up largely of Presbyterians until the majority, relaxing their vigilance, allowed their representation to drop to seven. It was at this time, in 1818, that Dr. Horace Holley accepted the presidency of the university; and with his coming the institution entered upon a period of prosperity, increased student attendance, and enlarged reputation. In February of that year the legislature changed the act of organization; the old board was turned out, and there

---

[2] Robert Peter, *Thoughts of Public Education in Kentucky, with Special Reference to Normal Schools, the State Agricultural and Mechanical College, and the Trusts of Transylvania University* (Frankfort, 1877), 15-16.

were appointed in their places "a set of men," a hostile critic charged, "not one of whom, whatever other merits they might have had, made any pretense at religion." It is in this last sentence that the controversies which followed the coming of Dr. Holley are fully foreshadowed.[3] During the twenty years before the Holley regime, the student body had never reached an enrollment of one hundred; and only twenty-two persons had been graduated from Transylvania. As contrasted with these meager figures, the university from 1818 to 1827 conferred more than six hundred degrees upon 558 graduates.[4]

With the departure of Dr. Holley in 1827, Transylvania was the center of conflict and religious controversy seriously affecting its growth and service to the state. A series of presidents followed who soon resigned after attempting the conciliation of the opposing forces. The reorganized university managed to keep some eminent men on the staff of the medical school, and the law school was revived. These schools, however, enjoyed but a brief period of real growth. Several times, the citizens of Lexington rallied to the call for help, as in 1838-1839 when eighty citizens contributed one hundred dollars each and the city of Lexington raised seventy thousand dollars for Transylvania. In 1820 Governor John Adair said in his address to the legislature: "By aiding our university, by putting it in its power to become useful in every department of science which it is prepared to teach, you will promote the real interest of the community at home, and give dignity and weight of character to the state abroad."[5] The tone of the official utterances changed markedly when Governor Joseph Desha declared in his message to the legislature: "But there can be no improvement in one University, which will make it the means, to any considerable extent, of promot-

---

[3] Robert Davidson, *History of the Presbyterian Church in the State of Kentucky* (New York, 1847), 292-300.
[4] Sonne, *Liberal Kentucky*, 255-256.
[5] Kentucky, General Assembly, *House Journal, 1820*, 13.

ing the great object which the State must have in view."[6] This message shows a confusion in the mind of the chief executive about common schools and higher education which he regarded as conflicting. Such an attitude was reflected in the declining interest of the state government in Transylvania University.

Another period of denominational control of Transylvania University began in 1842; the trustees persuaded the Methodist Church to take over the institution. Dr. Henry B. Bascom was appointed president, and almost immediately there was a revival in interest and an increase in student enrollment. Again sectarian controversy raised its head; and with the supplementary force of internal disputes, the student body was reduced in numbers, and the period of Methodist control came to an end within eight years. Before the Methodist regime, the trustees had tried Baptist, Episcopal, and another Presbyterian direction. The state had lost interest in the institution, so the trustees attempted to raise funds in the town of Lexington and among such friends as Transylvania had in the state and elsewhere. When the General Conference of the Methodist Episcopal Church, South, gave up the direction of the university, the management of the institution was left on the doorstep of two Kentucky conferences. This management was brief indeed, and the trustees had their orphan educational child again on their hands in 1850. The only way out of the dilemma which confronted the trustees was to appeal to the state; and by an act of March 10, 1856, Transylvania was converted into a State Normal School. Many suggestions had been made about the training of teachers as early as 1821 by Professor Peers, and later with still more eloquence by Dr. Robert J. Breckinridge. Under the new arrangement, the board was to consist of the former trustees and the principal state officers. The financial support from the state was fixed at $12,000 annually, an arrangement

---

[6] *Ibid., 1825,* 17.

that continued but two years, leaving the school at the end of the time in a hopeless condition. The failure of the state to maintain its obligation to support the new arrangement was due to the illegal use of the school fund for the support of the institution and the reluctance of the legislature to provide the money by taxation. The medical school and the law college continued until the Civil War had begun. Efforts were made by the trustees to have the state accept the college and its property as the basis of a land-grant institution provided for each of the states by the Morrill Act of 1862, but this was not to become an accomplished fact until the roundabout process of establishing Kentucky University had brought consolidation in 1865.[7] The war scattered the equipment and library of Transylvania; and the great dream of its founders vanished. Three times Transylvania had been on the verge of a real university career; and three times it had failed to reach the heights. Amalgamated with Kentucky University in 1865, once more, after thirteen years of a co-partnership, a university plan was again retarded by sectarian quarrels and bickerings. The story of that period is left for another chapter.

With the severance of the Agricultural and Mechanical College from Kentucky University in 1878, the latter became in reality only a college of liberal arts. On the same date the law college was closed, not to be opened again until 1892, and finally to be dropped from the college organization in 1912. Meantime, Charles Louis Loos continued as president for seventeen years, ending his administrative services in 1897. By the close of the century the university, formerly Transylvania, had brought into its circle of organization a College of Liberal Arts, a College of the Bible, a Normal College, a Commercial College, and the Medical College of Louisville. Some of these, according to the spirit of the times, were given a place in the institution merely to attract students. Kentucky University became Transylvania College in 1907, an act which

---

[7] Alvin F. Lewis, *History of Higher Education in Kentucky* (Washington, 1899), 35-82.

resulted in the passing of the Medical School in 1912 and the Academy in 1914. The College of the Bible, long affiliated with Transylvania College and under the same president, came to an agreement with that college and elected a president of its own in 1938. Dr. Stephen J. Corey was placed at the head of the Bible College, which had in the meantime become a graduate school for the training of ministers. Under the presidency of Dr. K. B. Bowden, in 1947 a site for the Bible College was purchased opposite the campus of the University of Kentucky. Dr. Raymond F. McLain became president of Transylvania College in 1939. The long struggle to reach university status was at last given up; soberly and earnestly the institution now entered upon the career of a high-grade college of liberal arts.

In 1818 the Presbyterians on the Board of Trustees of Transylvania University, regarding influences in Transylvania as dangerous to the young men preparing for the service of the church, resolved to establish an institution free from all contaminating doctrines. The Rev. Samuel K. Nelson, later president of Centre College, was the leader in this movement; and through his enthusiasm for the new college, called Centre, the Synod of Kentucky agreed to be its sponsor. Application for a charter was made to the legislature and was granted on terms unsatisfactory to the Synod, since the college was not placed under the Synod but under a self-perpetuating board composed of prominent public men. The charter bore the date of January 21, 1819. Locating the institution at Danville, Kentucky, it declared that "no religious doctrines peculiar to any one sect of Christians shall be inculcated by any professor in said college."[8] Such a restriction upon theological instruction made the college a general educational enterprise and did not please the rank and file of the church. In consequence, efforts to raise funds brought meager results. The Synod of Kentucky was stirred to its depths by a sermon

[8] Kentucky *Acts, 1818-19*, 618-621.

preached by President Holley on the occasion of the funeral of James Morrison, the benefactor of Transylvania; and, as a consequence of his views, the Presbyterians determined to establish a school of their own. With the consent of the state and the return of the money received for support of the college from the Harrodsburg branch of the Bank of the Commonwealth, the former charter was modified in 1824 and the Synod was given control. By 1830 considerable funds had been raised, and the Presbyterians had for the first time under their direction a strictly denominational institution. A medical department was established at Louisville in 1833, and a law college was added sixty-one years later. In time, Centre College took on some of the characteristics of a university.

The theological seminary, which in 1853 had been made a part of Centre College at Danville, was united in 1901 with the Louisville Theological Seminary (previously established by the Southern Presbyterian Church in 1893) under the name of the Presbyterian Theological Seminary of Kentucky. In May, 1927, the name of the union organization was changed to the Louisville Presbyterian Theological Seminary. This institution is well housed in a beautiful quadrangle on Broadway in Louisville. Since 1920 the presidents who have served the seminary are Charles R. Hemphill, 1910-1920; John W. Vander Meulen, 1920-1930; John B. Cunningham, 1930-1936; and Frank H. Caldwell, since 1936.

The seminary has developed a well-organized system of field work under which a good deal of attention is given to rural churches. A group of churches in southern Indiana furnishes an opportunity for seminary students to work among rural people under the supervision of an experienced director.

The affairs of Centre College paralleled the history of other colleges in Kentucky. The institution was injured by a schism in the church in 1838, and later by the controversy arising from questions involved in slavery. Efforts to increase the endowment, especially in the period 1840-1853, resulted in considerable prosperity for Centre. Its prestige and importance were multiplied by the establishment of the Danville Theological Seminary in 1853. The Civil War interrupted new efforts to increase endowments, but the operations of the college were not materially disturbed by the war. New buildings were added to the campus in 1872; the faculty was increased, and considerable equipment and many books were purchased at that time. The matter of control, so troublesome through the earlier years, had been straightened out; and with the material additions to plant and equipment, as well as an enlarged faculty, the institution hoped to enter upon a new period of prosperity.[9]

But again theological controversy, which had been a cause of disturbance so many times in the history of higher education in Kentucky, broke out in the Presbyterian Church. The Synod of the Southern Presbyterian Church felt that the control of Centre College had passed out of its hands when the courts, to which the northern and southern branches had appealed, awarded the property and endowments of the college to the northern branch of the Presbyterian Church. The Southern Synod accordingly determined, at a meeting held in Louisville in November, 1871, to establish a college under its own control. The simple plan for a college was widened under the influence of citizens who thought there was a place in the state for "a broad and comprehensive University." At a meeting held in Lexington, May 7 and 8, 1872, the verbal spark was applied to the enterprise. "It is the sense of this convention," the resolution read, "that steps be taken to at once establish on a broad and liberal basis, an institution of the highest order under the auspices of the Synod of Kentucky, and thus carry out the earnest wishes of the fathers as demonstrated by the establishment of Centre College now lost to the Church."[10] The loss was the result of differences of view occasioned by slavery and sympathy for the Confederacy. So again, another institution, called Central Uni-

[9] Lewis, *History of Higher Education in Kentucky*, 110-121.
[10] Central University *Catalogue* (1894-95), 4.

versity, sprang from religious and political differences. This institution continued until 1901, when it was merged with the present Centre College at Danville.

The legislature, ever ready to grant charters to any educational enterprise, was quite enthusiastic over the birth of Central University and passed the act required for its incorporation on March 3, 1873. All departments of a university were authorized, and a faculty of theology was created. The charter provided for six preparatory schools to be established in different parts of the state. Before 1891 only one such school had been created; a second was added in that year at Jackson, called the Jackson Collegiate Institute and later Lee's Junior College; in 1892 the Hardin Collegiate Institute at Elizabethtown increased the list; and a fourth, at Middlesboro, named the Middlesboro University School, was started in 1896. It was not until 1873 that a site for Central University, at Richmond, Kentucky, was secured, money raised, and a building erected. The town of Richmond, anxious to have the university established there, raised more than a hundred thousand dollars. Additional funds came from many persons; so Central University had $220,000 with which to begin its career. Under the able and earnest direction of Chancellor R. L. Breck, the university took form, and to its doors a considerable body of students came. In the period of financial disturbances of the seventies, the institution passed through dark days. The coming of Dr. L. H. Blanton to the chancellorship in 1880 raised the hopes of the friends of the university, and considerable sums were added to the endowment. Again, in 1883, a depression suspended the endowment collections, but an earnest seeking of funds brought the university property and endowment to the value of $325,000 by 1896. Central University then had two buildings, a considerable library and equipment. A College of Dentistry was established in Louisville in 1887, and a start made on a School of Theology in 1891. The university was progressing, though handicapped for funds; the student body had reached nearly a thousand in 1898; and at that time the organization included several colleges: arts, law, dentistry, and medicine.[11]

An underground current to unite Central University with Centre College had manifested itself again and again. Several things had worked against the new institution, not only the financial depressions of the seventies, eighties, and nineties, but the fact that its location was so close to the new state college at Lexington. The disagreements also in the Presbyterian state Synod concerning the support of Central University made the future success of the school very doubtful. The conferences for a consolidation were brought to a conclusion in 1901 when Central University was united with Centre College under the name of Central University, at Danville. In 1918 the legislature changed the name, however, to Centre College. The colleges of law, medicine, and dentistry located at Louisville were given up, and Centre College entered upon an increasingly effective and growing period devoted to a program of liberal arts and sciences. On May 9, 1926, the Kentucky College for Women was consolidated with Centre under the name of Centre College of Kentucky. Through the leadership of President Robert L. McLeod, a new endowment has been secured and additional buildings erected on the campus for a larger Centre.

While the Presbyterians struggled to develop a university under their own control, the southern division of the church began in the eighties to emphasize the establishment of secondary schools and colleges. In 1850 a number of churches of this denomination in Louisville which had developed parochial schools gave them up in view of the growth of the public schools in that city. But conditions in the southeastern part of the state caused the Ebenezer Presbytery of the Kentucky Presbyterian Synod to establish a junior college at Pikeville in 1888. Under the administration of Dr. J. T. Record the institution grew to serve the youth in the Kentucky mountains.

[11] Lewis, *History of Higher Education in Kentucky*, 193-210.

Dr. Record died in 1935. The president of the institution today is A. A. Page. In Jackson, Kentucky, Lee's Collegiate Institute was created as a preparatory school for Central University in 1884. Twelve years later the Institute was turned over to the Presbyterian Synod, and it has continued as a junior college. Dr. J. O. Van Meter served as president for many years until he resigned in 1948. In these and other educational ventures, the Presbyterian educational policy in Kentucky, through more than a century, has embraced parochial schools, secondary schools, junior colleges in the mountain area, and finally the consolidation of Centre College and the maintenance of a theological seminary in Louisville.

Baptists in Kentucky established many secondary schools in the state and several colleges during the nineteenth century. A list of such institutions, prepared in 1931, shows thirty-six private Baptist schools and twenty-eight denominational schools. Of this amazing number, only four institutions of college level now remain.[12] As the public high schools developed, the denominational groups quite wisely allowed the closure of the academies which they had created to meet pioneer conditions. As those conditions changed educational needs were materially altered. The colleges referred to are: Georgetown College, Cumberland College, Campbellsville College, and Bethel College. One alone of this group, Georgetown, is accredited as "a senior college." It began as a private school under Baptist auspices in 1787 with Elijah Craig of Georgetown as teacher. In 1798 Professor Craig's classical school was united with Rittenhouse Academy, which had received a land endowment of six thousand acres of state land. This academy, in turn, was absorbed by Georgetown College in 1829, and was incorporated under the name of the Kentucky Baptist Education Society. Issachar Pawling was the first benefactor of the college; his gift of $20,000 gave the new venture a considerable impetus. President Joel

---

[12] Louis B. Traylor, "Baptist Education in Kentucky" (M.A. thesis, University of Kentucky, 1931), 22-25, 28-31.

S. Bacon accepted the post of leadership after three other men, having looked at the place, refused to take up the burden. After a brief administration, he was succeeded by a number of able and conscientious men who, often under great difficulties, kept the school going. In 1851 the charter of the college was changed fundamentally by substituting an enlarged Baptist Education Society for the former close corporation of twenty-four members. Any member of the church who contributed $100 to the Baptist Education Society acquired the right to vote for the trustees of the college, who in turn selected the president and faculty. This plan was unique in college administration and likely to succeed fairly well if the members of the society were of one mind and not given to interfering with the work of the institution. During the first seventy years of its history, the college had eleven presidents, whose average term of service was something more than six years.[18] From Georgetown College a considerable number of graduates have entered business and professional pursuits in the state and nation, acquitting themselves well. The president at this writing is Dr. Samuel Hill.

In 1886 a small group of men representing eighteen Baptist churches came together in a little mountain chapel in eastern Kentucky. Those who attended the meetings were interested in providing an academic education for the children of an area where there were but few institutions offering college instruction. The following year, at Bethlehem, the Mt. Zion Association began the work of collecting funds, with the result that the Williamsburg Institute was opened in that town in 1889. The name of the institution was changed to Cumberland College in 1913. From the first, the sponsors sought adequate endowment; and after a long and difficult struggle a college of junior standing emerged with endowments of a half million dollars and an attractive campus with a number of modern buildings. The college is governed by

[18] Lewis, *History of Higher Education in Kentucky*, 140-165.

a self-perpetuating board of trustees who are independent of the Baptist Education Society.

The Baptist denomination in the South had no theological seminary when the Baptist Convention was constituted in 1845. At a meeting in Louisville in 1857 a decision was made to establish a school for the education of ministers, which resulted in the opening of a seminary at Greenville, South Carolina, in 1859. The coming of the Civil War retarded the institution to such a degree that further operation was suspended in 1862; a new start was made three years later under great difficulties. In 1877 the institution was moved to Louisville. Slowly funds were found with which to erect buildings in that city. These were occupied in 1888. Nearly thirty years later the school moved to a new campus on the outskirts of the city and there found a home in beautiful surroundings and well-designed buildings. From 1859 to 1888 James P. Boyce served as president. He was succeeded by John A. Broadus, who continued as head of the institution until 1895. He was followed by William H. Whitsitt, 1895-1899; E. Y. Mullins, 1899-1928; John R. Sampey, 1929-1942; and Ellis A. Fuller, who has served as president since Dr. Sampey's retirement in 1942.

The Methodist Church in Kentucky was the first of the denominations to establish an institution of learning. This was done under the auspices of Bishop Asbury in 1780, on the banks of the Kentucky River in Jessamine County. The difficulties of Bethel Academy were great, and the project was abandoned. Then, as President E. H. Pearce of Kentucky Wesleyan College said in his inaugural address of 1895, "The journeying ark of educational purpose of the [Methodist] church fathers in Kentucky found rest for a time" at various places, "first at Bethel—then truly in a western wilderness—then at Augusta, then at Lexington, then at Millersburg, and finally at Winchester on the one hand, and Nashville, Tenn., on the other, for Vanderbilt University is the adopted institution of the Louisville Conference, the western portion of the old Kentucky Conference of the Methodist Episcopal Church."[14] (Later, in fact much later, 1915, Vanderbilt University was freed from church control.) Bethel Academy having been abandoned by the Methodists, the idea of a college in northern Kentucky took shape in the establishment of Augusta College in 1821, on the foundation of Bracken Academy. A charter was obtained in 1822; after a quarter of a century of service, the college was abandoned. The Methodists, after giving up their control of Transylvania University in 1850, were without an institution of higher learning. Meantime, the church had been split by the slavery controversy. The southern branch began to make plans for a college, and the conference instructed the citizens of Millersburg to assist in the proposal. In 1823 the Ohio and Kentucky conferences of the Methodist Church had started an institution on the Augusta campus, but the Ohio group withdrew when differences over slavery became acute, and the Kentucky Methodists showed little interest in the school after acquiring Transylvania. After the Civil War the old Augusta College came under the direction of the northern branch of the church, which in 1886 acquired the property of Union College at Barbourville; the collegiate efforts of Augusta then came to an end. Kentucky Wesleyan, the Southern Methodist college, continued at Millersburg until 1889, when lack of endowment induced the commissioners appointed by the church to accept the offer of the citizens of Winchester, who agreed to provide a site of eight acres and $42,000 to erect buildings and purchase equipment. As the years have passed, the struggle of the college to keep going has been conducted by able men; but the institution has faced many problems arising from lack of funds. Now, after nearly one hundred years of separation, the two branches of the church have been united, a union that should reduce friction and bring greater support to the effort of the denomination to maintain institutions of college rank.

[14] *Ibid.*, 125-126.

With the same motive in mind that has been influential in establishing church colleges, the Sue Bennett Memorial School was established at London, Kentucky, by the women of the Methodist Episcopal Church, South, in 1896. After passing through various experiences, the school entered upon a promising career as Sue Bennett College. Miss Oscie Sanders is now president.

At Wilmore, Kentucky, is located Asbury College, founded in 1890 by the Rev. John Wesley Hughes. The college is nominally Methodist. By the constitution, the self-perpetuating board of trustees is bound to operate the college on the doctrinal standards set up and taught by John Wesley and his immediate followers. The institution is coeducational. Dr. Henry C. Morrison, who served as president for many years, was succeeded by Dr. Lewis R. Akers. In 1933 Dr. Morrison returned to office, continuing until 1940, and was followed by Dr. Z. T. Johnson. The college has a considerable campus, large farm lands, and buildings and equipment valued at a million dollars.

Bacon College, destined to play an important part in the history of Kentucky University, was founded by the Disciples of Christ in 1836. This college, like many colleges started in Kentucky, resulted from a controversy. This one led to the resignation of Professor Thornton F. Johnson from the faculty of Georgetown College. A charter similar to that granted to Centre College was issued to Bacon College by the legislature in 1837. The trustees voted to accept the invitation and financial assistance of the citizens of Mercer County, and the first session was opened in Harrodsburg in 1839.[15] The new college, named in honor of Sir Francis Bacon, continued with varying fortunes until 1850. In 1847 the records show 180 students in attendance; yet suspension of the college came at the middle year of the century after its friends had given up all hope for its future.

[15] A. W. Fortune, *The Disciples in Kentucky* (St. Louis, 1932), 182-184, 187, 193-196.

Five years later, the interesting figure of John B. Bowman came into the history of education in Kentucky. His idea was to establish a new institution, "more liberal in all its appointments—permanent in its nature—and auxiliary to the cause of sound morality and pure religion in our State."[16] A new charter placed the government of the institution in the hands of a board of thirty curators, two-thirds of whom were required to be members of the Christian Church in Kentucky. Bowman was energetic in his solicitation of funds for the new Kentucky University. A preparatory department was started in 1857. The institution made good progress, which was interrupted by the loss of the college building by fire in 1864. When this disaster became known, propositions were received from Louisville, Lexington, and Covington. The offer from Lexington was one not easily refused since it provided that the trustees of Transylvania University convey all its property to Kentucky University on the one condition that the institution be located in Lexington. The question of the state's acceptance of the land-grant provisions of the Morrill Act by founding an agricultural and mechanical arts college had been neglected by the legislature. It was, therefore, proposed that a College of Agriculture and Mechanical Arts, financed by Federal funds, be made a department of the university. To do this it was necessary to provide buildings, an experimental farm, and scholarships for three hundred students. By the prompt action of Colonel Bowman, not only was $100,000 raised for the agricultural college, but an additional $30,000 was collected before the legislature adjourned. Thus Kentucky University was revived and, under the joint management of a board representing church and state, began a history lasting thirteen years before the state withdrew from the partnership in 1878.[17]

[16] Lewis, *History of Higher Education in Kentucky*, 85-86.
[17] *Ibid.*, 86-91.

Unlike the other educational institutions in the state, Berea College had its origin without aid of denominational support. The Rev. John G. Fee, who accepted the tenets of the abolitionists' cause, became the pastor of Berea Church, founded in 1855. The school based on the founder's views was started in the same year; its work appealed to an increasing number of friends. The constitution adopted in 1859 said that "This college shall be under an influence strictly Christian, and, as such, opposed to sectarianism, slaveholding, caste, and every other wrong institution or practice." Due to the feelings engendered by John Brown's Raid and the state of public opinion following that event, the school was closed and those connected with it left the state, but in 1865 another charter was secured and the institution was reopened as Berea College.[18] The admission of Negro students resulted in the withdrawal of some of the white students, but the school grew in numbers and continued to admit colored students until the passage of the Day Law in 1904. Under able leadership all through its history, Berea College has made friends and steadily increased its endowment, buildings, grounds, and equipment, until today it has an extensive plant, a large student body, and a wide circle of influence. The plan of educational courses includes the studies of liberal arts and sciences, and adjunct departments of industry, commercial training, teacher training, music, and art. Each student is required to work at least a minimum number of hours each week, and many students are thus able to pay their expenses. Under this policy, the college has established several industries that provide employment for students. Thus Berea College, situated as it is in the foothills of the Kentucky mountains, has devoted its best efforts toward helping the young people of that area to obtain an education. Its work and influence have grown even wider through the extension of its instruction to the adult population and to students in other parts of the

[18] *Ibid.*, 183-185.

country. For twenty-eight years Dr. William G. Frost led this college into new fields of service with a spiritual vision that brought far-reaching results. His great work was taken over by William J. Hutchins in 1920, who was president for nineteen years. Dr. Hutchins was succeeded by his son, Francis S. Hutchins, in 1939. Both men have maintained the ideals of their predecessor with gratifying results.

Higher education in Kentucky under the direction and control of the Catholic Church began with the founding of a little school in Marion County in 1812. Those interested in the establishment of the school for young women became the nucleus of a sisterhood which adopted the name of "Sisters of Loretto" or the "Friends of Mary at the Foot of the Cross." This sisterhood grew apace and founded many schools, not only in Kentucky, but in other states as well. By a charter granted in 1829, Loretto Academy became the Loretto Literary and Benevolent Institute. Nazareth Academy, later Nazareth College, began its history in Nelson County in 1814, and developed in attendance and equipment into a large and well-directed college on a campus located near Bardstown, Kentucky. Early in the century, in the year 1811, the Catholics established a college for priests which found a site near St. Thomas, and later in Bardstown in 1819. This institution, St. Joseph's College, developed an excellent course of study which drew students from the South and Middle West. The Civil War interrupted the growth of the college, with a resultant cessation of operation for several years. The Jesuits withdrew from the management of the college in 1868 and were succeeded by a faculty composed of the secular clergy. The presence of St. Mary's College in an adjoining county brought questions of competition and duplication with the result that the Bishop of Louisville closed the school in 1890 and made St. Mary's College the official successor of St. Joseph's.

In 1821 Father William Byrne opened a school near Lebanon, Kentucky, and called it St. Mary's Seminary. Without funds, he was able by diligence, integrity, and purpose to build the school into one that was accepted by those who sought thorough instruction. "He was president, chief disciplinarian, principal professor, procurator, missionary, everything at the same time." Upon the death of Father Byrne in 1833, the Jesuits came into exclusive control and reorganized the college. The brotherhood continued to direct the institution until 1846, when the secular clergy took over its management. Meantime, the school had acquired wealth, equipment, and reputation. In later days the college devoted its efforts to the training of young men for the priesthood.[19]

Today, the Catholic Church has a college to which young men may go, Villa Madonna, in Covington. In the main, the energies of the church have been directed to the maintenance of excellent secondary schools for boys, and two- and four-year colleges for young women which include Nazareth, Ursuline, Sacred Heart, Villa Madonna, St. Joseph's, and St. Catherine's Junior College. The only church organization in Kentucky that maintains college, secondary, and elementary instruction is the Roman Catholic Church. These institutions and schools are located mainly in the larger urban centers, such as Louisville, Covington, Lexington, and Owensboro. The story of the struggle for more than a century to establish a church school system is an interesting one, though part of it only can be told in these pages.[20]

In 1884 there were thirty-one Catholic institutions enrolling 5,747 pupils in the city of Louisville. Fifty years later the number of parochial schools under the Catholic School Board had doubled, and the enrollment had increased nearly 300 per cent. These schools of secondary education are in the charge of the Sisters of Loretto, Sisters of Charity, Sisters of St. Dominic, the Ursulines, Sisters of Mercy, and the Xaverian Brothers; while the elementary schools were started and maintained as parish enterprises. As far back

[19] *Ibid.*, 133-136.
[20] Louisville *Times*, May 1, 1934.

as 1831 the first Catholic school was established under the pastor of the St. Louis church, the Rev. Robert Abell. To the work of managing the school, Mother Catherine Spalding, who had been cofounder of the Nazareth community, was called. The school became known as the Presentation Academy. St. Benedict Academy, started in 1842 by the Sisters of Loretto, became Loretto High School in 1925. The Jesuit Fathers appeared in Louisville as early as 1836, remaining until 1849; and after disposing of their property, they established a college which they called St. Aloysius College. They sold the property in 1858 and retired from the Kentucky field.

The work in secondary education for boys was taken up by the Xaverian Brothers in Bruges, Belgium, who after various vicissitudes established St. Xavier Institute in Louisville in 1864. The Sacred Heart Academy, located on the Lexington Road near Louisville, began its history when the Ursuline Sisters established an academy for girls in 1859. Favored by a considerable growth, the school has extended its offerings to the junior college level of instruction. Other sisterhoods of the Catholic Church have established academies in Louisville. Holy Rosary Academy began its career in 1867, under the fostering care of the Sisters of St. Dominic; and the Academy of Our Lady of Mercy was originated in 1871 in the parochial school carried on by the Sisters of Mercy. These schools offering secondary instruction have had a history of more than sixty years. A sharp line is drawn between the schools established by Catholic orders and the parish schools. In the latter, the elementary instruction of the children was given by the sisterhood which provided teachers. In other cities of the state, the Catholic parochial schools were established on much the same basis as that of the schools located in Louisville. Since that city has the largest urban population in Kentucky, it possesses the most extensive parochial school system in the state.

A CENTURY OF SECTARIAN EDUCATION 101

In Lexington there are two academies: one for boys, St. Paul's Latin School, and one for girls, St. Catherine's Academy. Each of the two larger parishes maintains and directs a parochial elementary school. At Bardstown there are Nazareth College and Nazareth Academy, with a parish school also in the town. Wherever a considerable population of Catholics is located, the church endeavors to supply educational facilities in which religious instruction may be given.

Information regarding the schools maintained by the Catholic Church in Kentucky is not fully available to the inquirer. The latest aggregate figures showing attendance and instructional staffs come from the United States Office of Education. These figures are for the year 1937-38, and, though now ten years old, are the best available.[21] There were in the state in that year 181 Catholic elementary schools with staffs of 989 persons, religious and lay. The enrollment was given as 16,784 boys and 16,716 girls, or a total of 33,500. The secondary schools numbered 46; the staffs, 394; and the enrollments, 6,266, of which 2,516 were boys and 3,750 girls.

To make the picture more nearly complete, a few additional statistics may be quoted. The State Department of Education reports seventy-four private secondary schools. Of this number, 62 per cent are Catholic. The rest are, in the main, church schools located in the mountain region of the state, though there are a few schools such as the Kentucky Military Institute at Lyndon, the Millersburg Military Academy, and Sayre School in Lexington that are in private hands. Of the junior colleges in Kentucky, three are municipal, six are Protestant maintained, and five are Catholic owned and directed. As standards of instruction have advanced and teacher training has grown in effectiveness, both private and church schools have improved their instruction, equipment, and teaching staffs. In consequence, many of these schools

---

[21] U. S. Office of Education, *Statistics of State School Systems, 1937-38*, Bulletin 1940, No. 2, Chap. 2 (Washington, 1941), 171.

are recognized and placed upon standard lists of the state department and the Southern Association of Colleges and Secondary Schools.

The Sisters of Notre Dame of Covington, Kentucky, have been active in educational work since 1875. When they first came to the United States, at the invitation of the Most Reverend Augustus Maria Toebbe, Bishop of Covington, the diocese was just twenty-one years old. Upon their arrival, the sisters were given charge of the parochial school of "The Mother of God Parish." Within a year's time, they had staffed parish elementary schools in the following places in Kentucky: St. John's and St. Augustine's, Covington; St. John's, Carrollton; St. Augustine's, Augusta; St. Stephen's, Newport; Sacred Heart School, Bellevue; St. Mary's, Alexandria; St. Joseph Orphanage and St. Joseph School, Cold Spring. Later this sisterhood took charge of schools at St. John's, John's Hill, and St. Agnes, at Park Hills. All of these schools are on the elementary level. Enrollments in the beginning were small, usually ranging from twenty to fifty pupils. Very soon, however, the numbers increased; and to-day the enrollments have reached several hundred in some of these schools.

From the outset, the curriculum included not only the rudiments of formal knowledge—religion, grammar, reading, writing, spelling, and arithmetic—but also geography, history, music, nature study, drawing, needlework, and painting.

In the year 1875, when the sisters first arrived in Covington, they purchased a four-story building for residence and at once opened a small private academy. This marks the beginning of Notre Dame Academy, northern Kentucky's largest private school for girls. Besides academic subjects, the Academy conducts classes in sewing, cooking, music, art, science, secretarial studies, dramatic art, and physical training. In 1938 Notre Dame Academy was selected as the practice-teaching school for the students of Villa Madonna College who majored in secondary education. This selection required that the heads of the various departments at the Academy be certified critic teachers. Since 1928 Notre Dame Academy has received an "A" rating from the Southern Association of Colleges and Secondary Schools. In 1943 the Academy was evaluated by a selected staff of the Southern Association and given the rating "Superior."

In 1928, at the instigation of the late Most Reverend Francis W. Howard, Bishop of Covington, the Sisters of Notre Dame, together with the Sisters of St. Benedict and the Congregation of Divine Providence, opened a diocesan college and teacher-training institute, known as Villa Madonna College. At present the Sisters of Notre Dame staff the following departments: science (chemistry, biology, and physics), history, and art. Until 1944 Villa Madonna College was available to women only; since 1945, however, it has opened its doors to men. The College confers the Bachelor of Arts and the Bachelor of Science degrees and teachers' certificates for educational work in Ohio or Kentucky, on both the elementary and secondary levels.

The Sisters of Notre Dame, Covington, maintain a trained staff of teachers in all levels of education: elementary, secondary, and college; and, while holding fast to their fundamental beliefs and ideals, they are endeavoring to keep pace with modern trends in education. From their convent on Dixie Highway, they also staff a number of large and small schools in greater Cincinnati and a mission field in Alabama and in Nebraska.[22]

Within a radius of twenty-five miles about the city of Covington there are a considerable number of parish schools and colleges under the various organizations of the Catholic Church. "During its seventy-nine years of work, the community has been placed in charge of thirteen parish schools

---

[22] Notes from the Rev. Thomas A. McCarty, Dean of Villa Madonna College, March 4, 1947.

and one catechistical school in the Diocese of Covington."[23] The enrollment of these schools in 1938 was 2,857. The first definite course of study issued by the community appeared in 1906. In 1918 improvement in the study course and uniform textbooks were prescribed. Five years later a diocesan school board was organized and a course of study drawn up for the use of all the Catholic elementary schools in the diocese. Thus, according to the writer of the thesis quoted above, the plan of study "fulfills the requirements of the Kentucky State Board of Education, and in following it every effort is made toward the improvement of methods and means, in order to obtain the best results in teaching." The schools under the diocesan board are making progress; but as in other schools, both public and private, there is need for better equipment, efficient supervision, and extended teacher training.

This chapter has shown the drifts and trends of church-directed education within the state of Kentucky; though space does not permit further consideration of the part which every college and school has played throughout an active century of sectarian education, the main story has been covered. Now and then, a man inspired by vision started a school in the wilderness which through the devotion of himself and his followers grew into a college. Denominations seeking to impress youth with the purposes of a Christian life did not rest until they had colleges under their own control.

When there was no adequate public school system, before the middle of the nineteenth century, literally hundreds of elementary schools were set up in the towns and villages of the state by private organizations, churches, and individuals. The colleges too were numerous, and many were born only to die. Those that were hardy enough to weather the difficult years often suffered destruction of buildings by fire, loss of endowments, constant changes in presidents and faculties, and

---

[23] Sister Mary Catherine Bramlage, O.S.B., "Origin, History, and Educational Activities of the Benedictine Sisters of Covington, Kentucky" (M.A. thesis, Notre Dame University, 1938).

schisms in the churches that should have fostered and supported them. The sifting process of time, the better understanding of educational procedure, an increasing support of private and public institutions, and a growing tolerance among religious sects have removed many obstacles which confronted education in the state during the past century. Thus the outlook and opportunities for advanced learning in Kentucky show more promise today than at any previous time in history, even in the face of the difficulties following World War II.

CHAPTER VII

AND FINALLY A STATE UNIVERSITY

THE REAL part taken by the State University in the history of education in Kentucky may be said to have begun in 1878, when the legislature re-created the Agricultural and Mechanical College after separating it from Kentucky University and placed the new institution under complete state control. Prior to that time, the educational institution established by the provisions of the Morrill Act of 1862 had been amalgamated with Kentucky University, which started a promising career in 1865 with the union of Transylvania University and Bacon College and the use of the funds provided by the Morrill Act. In 1863, a year after the passage of the Morrill Act, the legislature of Kentucky enacted a law making the members of the State Board of Agriculture a body of commissioners to examine and report to the next General Assembly upon the advantages and inducements to be offered for the location of the state agricultural college.[1] The commissioners advertised for bids, but none were received except that of Transylvania University. Again the commissioners advertised, but with the same result. This time they agreed to recommend the acceptance of the Transylvania offer. A bill was reported agreeing to the proposal, and the State Senate voted favorably; the House, however, listening to suggestions for delay, failed to pass the bill.

In 1865 the governor approved an enactment consolidating Transylvania University with Kentucky University; a few days before, a bill had passed which made the Agricultural and Mechanical College part of Kentucky Uni-

[1] Kentucky *Acts, 1863,* 370.

versity. By these two acts, a paper university came into the possession of Transylvania which secured practical control of the new agricultural college. Thus the use of a considerable foundation for the land-grant college went over to the maintenance and enlargement of a sectarian institution. With this arrangement began a trial of state and church control that led to controversies and the final withdrawal on the part of the state, with a loss of everything that had been put into the new enterprise by the state except the land grant from the Federal government. It is difficult from the vantage ground of today to understand such maneuvering. The idea of a state institution of higher learning free from denominational control was not grasped by the leaders of that time, for denominational direction of Kentucky University was close to the hearts of those who sponsored it.

At least it may be stated that John B. Bowman, the regent of the university, saw rather clearly the possibilities of the incorporation of the land-grant college as one of the colleges of his Kentucky University. Later, the regent said that "I entered into this arrangement upon my individual responsibility, and without the knowledge or action of its curators, and against the almost unanimous judgment of the special friends of the Institution." His object, Bowman further declared, was "to build up eventually, a great, liberal institution, which while under the auspices of the Christian Church, was to be unsectarian and unsectional; to cheapen and widen the system of higher education, so that the humblest youth in all the land could enter it, and receive such education, general or technical, as would qualify him for any business of life."[2] The act to establish an agricultural college stated that Kentucky University should provide $100,000, in addition to the funds and properties belonging to Transylvania, with which to buy a farm and erect college buildings thereon.[3]

[2] Merry Lewis Pence, "The University of Kentucky, 1866-1936" (manuscript, Lexington, 1936), Pt. I, 8. [3] Kentucky *Acts, 1865,* I, 45-48.

Regent Bowman at once went to work to raise the money required by the act. In three months' time he had secured a total of $112,000. The donations, for the most part, were made by citizens of Lexington and Fayette County. With these funds the Regent purchased the Henry Clay estate for $85,000 and Woodlands, 109 acres belonging to J. B. Tilford, the two tracts making a farm of 433 acres on the edge of Lexington. Meantime, the Federal land scrip belonging to the agricultural college was sold at fifty cents per acre, yielding $165,000. This sale was a great disappointment to the friends of the college, who expected at least $330,000 for the endowment. The state received the money and, in characteristic fashion (as it had done in 1837 with the schools' share of the surplus revenue distributed by the Federal government), placed it in the state treasury, spent the amount, and issued a perpetual 6 per cent bond to the curators. When the institution, called Kentucky University, was opened in October, 1865, the three colleges, Law, Bible, and Arts and Sciences, were ready to receive students. The following year, the Agricultural and Mechanical College was organized and became a part of the new university. Under such arrangements the agricultural college began its history as a part of Kentucky University. The first president was Dr. John Augustus Williams, who served one year and then resigned to accept the presidency of Daughters' College at Harrodsburg. His successor, Joseph Desha Pickett, occupied the office for two years; and in 1869 Dr. James Kennedy Patterson was elected to the presidency. He served through the Kentucky University period ending in 1878 and through that of the State Agricultural and Mechanical College, 1878-1908. Dr. Patterson retired in 1910, two years after the legislature had created the State University of Kentucky from the agricultural college and its associated activities.

The interest of the leading farmers of the state in the establishment of a college of agriculture goes back as far as 1838, when the newly formed State Agricultural Society, meeting in Frankfort, appointed a committee to draft resolutions calling on the legislature to support a school for the instruction of the sons of farmers in the art of agriculture.[4] The committee consisted of James T. Morehead, John Lewis, C. J. Blackburn, and Thomas B. Stevenson. The recommendations proposed by the committee quoted with approval a memorial of Charles Lewis Fleischman, a graduate of the Royal Agricultural School of Bavaria. This document had been printed by order of the Congress of the United States for distribution among the people.

"In order," the Bavarian said in his memorial, "to diffuse the science of agriculture properly, so that every branch would affect all others advantageously and the whole system of this important science become perfected, it was found necessary to erect SCHOOLS and educate young men scientifically and practically. Such schools were established on large, properly conducted farms, where all the sciences were taught connected with agriculture, illustrating the practical manipulations in the fields, barns, stables, &c., together with the use of all the implements and machines as well as all the minutest branches of husbandry.

"Deeply impressed therefore, with these considerations; your memorialists pray the passage of a law establishing and endowing a SCHOOL OF AGRICULTURE for the State of Kentucky, in which the theory and practice—the science and the art of agriculture in all its departments—may be thoroughly taught to the sons of the state who may desire a finished education to fit them to pursue intelligently and successfully, the dignified and independent profession of husbandry. Such an institution, in point of fact, would be a most important part of the system of internal improvement; and the appropriation of only four thousand dollars a year for thirty years, it is confidently believed, would not only command the funds necessary to obtain a suitable farm, erect the

[4] *Franklin Farmer* (Frankfort, Kentucky, 1838-1840), I (1838-1839), 257; II (1839-1840), 156-157.

proper buildings, and pay the professors, but return the principal together with the whole of the annual appropriations at the end of that time, leaving the school in a situation to need no further endowment or aid whatever, but capable of sustaining itself in its high station of utility to the people of the Commonwealth. The data on which this statement is submitted, will be respectfully presented to a committee of the Legislature, by your memorialists. And surely, if the object prayed for is thus easily attainable, the agricultural interest of Kentucky, which pays nearly all the revenue of the state, which gives it stability and prosperity at home and credit abroad, makes but a small claim on the Legislature to accomplish so desirable an improvement in the condition of far the largest class of community and in the modes of productions of husbandry, and which will favorably affect the interests of every class of people. All of which is most respectfully submitted and your memorialists, as in duty bound, will ever pray."[5]

Evidently the memorial made some impression upon Governor Charles A. Wickliffe since he commented on it and the work of the State Agricultural Society in his message. "Kentucky is," said he, "and must ever be, an agricultural state." Governor Wickliffe was the last governor to suggest instruction in agriculture and the appropriation of money to support it until 1863, when Governor James F. Robinson called the attention of the legislature to the Morrill Act and the wisdom of accepting the offer of the Federal government.

The new university, made up of varying educational segments under the control of a Board of Governors, two-thirds of whom were to be communicants of the Christian Church, gathered momentum and reputation in the first five years of its history. The resources of the institution increased rapidly. Transylvania brought to the union buildings and grounds valued at $100,000, and cash of $70,000. The land

[5] *Ibid.,* II (1839-1840), 157.

allotment of the Agricultural and Mechanical College produced $165,000, which with donations and lands gathered by John B. Bowman made a total of nearly a million dollars.[6] In 1868 and 1869 the enrollment of Kentucky University reached a high point. The number of students in the latter year was 772, of whom 300 were enrolled in the Agricultural and Mechanical College. Evil days were soon to fall upon the university, for in ten years the attendance in all the colleges of the institution dropped to 196 students. The cause of this decline was the division among the officers, professors, and friends of the university over sectarian questions. With the spreading of the quarrels to the whole state, the regent, Dr. Bowman, was involved. The controversy became so bitter and personal that the very existence of the university was seriously menaced.

As early as 1867 the legislature showed some interest in the state's part in the university, for a resolution was adopted authorizing the appointment of a committee to investigate the affairs of the Agricultural and Mechanical College to ascertain whether the law creating it was being disregarded and if the institution was controlled by a religious sect for sectarian ends and purposes. "This," the resolution stated, "is giving great dissatisfaction."[7]

The records show no report from that committee; but in the session of 1872 a committee of five was appointed to ascertain for the Assembly whether the contract between Kentucky University and the state was being complied with. "We are of the opinion," said the committee when it made its report, "that the contract has not been violated, and in view of that opinion, it is not desirable to take the interest on the agricultural fund from the University . . . which would be an attempt to injure a great college which is not only nonsectarian, but broad, catholic, and comprehensive in its spirit

[6] Mabel H. Pollitt, *A Biography of James Kennedy Patterson* . . . (Louisville, 1925), 86-87.
[7] Kentucky *Acts, 1867*, I, 76.

and scope."⁸ It is to be doubted that the report was in accordance with the facts, because the feeling in the university and in the public mind had increased in bitterness. Meantime, Regent Bowman was losing ground and the university was on the downgrade. The matter came up again in 1874, but it remained for the legislature of 1878 to take drastic action. The resolution adopted declared it was most important to know what was going on; to that end a committee of twelve was appointed to visit the Agricultural and Mechanical College with full power to take the testimony of any and all under oath.⁹ The committee made an extended report recommending that the union between the College of Agriculture and the university be dissolved. An act was passed March 13, 1878, repealing the previous legislation authorizing the union, and providing that the "said Agricultural and Mechanical College shall forever remain a State institution, free from all ecclesiastical entanglements or control." This legislation was far in advance of any action taken by the lawmakers for the benefit of a college owned by the state.¹⁰ The lessons of the past had brought some light to the people of Kentucky who looked forward to a progressive commonwealth.¹¹

Between the date of separation and the location and establishment of the new State College there was much to be done. An agreement was made to continue the college on its former location; the university consented to accept the work of the college; and the college, in turn, was to share some of its instructors with Kentucky University. The commission created under the act of 1878 met in Louisville, August 14, 1879, for the purpose of examining proposals for the

---

⁸ *Ibid., 1871-72*, I, 98; Kentucky, General Assembly, *House Journal, 1871-72*, 910.

⁹ Kentucky *Acts, 1877-78*, I, 155.

¹⁰ *Ibid.*, I, 46-51.

¹¹ Detailed information may be found in the following typed histories and reports in the University of Kentucky Library: Robert Peter, "Kentucky University and Transylvania University"; Merry Lewis Pence, "The University of Kentucky, 1866-1936"; and George Roberts, "University of Kentucky, a Brief History, Its Organization and Its Function in the Commonwealth" (Lexington, 1933).

permanent location of the new independent Agricultural and Mechanical College. The offers came from Ogden College in Bowling Green and from Lexington. The latter location was accepted since, in the opinion of the commissioners, it offered the most advantages. Lexington agreed to give $30,000 in bonds and the city park of fifty-two acres; Fayette County supplemented the offer by agreeing to provide the proceeds from the sale of $20,000 in bonds. By legislative act, the offers of Lexington and Fayette County were accepted, and a board of trustees was created to govern, administer, and control the college. The board consisted of the governor, twelve men, "discreet, intelligent and prudent," who with the advice and consent of the Senate were appointed for a six-year term, and four alumni to be appointed for a similar term when the graduates of the college should exceed one hundred. In the act was a provision entitling each state representative district to send two properly prepared students to the institution free of tuition.[12] This arrangement continued until it was declared unconstitutional by the Court of Appeals in 1917.[13] In addition to the legislative scholarship, each county in the state was entitled to send students who had been engaged in teaching to the college without the payment of tuition. To provide funds for the conduct of the college, an act authorized the levying of a tax of one-half cent on each one hundred dollars of real and personal property valuations in the state.[14]

Now that the separation from Kentucky University had been made legal in 1878 by the General Assembly in a series of acts, and the Court of Appeals had ruled against the claim of the college for the lands and buildings provided by the money raised by Regent Bowman, the State College was without a home where its work could be carried on. The executive committee accepted the offer of the Northern Bank of Kentucky, receiving $54,062.50 for the bonds issued by the city

[12] Kentucky *Acts, 1879-80,* I, 28-42.
[13] Barker, President, et al. *v.* Crum, et al., 177 *Kentucky Reports* 637.
[14] Kentucky *Acts, 1879-80,* I, 137-138.

of Lexington and the county of Fayette. With funds from the land grants and the proceeds of the half-cent tax, the institution's operating costs were provided for. The executive committee of the board was directed to submit plans, specifications, and estimates for a president's house and three college buildings. On October 28, 1880, the cornerstone of the main building was laid. The construction went on slowly owing to the inability of the college to make regular payments. Finally, the funds were exhausted; and President Patterson, determining to push on with the construction, pledged all his savings to support a loan of $7,000. With this new stimulus considerable progress was made, and the college was able to move into its new quarters by February 13, 1882.

Such an event was not allowed to pass unnoticed; and promptly, on February 15, a notable program of dedication was carried through with a procession, speeches, and a banquet. On the day of the dedication, "the sun rose bright and beautiful," wrote the scribe who reported the event. And it "smiled benignantly upon the occasion of the assembling of so many distinguished guests in the city for the purpose of inaugurating the new Agricultural and Mechanical College." It was a great day, ushered in by the procession headed by the college trustees and the faculty, followed by Currier's band from Cincinnati and the cadet corps. Then came the carriages containing Governor Luke P. Blackburn, Lieutenant Governor Cantrill, Governor Meriwether, Speaker Owens, Senators Robbins and Edwards, Representatives Clarke and Jones, and not least of all, the Honorable Henry Watterson, orator of the day. The Lexington Light Guards followed, with invited guests and citizens bringing up the rear. Orator Watterson was eloquent as always: "I say that Kentucky cannot escape her destiny which is fixed by her geography. That on this account, higher standards of education and the more general instruction of the masses are indispensable to the development of our material resources, and that our future absolutely depends, for good or ill, upon the direction which is given to this development." Governor Blackburn approved heartily of the new educational adventure, saying so in the address which followed Henry Watterson's oration. Senator Beck also spoke, as did the Honorable J. H. Mulligan. "The day closed with a banquet which was a magnificent affair at the Hotel Phoenix."[15]

It was Superintendent H. A. M. Henderson who, in his report dated June 30, 1879, attacked the new setup of the Agricultural and Mechanical College by declaring that the support of the institution rested upon the school funds of the state and "was not justified in the dedication of our resources to the support of academies and colleges." This protest against the college was followed by others, in particular one appearing in the Louisville *Courier-Journal* showing that the same spirit and motives were still at work which had dominated education in the evil days when so much harm had been done to Transylvania University.[16] The protest was centered on the half-cent tax and declared that "it was bad enough to tax the many for the few; it was still worse to tax the poor for the benefit of the rich." The matter was brought before the legislature on January 22, 1882. President Patterson, unable to secure first-class legal talent, took on the role of advocate for the cause of the college and made a remarkable speech that cleared the mind of the legislature and gave its members a vision of the educational policy the state should follow.[17]

The controversy was not ended by this incident, however, for Judge William Lindsey appeared before the Legislative Joint Committee, on the evening of January 25, to argue against the constitutionality of the half-cent tax. Five days later, President Patterson answered the argument of Judge Lindsey; and the consensus was that the tax would not be repealed. Repeatedly, in the sessions of the Assembly, bills were presented to repeal the tax. Following the hearings

[15] Louisville *Courier-Journal*, February 16, 1882.
[16] *Ibid.*, November 18, 1891.   [17] Lexington *Daily Press*, January 22, 1882.

referred to above, such a bill was introduced in the House, February 23, 1882. That bill was defeated and a similar bill in the Senate suffered the same fate. Again in 1884, 1888, and 1890 bills were offered by opponents of the college, either to dissolve the college or to discontinue the state's support; these bills, however, were defeated. From 1890 on into the next century, bills were enacted by the legislature authorizing the appointment of investigating committees to look into the management of the college and, particularly, to inquire about the expenditure of moneys. In the 1890 report of the investigating committee, the income of the institution was shown to be $39,300, including $15,000 from the Federal government for the maintenance of the Experiment Station. The value of the buildings and grounds was estimated at $293,000.[18] From time to time criticisms appeared in the press reflecting on the conduct of the college or its failure to meet everyone's expectations. As late as 1907 the president said in his report to the Superintendent of Public Instruction, "During the earlier years of the existence of the college, the matriculates of the preparatory department far surpassed in numbers those in the college proper." The ratio was four to one; but as high schools grew in number and attendance, the college student body materially increased. In 1907 the income of the institution had multiplied nearly five times and amounted to $190,457.

A suit had been entered in the Chancery Court in Louisville against the payment of the half-cent tax; and in the Magoffin County Circuit Court a similar suit had been brought. In both courts the validity of the tax was upheld by the presiding judges. Both decisions, rendered in 1882, were carried to the Court of Appeals which held the case until December 9, 1890, when the court, with one dissenting opinion, upheld the decisions of the lower courts.[19] It was fortunate for the welfare of the college that the decision of

[18] Kentucky *Acts, 1890,* ch. 5.
[19] 91 *Kentucky Reports* 6.

the Court of Appeals was made public on the eve of the meeting of the fourth constitutional convention. Despite the court's decision, efforts were made to have the convention frame a section in the new document prohibiting aid in behalf of public higher education. The section dealing with education approved of the half-cent tax for the support of the college and confirmed its continuance and location within the city of Lexington. Thus twenty years of controversy over the legal status of the State College came to an end. Mutterings about ungodly institutions were still to be heard, and opposition appeared in legislative sessions; but the hostility to the college from sectarian sources became weaker and weaker until by 1900 it had ceased to be impressive. The people had adopted the idea that public higher education and church-related enterprises in the field of education could work together, each supplementing the efforts of the other. Particularly was this true as the demands for professional training grew with the rapid industrial development of the nation. The church-related colleges have come to recognize the changing conditions and to realize that most of them cannot offer the technical training and graduate studies so important today.

The acceptance of the Morrill Act placed the obligation upon the state to support the Agricultural and Mechanical College, which after many ups and downs was fully recognized by the legislation of 1878 and 1880. It was certain, as the land-grant colleges came to realize their specific purpose, that attention would be given to the application of science to agriculture. Prior to the time of the passage of the Hatch Act, the executive committee of the college had ordered by resolution the establishment of an experiment station. Professor M. A. Scovell was appointed director at a salary of $1,500, and Dr. Robert Peter was made professor of chemistry. The legislature, in 1886, had recognized the station and passed an act regulating the sale of fertilizers. The fees for analysis and those from the sale of identification tags were to be paid to the treasurer of the college for the support of the station. In 1887 the United States Congress passed the Hatch Act providing for the establishment of an agricultural experiment station in each of the states and territories. Additional Federal support was provided by the Adams Act in 1906, which brought to each station $30,000 annually. The legislature promptly accepted the Federal grant at the first session following its passage.[20] Further legislation for the benefit of the land-grant colleges was enacted with the passage of the Nelson amendment in 1908, by which $25,000 was added annually to previous appropriations from the Federal treasury. These additions to the station's support were markedly increased by the fees from the pure seed law and by an annual appropriation of $50,000 provided by the legislature.[21]

With growing equipment, enlarged farm areas, and a better trained staff, the Kentucky Experiment Station has made great progress throughout the years. Many experiments in agronomy, animal husbandry, horticulture, plant breeding, and farm management have been of tremendous value to the farmers of the state. The work done by the trained experts, men and women of the staff, has received both national and international recognition. For twenty-seven years Dr. Scovell served ably as director; he was followed by Dr. Joseph H. Kastle, whose term of direction ended with his death in 1916. In 1918 Dr. Thomas Poe Cooper was appointed the new director, and under his management the station has grown in reputation and in the amount of work accomplished. The First World War brought heavy responsibilities to the station which were later increased by the depression, and again by the new demands for conservation and food production imposed by the Second World War. To the station, property was added by the gift of E. O. Robinson and F. W. Mowbray in 1924, a tract of 15,000 acres in Perry, Breathitt, and Knott counties. Here a substation has now been established where much important work has been done. In the western end

[20] Kentucky *Acts, 1908*, ch. 11, p. 42.
[21] *Ibid., 1912*, ch. 26, p. 134.

of the state, at Princeton, a second substation was located in the same year; and by these provisions the state has come into the possession of a well-rounded agricultural experimental system.

Supplementary to the acts establishing the experiment stations, Congress passed in 1914 what was called, after the authors, the Smith-Lever Act. The purpose of this law was to bring the work of the stations to the attention of the farmers so that the information worked out by the experts might be carried into the practice of agriculture. As time passed, Congress increased the appropriations for the conduct of agricultural extension which were met in part by the state, resulting in a great increase in the number of county agents and home demonstration agents. This work has spread over the entire state so that every county is now provided with an agent. The passage of the various Federal acts providing for the regulation of production and the conservation of lands in 1931-1938 have increased the work of the Kentucky Division of Agricultural Extension. The staff today is a large one, but through the organization of the Agricultural College, the present Station, and the Extension Division under one direction, the work in agriculture has proven to be of great advantage to the state.

As far back as 1897 the proposal to change the name of the institution from that of college to university had been concurred in by the board of trustees. It was not until a meeting of the board on December 10, 1907, that a committee, appointed the year before, made a report based upon the results of a conference with the curators of Kentucky University. Unless the curators would accept an arrangement for the change of name, the State College could not assume the title, University of Kentucky. It was agreed that Kentucky University should surrender its name upon the payment of $5,000 with which to meet the costs of advertising and printing occasioned by this change. After more than a half century of effort, the transfer of name was recorded in a long legislative chapter, giving the institution a university status.[22] During four-fifths of this long period, the college had been guided by President Patterson, ably and aggressively. Two years later, in 1910, Dr. Patterson presented his resignation, an interesting document in which he included requests for a retirement salary, status as a president emeritus, a place on the Board of Trustees and in the faculty, the privilege of representing the university at various meetings, and the right to occupy the presidential house upon the payment of an annual rental. All of these requests were granted; and Judge Henry S. Barker, upon the expiration of his term on the Court of Appeals, assumed the duties of president on January 1, 1911.

During his presidency, Dr. Barker was confronted with many difficulties. A controversy with his predecessor and the withdrawal of the Carnegie Foundation for the Advancement of Teaching from the consideration of the university as a member of the pension plan added to the problems of the institution. "These effects with their cause and all coupled with various evil conditions that had arisen in the University resulted in great harm to this institution."[23] Such was the comment of a member of the staff who served the university with ability and loyalty during these difficult years, but it may be said in all fairness to Judge Barker that the opinion of the commentator referred to above was a severe one. When President Patterson retired, he placed in his resignation certain conditions and asked for privileges which brought him into university policy as a critic despite the fact that President Barker was the choice of Dr. Patterson, who preferred him over the campus candidates for president of the institution. In his criticism of his successor Dr. Patterson contended that he was not a man of education and did not have the will to deal with the problems then confronting the university. All of this was known before the election of Judge Barker as president of the university. His friends said he had two

[22] *Ibid., 1908,* ch. 3, p. 4.
[23] Pence, "The University of Kentucky," Pt. III, 11.

weaknesses: one, kindness of heart, and the other, too great a disposition to delegate authority to the deans and the business agent. Failing to hold on to the purse strings of the university funds, the new president lost much of his control of institutional policy, which brought on conflicts between the deans of the colleges. In addition, his predecessor proved unwilling to keep hands off and in various ways stalled and checked the new administration. During the Barker regime, attendance of students doubled, while the president preached good will and urged the promotion of agriculture in the state. President Barker had fine qualities which under other circumstances would have carried him on to a helpful administration, but the conditions of his appointment and hostile trustees, faculty, and alumni limited and hampered the work he so earnestly desired to do.

At the meeting of the board of trustees on January 17, 1917, the chairman, Governor A. O. Stanley, announced that he would appoint an investigating committee, "since there were maladjustments seriously affecting the welfare of the institution." The members of this committee were Robert G. Gordon, J. A. Ammon, H. M. Froman, J. I. Lyle, and James W. Turner. At its meeting in Frankfort, February 17, 1917, the committee concluded that, in order to make an intelligent recommendation to the board, it should have the benefit of a study of the university by competent college men. The dean of the College of Liberal Arts and Sciences, University of Illinois, Charles K. Babcock, Thomas F. Kane, president of Olivet College, and Charles M. McCann, of the University of Illinois, were asked to make the study. The board's committee took its commission seriously, held many meetings, and interviewed 150 persons; its report was combined with the findings of the Survey Commission. The investigating committee approved the report with three exceptions: first, the continuance of Dean Anderson as head of the combined College of Engineering; second, the retirement of Dean Rowe at once; third, the continued residence of

President Patterson on the campus. The investigating committee recommended the retirement of President Barker to take effect on the first day of September, 1917.[24] Meantime, a committee appointed by the board was authorized to find a successor to Judge Barker. This committee was composed of R. C. Stoll, chairman and trustee; R. G. Gordon; F. M. McKee and J. I. Lyle, trustees; Dean P. P. Boyd; Professor W. E. Freeman; and George Roberts, acting dean of the College of Agriculture. At a special meeting of the board of trustees, August 15, 1917, the nominating committee made its report and recommended Dr. Frank L. McVey, president of the University of North Dakota. President McVey accepted the position by letter, August 27, 1917, and began his service of twenty-three years in September, 1917. In 1940, he retired from office and was succeeded by an acting president, Dean Thomas P. Cooper, who continued in office one year. Dr. Herman L. Donovan, president of Eastern State Teachers' College, was elected to the office of president of the University of Kentucky in 1941. President Donovan began his presidency on July 1, 1941.

The report of the Survey Commission, 1917, was both a charter and a guide; for the document suggested what measures must be taken to shake the institution out of its lethargy and to enlarge its service to the state. When President McVey came to the university, the First World War was in its third year; and in the following April, 1918, the educational institutions of the country were called upon by the Federal government to contribute to the national defense. In that effort, the University of Kentucky conducted a Student Military Training Corps and, as an additional service, instructed men in motor mechanics, electricity, carpentry, and military science. More than three thousand men were trained at the university, and many of her alumni and students entered the armed forces of the nation. The peace which came in

[24] University of Kentucky *Bulletin*, X, No. 5 (July, 1917).

November, 1918, found the campus torn up, ugly wooden buildings marring the grounds, the student body scattered, and the curriculum disorganized. These difficulties, however, were met rapidly, and a semblance of order and neatness was soon restored on the campus. In the meantime, the people of the state were showing a willingness to co-operate in the growth of the university. The legislature meeting in 1918 granted funds for the university, the first real appropriation since 1907 when $200,000 had been appropriated for buildings.[25] In 1924 additional support was provided in Chapter 116 of the Kentucky Acts by granting a part of the inheritance taxes for the maintenance of institutions of public higher education. Two years later the proportion was increased; and these institutions had for the first time in their history a considerable income. With the passage of the Reorganization Act and the establishment of a real budget system, the institutions were placed upon biennial appropriations which fell much below that which they had received under the direct tax for their support. As the state becomes more prosperous and the state debt is no longer a menace, the support for the university should more nearly meet its growing demands.

In its seventy-five years of history, the university has passed through the stages of what would now be called a junior college, 1865 to 1882; a college with three principal divisions of Arts, Engineering, and Agriculture, 1882 to 1907; a small and limited university, 1907 to 1920; and finally, into the larger status of a real state university, with graduate work and research provided. In 1917 there was a library of 22,000 volumes, a student body of 1,204, a farm of 254 acres, and eleven buildings. In 1945 the library had become the largest one in Kentucky with 367,000 volumes; the campus had grown to 106 acres; the experiment farm at Lexington, to 605 acres; the substation at Quicksand, to 15,000 acres; and the Princeton substation, to 519 acres. The buildings devoted to educational purposes numbered forty-two; the staff of

---

[25] Kentucky *Acts, 1918*, ch. 4, pp. 11-15.

teachers, experts, and experiment station and extension workers had increased to 800 persons. The income of the university from all sources and for all purposes was approximately $2,400,000. From 1917 to 1945, the course offerings had been materially increased in the seven colleges composing the university, and the student body had grown to 6,242. Progress had been made in the number and equipment of the laboratories; this statement applies also to the museums and the materials gathered within them. A real pride in the university has taken the place of the opposition and criticism of earlier days. It has become in reality a great state university, although faced still with many problems and with much yet to be accomplished in service to the state which founded it.

A second world war befell the country five months after Dr. Donovan had begun his work as president of the university. The governments of the states and of the nation again called upon the universities and colleges to aid the war effort. The record of the University of Kentucky in the last great conflict is an honorable one and presents an amazing story. Much of what was done during this war period was due to the leadership, courage, and farsightedness of the new president who has given his strength and ability at all times that the university might be worthy of the trust placed in it by the people of Kentucky.

CHAPTER VIII

THE FALLS CITY EVOLVES AN URBAN UNIVERSITY

To FIND a word that will describe the history of the University of Louisville, a seat of learning that began with an idea and became a fact, is not an easy procedure. The dictionary gives as a synonym for "evolve" the word "disentangle," which describes more than any other word what took place in the development of the University of Louisville.

In 1937 this university celebrated its one-hundredth anniversary with an interesting and effective program of lectures, exhibits, and convocations. It is a far cry from this date to the land-grant period and the sordid story of medical education when the university gathered the numerous medical colleges operating in the city into one effective medical school. In a lesser degree, the law school situation in Louisville passed through much the same course, and also the dental school, organized as a proprietary institution and acquired by the university in 1918. A College of Arts and Sciences did not come into the orbit of the university until 1907. Consequently, the University of Louisville at the opening of the century consisted only of a medical school and a law school. These went on their way with little or no recognition of a joint purpose, though ostensibly under the auspices of the same board of trustees.[1]

In true American style, a remote date for the origin of the University of Louisville has come to be established in the public mind; and so, by courtesy, that institution is referred

---

[1] Kentucky Writers' Project of the Work Projects Administration, *A Centennial History of the University of Louisville* (Louisville, 1939), 117.

to as the oldest urban university in this country. As a matter of fact, its beginnings are really centered about the year 1907. Strangely enough, that very year the State Agricultural and Mechanical College was reorganized and became the State University of Kentucky. What happened in Louisville was not unlike what had taken place in the development of other institutions of higher learning in Kentucky and elsewhere.

There is a definite purpose in making this comment on early origins since the acceptance of remote dates of establishment raises the question: Why did such an institution take so many years to develop into an effective educational agency? The answer is that very few schools actually had their beginnings at the dates given by the traditionalists. It was natural enough that leaders among the pioneers should wish to have a school where promising youth could acquire some college and professional training without going to distant places. Itinerant schoolmasters encouraged such ambitions, and legislatures made grants of land to give some support to the schools that were established to meet the hopes of the people. However, little in the form of taxes, contributions, or fees was forthcoming to maintain these educational ventures. So the proprietary type of professional school came into existence to meet the need and to supplement the incomes of those who taught in them. Many institutions supported by churches languished or passed through short periods of progress only to fall by the wayside; others were revived and continued their difficult existence in the hope that better times would come.

Harrodsburg is generally conceded to have the honor of being the first permanent town in Kentucky. Nevertheless, Louisville claims that it was the first town located and laid out with future settlement in mind. In July, 1773, Captain Thomas Bullitt, acting under a commission from William and Mary College, surveyed a tract of land, 2,000 acres in extent, opposite the Falls of the Ohio, and there laid out a town site. The surveyed land was not appraised by the county surveyor, but Lord Dunmore gave it to his friend Dr. John Connolly in 1773. Many colonists followed General George Rogers Clark when he built a stockade and cabin on Corn Island in the Ohio River. This was in 1778. During the succeeding winter, the settlers moved to the mainland and established themselves within the present site of Louisville. Having organized a town government in 1779, this practical move was followed by an act of forfeiture in which it was declared that the British sympathizer, Dr. Connolly, was deprived of his rights by the Virginia legislature in 1780, and the name of the town was changed to Louisville in honor of the King of France, Louis XVI. The town grew apace, for the Falls of the Ohio forced a transfer of passengers and freight going either downstream to points farther south or to places on the upper Ohio. Such a break in transportation soon made Louisville a place where accommodations for travelers, warehouses and storage facilities, boat yards, construction of barges and the repair of shipping, and trafficking on the river developed into flourishing industries. Louisville was engaged in laying a broad foundation for a business and manufacturing development that would make the city not only the largest municipality in the state but would create contacts and commercial relations in the South.

When the steamboat had succeeded the heavy barges and the keel craft laboriously propelled by the muscle power of tough and seasoned men, the Falls of the Ohio were more of an obstacle and danger than in the earlier days of the river traffic. In 1811 the steamer *City of New Orleans* traveled the Ohio and Mississippi rivers to the Crescent City. In 1815 the *Enterprise* was the first steamer to make the upstream journey. Such demonstrations in the annihilation of distance and the reduction in time consumed in making the voyages raised anew a demand for a canal around the Ohio falls. It was not until 1830 that the canal was finally completed. Progress in the opening of the river trade gave Louisville predominance over its rival, Lexington, located eighty miles to the east in the center of Kentucky. The river continued to be the main means of transportation for the growing city until 1859, when the Louisville and Nashville Railroad Company ran its first train over the rails to Nashville.[2] Louisville, on the Falls of the Ohio, possessed a natural monopoly of trade that gave the new city many advantages, which in turn attracted ambitious and adventurous men who were quick to see the possibilities of the place. Favored later by freight rates established on the principle of water competition, the city grew in wealth and influence. The emphasis in Louisville was placed on business, and the energies and thoughts of the leading men were on their industrial enterprises, which may account for the intermittent and rather unsatisfactory progress of education in that city. An examination of the catalogues of Yale and Princeton colleges in 1850 would show that the well-to-do Louisville businessmen were sending their sons to schools in the East. In no other way is it possible to explain the lag in the development of a college in Louisville on a broad and liberal basis; for there was money in the city and culture among many of the families who dwelt there.

Writing in 1826, Timothy Flint, a great letter writer, missionary, traveler, and teacher, tells of stopping at Louisville on his way north from New Orleans. "Louisville has grown to be a fine town," said he. "The ware-houses, the stores, the smell at the landing even, the ship-yards, all indicated the mercantile character, the great and growing importance of the place."[3] In contrast to this statement, in an earlier letter to his family in Massachusetts, Flint wrote of Lexington: "It is not so large and flourishing as Cincinnati, but has an air of leisure and opulence, that distinguishes it from the bustle and occupation of that town. In the circles where I visited, literature was most commonly the topic of conversation. The window-seats presented the blank covers of the new and most interesting publications. . . . The uni-

[2] Thomas D. Clark, *A History of Kentucky* (New York, 1937), ch. 11, *passim.*
[3] Timothy Flint, *Recollections of the Last Ten Years* . . . (Boston, 1826), 377.

versity [Transylvania], which has since become so famous, was, even then, taking a higher standing, than the other seminaries in the western country. There was generally an air of ease and politeness in the social intercourse of the inhabitants of this town, which evinced the cultivation of taste and good feeling. In effect, Lexington has taken the tone of a literary place, and may be fitly called the Athens of the West."[4] Transylvania University, highly praised by Timothy Flint, was soon to pass through a bitter controversy so devastating in its effects that it suffered for years from the dissensions among its friends and supporters. Meanwhile, the city of Louisville, engrossed in business, left the founding of a university to a vague and uncertain future.

Among the many grants of land from the public domain for schools, one was made to Jefferson County in 1798. The acreage received was six thousand in extent; but the supporters of this cause, having in mind that funds were needed to equip a school, secured the passage of another act in the same year authorizing a lottery to raise $5,000 in addition to such money as might result from the sale of the land endowment. The seminary provided by these funds was not established until 1816 when it attained an enrollment of about fifty students under the principalship of Mann Butler. The seminary did not prosper since the city council of Louisville asked the state legislature to apportion the lands and funds belonging to Jefferson Seminary for the use and benefit of the public school.[5] With both hands holding gifts for different parts of Jefferson County, the legislature gave the city the old seminary building and a lot of two and a half acres; the rest of the property was given to the county orphan asylum at Middletown. Even this gift was tardily made, for the transfer was not completed until 1844. Perhaps this date has some significance due to the fact that the Collegiate Institute of Louisville, started in 1837 with some promise of success, finally

[4] *Ibid.*, 67-68.
[5] Kentucky Writers' Project, *Centennial History*, 11-12.

ceased to carry on when the entire faculty resigned. The new charter of 1846 repealed the act of 1840 by which the institute had been established, and in its stead authorized the creation of a department to be called the Academic Department of the University of Louisville.

Legislation does not necessarily carry financial support. Matters drifted along with complaints from the board of trustees that they could not maintain the department on fees alone. Appeals were made to the city authorities for endowment and annual support, but deaf ears were turned to this suggestion when the city council asked the state legislature to designate, in a new city charter, the public school board as Trustees of the University of Louisville. The charter was authorized by the legislature, but the courts decided that the university was an independent institution and did not come within the authority of the charter. In the meantime, the city school board took over the academic department, leaving it nominally a part of the university but actually a city high school. Satisfied with the success they had made of the school, the board asked the legislature to sever these tenuous relations with the university and to create a Male High School with the right to confer A.B., B.S., and M.A. degrees. "So," says the Centennial historian, "the effort to establish a college or an academic department in the university had been defeated at every turn. It was not until the professional schools, which were self-sustaining, and until the public more fully and generally appreciated the necessity for a liberal arts background as a prerequisite to the professional career, that the Academic Department, which is known today as the College of Liberal Arts, acquired the public support necessary to sustain it. That time did not arrive until the first decade of the next century. Until then the history of the University of Louisville is the story of the departments of medicine and law."[6]

During the sixty-five years from 1835 to 1900, the city of Louisville harbored no less than eleven medical schools

[6] *Ibid.*, 19-20.

of one sort or another. In the main these early schools were conducted on the lecture principle with no laboratory or clinical aids to instruction until the latter part of the period. Among these institutions may be named the more important ones: the Louisville Medical Institute, 1837; the Kentucky School of Medicine, 1850; the Louisville Medical College, 1869; the Hospital College of Medicine, 1873; the Southwestern Homeopathic Medical College, 1892; and the Medical Department of Kentucky University, 1898. The reasons for the large number of institutions situated in Louisville with the purpose of forwarding the ambitions of youth seeking careers in the medical profession are to be found in the central location of the city, the low requirements for admission to the practice of the healing art prevailing in the state, the expectation of making money from the operation of the schools by those who gave the instruction, and, finally, the ambitions of colleges in other parts of the state to round out their offerings with courses in medicine. Thus, Central University, Centre College, and Kentucky University had medical departments in the city of Louisville at some time in their history. It was a day of keen competition, with no holds barred from the use of practices to attract students that are now regarded as highly unethical. Yet such methods prevailed for fully sixty years before more intelligent and ethical considerations could be used in working out the medical school situation in Louisville.

The College of Medicine of the University of Louisville began its long career with the establishment of the Louisville Medical Institute by a legislative act passed in 1833. As a matter of fact, this paper organization was regarded as a legal basis for a real medical school. Before the school was really started and engaged in teaching medicine, a controversy was raging over the transfer of the Transylvania College of Medicine from Lexington to the larger city. The proposal to found a medical school in the Falls City raised the ire of the Transylvanians, further increased by a paper by Dr. Charles

Caldwell in the *Transylvania Journal of Medicine and the Associate Sciences* (1834). The outcome was climaxed by a proposal from Louisville to the Lexington medical school that it move to Louisville. For those days $40,000 and a location were regarded as an attractive offer, but the people of Lexington and the Transylvania trustees bitterly opposed such a move even though more clinical facilities were to be had in Louisville. They felt that a good school could be operated in Lexington. This opposition brought the negotiations for removal to an end, but the controversy raged on for several years in picturesque and vituperative language, sadly marring relations between the two cities. It was on March 30, 1837, that a mass meeting was called in the Radical Methodist Church, Louisville. After considerable discussion, it was resolved to establish a medical school in Louisville; and the meeting called upon one and all, physicians as well as citizens, to support the new proposal. Four days later the city council passed a resolution authorizing the Louisville Medical Institute.

Some of the members of the faculty of the Transylvania Medical School transferred their allegiance to the venture in Louisville, which began its career in the upper room of the city workhouse; a new building was provided, however, the following year. After many vicissitudes, financial and otherwise, the Louisville Medical Institute became the medical department of the University of Louisville in 1846. Troubles and difficulties continued nevertheless; the loss of a building by fire, changes in the faculty, and keen competition made life hard for the school which persisted until 1891 when its efforts were rewarded by admission into the Association of American Medical Colleges. The increased demands upon medical schools and the rising standards required by physicians and the association had forced improvements in the instruction offered.[7]

[7] *Ibid.*, chs. 2-3, *passim.*

In 1907 the three remaining schools of the eleven that had existed at one time were merged with the University of Louisville Medical School; and by 1911 this institution was the only medical school in the state. In 1908 it claimed the largest attendance of any medical college in the United States. The boast that there were 706 students enrolled stimulated the attack in the report of the Carnegie Foundation for the Advancement of Teaching on *Medical Education in the United States and Canada;* this was not unexpected, and the trustees had already begun to remedy the situation. Published in 1910, the report dealt with every medical school in the country and so brought to light the many shortcomings of medical education in the United States. "To carry the school at all," said Dr. Abraham Flexner, who made the report, "a large attendance is necessary; but a large attendance implies a low standard. The situation is thus practically deadlocked." Continuing, Dr. Flexner declared, "The outlook is not promising; for there is no indication of such support, financial or academic, as would be required in order to reconstruct the institution on acceptable terms."[8]

There followed as a consequence of the findings in the report much searching of purpose by the board in charge of the school. From a definite statement of deficiencies formulated by the Council on Education of the American Medical Association, the leaders of the Louisville Medical School reorganized the faculty, improved the building, and lengthened the session. These changes were sufficient to bring the medical department a Class A rating in 1910. From that date, the Medical School and associated departments have advanced steadily. In the city hospital, the School of Medicine has installed highly satisfactory clinical facilities for the training of students. New laboratory buildings have been erected, and a considerable equipment has been acquired under Dean John Walker Moore and his associates.

[8] Quoted, *ibid.,* 87-88.

As long ago as 1887, the Hospital College of Medicine established a Dental Department with the Dean of the Medical School, Dr. James L. Howe, as its first dean. With him were associated eight instructors who made up the faculty. Only three, however, held the degree of Doctor of Dental Surgery. By 1900 this school was doing so well that it withdrew from the Medical School and became the Louisville College of Dentistry. It was organized as a stock company owned by the dean, William Edward Grant, who held the whole body of stock until he retired because of ill health. The school was then purchased by and transferred to the University of Louisville in 1918.

In the resolutions adopted at the meeting held in the Radical Methodist Church, March 30, 1837, it was stated that the college should consist of a medical school and a law department. In fact, such a school was included in the university organization when the city charter of 1846 authorized the establishment of a law school as one of the departments of the university. The University Law Department, through the years, moved from one dingy building to another until finally it was beautifully housed on the Belknap campus in a building provided by the gift of Mrs. Attilla Cox, in memory of her husband, and a grant from the Works Progress Administration in 1939. The school had its ups and downs, fostered though it was by some of the best legal minds in the city. The attendance was never large, in part because of the competition of night schools of law and adherence to fairly high requirements for admission. The process of raising the admission requirements and the lengthening of terms was of little assistance against competition until the teaching and methods of instruction were raised to the standards practiced in the better schools. The case system was introduced, new professors were added to the staff, and library facilities were greatly improved. Gifts from Bernard Flexner, Justice Louis D. Brandeis, and the Allen family brought the law department new facilities and new opportunities to work in the Legal Aid

Society of Louisville and to practice briefing in the service provided for lawyers in the city. The law school is now well housed, satisfactorily staffed, and equipped with good library facilities. It is, in fact, a worthy part of a revived University of Louisville.

While the medical and law schools could trace their history back to the first charters of the university and of the city, the College of Liberal Arts did not become an essential and vital part of the university until 1907, and even then it was hardly to be compared with the schools of that type in universities and colleges elsewhere. With the rising standard, supported by college associations and accrediting agencies, the medical and law schools were handicapped in their effort to maintain a two-year college requirement for admission to their courses when no general college training was to be had in the city. The General Education Board and the Carnegie Foundation for the Advancement of Teaching had agreed to furnish a half million dollars if a similar sum could be raised within the city. This was too much to expect, for the time had not yet arrived when Louisville would take pride in its university. Again the institution fell back on the slow and enervating process of establishing a College of Liberal Arts. The old building formerly occupied by the Kentucky University Medical Department was available, and here the new college was opened in the fall of 1907. In addition to the usual ground courses leading to an A.B. or a B.S. degree, the college offered some graduate work. Under the guidance of Dean John L. Patterson, the college made advancement, though funds were not forthcoming. After the appearance of the Flexner report in 1910, the city came forward with an appropriation of $10,000, which was raised to $25,000 the following year and made an annual contribution until 1916, when a tax for the support of the university was authorized by legislative act.

The library facilities in the early days had been meager indeed. Now progress in the work of the arts college and of the university was to be seen in the betterment of instruction, more facilities, and an added income. Recognition, too, of the arts college had come, so that it was now a member of the several accrediting agencies and a full partner in the university. Other advances in the development of the institution came on rapidly in the second decade. In 1925 the Speed Scientific School became a possibility with the gifts of William S. Speed and his sister, Mrs. Olive Speed Sackett. A School of Social Work, affiliated with the university and the Welfare League, was established in 1923. A School of Music, begun as an experiment in 1932, after a trial of three years with the co-operation of the Juilliard Foundation, was made a part of the university and fully recognized by the governing authorities as such. These and other advances came about, but in the meantime the legal and financial support of the institution left much to be desired. It was in this field that a businessman, afterward president of the university, A. Y. Ford, laid broad foundations for the future of the institution.

Arthur Y. Ford was the seventh and the first salaried president of the University of Louisville. The others had been deans of the Medical School, presidents of the board of trustees, or members of other departments who devoted but a nominal proportion of their time to the general purpose of the university. The first administrative move made by President Ford was the establishment of a central office. Heretofore, the office had been located wherever the president of the board of trustees transacted his personal business.[9] This simple fact may account in part for the languishing progress of the university during the years from 1837 to 1915. The problems confronting the new administrator were the consolidation of properties, betterment of the Medical School facilities by a far-reaching agreement with the City Hospital for clinical and laboratory work, and provision for adequate

[9] *Ibid.,* 142.

support of the university. These problems required the application of tact and careful management for their solution.

When President Ford died in 1926, the medical situation had been greatly improved; the university had acquired the Belknap campus; and the city had secured legislative permission to levy a tax of five cents on the assessed values of real property in the city for the support of the university, which sadly needed buildings and additional campus space. A proposed bond issue of a million dollars was submitted to the voters, but the proposal failed to carry. Submitted again, the bond issue carried in 1925 with the understanding that provision should be made for the college education of Negroes. This pledge was met in 1929 by the acquirement of the old Simmons University property and the erection of academic buildings for the college. In the meantime, a million-dollar campaign had been started which resulted in pledges of more than eight hundred thousand dollars. President Ford died in office and was succeeded by George Colvin, former State Superintendent of Public Instruction and later head of the Louisville and Jefferson County Children's Home. President Colvin threw himself into the endowment campaign with vigor, but his short administration was marred by contention and strife in the city and on the campus. The trustees, recognizing that the basis of the problems was curricular and administrative, asked Dr. Fred J. Kelly of the faculty of the University of Minnesota and Frank L. McVey, president of the University of Kentucky, to make a study of the situation and to report their findings. The reports were accepted by the board but not put into effect owing to the disturbing conditions then existing in the University of Louisville. Dr. Colvin died in 1928, and for a year Dr. John L. Patterson, dean of the College of Liberal Arts, took up the task of guiding the university and holding it together.

In 1929 the board of trustees invited Dean Raymond A. Kent of Northwestern University to become president of the University of Louisville. He accepted the position and took office on July 1, 1929. The new president was the first man to hold that office who combined business and administrative experience with a knowledge and understanding of education, public and private. The hope of immediate material progress under the new administrator was dimmed, however, by the depression that swept the country in 1929 and continued for nearly eight years. Nevertheless, the college for Negroes was under way by 1931 through the assistance of the General Education Board and the Rosenwald Fund. On the main campus, new buildings were erected, and much was done to beautify the grounds through grants made by the Works Progress Administration and Public Works Administration. Departments and curricula were restudied and reorganized. The colleges and scattered interests of the university were brought together, thus developing a unity of purpose in administration and future plans. The attitude of the city changed from one of skepticism to pride in its university. Notable gifts, both of money and collections, began to come to the institution on the wave of this awakened interest.

The status of the University of Louisville was brought into question in 1938 through a suit filed in the courts contending that the salary of the president could not exceed $5,000 under the constitutional provision which limited the salaries of public officials to that amount. Was the university a municipal enterprise, or was it a private institution with municipal affiliations? The case went through the Circuit Court, which gave an opinion favorable to the defendant. Also, the Court of Appeals confirmed the university's contention that it did not come within the constitutional provision on public salaries. It was inevitable that the status of the University of Louisville should be brought in question by some citizen, or group of citizens, who would demand court action to clear the position of the university. Just this happened in 1938, in *Kerr* v. *City of Louisville et al.* This case was an indirect attack on the status of the university, since it raised the question as to the character of its incorporation.[10] The contention was that the trustees of the university and the members of the Board of Education were state officers. In due time, the case found its way to the Court of Appeals. The charter of the university, authorized in 1846, had been amended in 1926, 1929, and 1934 for the purpose of correcting minor defects, and in the last instance to permit the university to borrow money and mortgage its property to the extent of one million dollars. In 1854 the Court of Appeals had rendered a decision which settled any doubt about the university's being a private corporation.[11] The court specifically stated that it had every characteristic of a private corporation. In fact, the decision meant "that the State even with the consent of the City of Louisville could not take away from the University the charter rights which it had acquired, or revest in the City control over the property donated by it to the University." This view is accepted by the court today.

Another question arose from the discussion of the case referred to above which involved the position of staff members of the university. Were they public officers and therefore subject to the laws and rules affecting public officers? The inquiry about public officers arose out of a case in which the question was raised whether a city manager was an officer within the meaning of Section 246 of the constitution.[12] Did this decision apply to the University of Louisville? If that institution were a private corporation, then the members of the staff of the university could not be regarded as public officials. By the decision of the Court of Appeals, the University of Louisville was cleared of legal difficulties, which relieved that university of further interference in its affairs. Meantime the equipment, campus, and buildings have been greatly augmented, and the organization and administration of the

---

[10] 271 *Kentucky Reports* 335.

[11] City of Louisville *v.* President and Trustees of the University of Louisville, 54 *Kentucky Reports* 515.

[12] City of Lexington *v.* Thompson *et al.*, 250 *Kentucky Reports* 96.

institution have been able to meet the difficulties of the war years and to respond to the demands and needs of a peacetime world.

President Kent died suddenly in 1943, after thirteen years of service in which the university made signal and important progress. His death was a shock to his friends and to the university which had relied confidently upon his leadership, a leadership which brought for the university a growth in number of students, equipment, plant, and income. As his successor, the board of trustees elected E. W. Jacobsen of the University of Pittsburgh. After holding the office for three years, President Jacobsen resigned in 1946 to assume the presidency of the College of the City of Los Angeles, and succeeding him Dr. John W. Taylor took office in 1947. The University of Louisville within twenty years had lost three presidents by death and one by resignation.

CHAPTER IX

THE COLOR LINE IN EDUCATION

THE INSTITUTION of Negro slavery precipitated the race question into the realm of education and into the economic and political affairs of the South. Though a border state where slavery persisted from territorial beginnings until the Civil War brought the institution of bondage to an end, Kentucky has been confronted throughout its history with problems involving the education of colored people living within its borders. Although the ratio of Negroes residing in Kentucky to the total population has steadily declined with each census since 1790, nevertheless the problem continues on with a new emphasis upon the adequacy of instruction and the opportunities for special training. In the 1850 census the Negro population amounted to 210,981 (slave and free colored), a ratio of 22.5 per cent of the total population. Eighty years later, 1930, the Negroes living in Kentucky were enumerated as 226,040 persons, a ratio of 8.6 per cent of the total population. Ten years later, 1940, a smaller number of colored persons lived in the state, and the ratio to total population had dropped to 7.5 per cent. This change was due to emigration to the large industrial centers outside the state and to a falling birth rate and a high death rate among the colored population living within the state.

A more limited migration had been going on for at least three decades within Kentucky, a movement from the rural areas to the wealthier and more densely settled parts of the state, especially around Louisville and Lexington. In these two places, nearly one-half of the Negroes in the state had found homes and better opportunities for employment by

1940. The race has made progress in many ways; on the whole, the economic status of the Negro has improved in the eighty years since the Civil War, and educational opportunities have increased considerably during the same period as shown by the decline in the percentage of illiteracy among the Negroes. The colored people have displayed a great eagerness to improve themselves and their children as shown in attendance at schools. Among these people there is a growing appreciation of real leadership and the desire to take advantage of the opportunities offered in the schools. Meager as these are in many communities, and they are seldom equal to the provisions made for white children, all such advantages provided have been used with enthusiasm by the colored people and their children.

The shifting of the Negro population from the rural areas has had a double effect: first, the increase in the opportunities for those who dwell in the larger towns; and second, the reduction of educational facilities for those colored people remaining in rural areas. This latter situation results from isolation of those Negro families living in country districts where transportation is provided for whites rather than for Negroes. In the matter of the length of the school term, there is no such discrimination; for the number of school days is the same for white and colored children. According to a recent study, more than a third of the Negro school population has a school term of nine months as compared with a fifth of the white school population.[1] The study referred to informs us that 25 per cent of the total Negro school population has only the minimum school term of seven months. In the matter of school buildings, the Negro children do not fare as well; for the school buildings in the rural areas were scored 83.7 points lower than the buildings used by white children. In the cities, the value of the buildings for Negro children was rated as about half the value of those provided

---

[1] L. E. Meece, *Negro Education in Kentucky* (Lexington, 1938), 61, 82, 122, 126.

for white pupils. The basis used for the comparison was the classroom costs. In the matter of the training of teachers in the elementary and secondary schools, there was but little difference. Very few white or Negro teachers had less than one year of college training for their preparation in the elementary field; and in the secondary schools, only one per cent of the Negro teachers had less than two years of college training. In teaching experience, the Negro instructors in the elementary schools had an average of three years more than the white teachers in the same level. In the secondary schools, the white teachers averaged approximately two or three years longer service than the colored teachers.

In all the southern states, a difference in salary payments for white and Negro teachers has been a practice of long standing under a dual system of education. In the rural schools of Kentucky, there is little variation in the salaries paid to the two groups of teachers. It is in the independent districts that the greatest difference is to be found. In twelve of the districts, both colored and white teachers were paid the same. The facts gathered by Professor L. E. Meece in the study referred to above indicate that there is a difference of 10 per cent in thirty districts, 20 per cent in twenty districts, and 30 per cent or more in twelve districts. Public opinion is changing, and the attitudes of school boards and administrative officers are tending toward a more liberal treatment of colored teachers.

The early attempts at the education of the Negro in Kentucky took the form of religious instruction. The Lexington *Kentucky Gazette* of October 17, 1798, printed a notice declaring that "A Sunday School is now open at Colonel Patterson's old house on High Street for use of the People of Color. Those who wish their servants taught, will please to send a line, as none will be received without."[2] It was in the same year that Kentucky adopted the Virginia

---

[2] Lexington *Kentucky Gazette,* October 17, 1798.

statutes for the treatment of those held in slavery. The act was a combination of previous laws and contained forty-three sections which set forth in detail the legal procedures in all matters relating to slaves, free blacks, mulattoes, and Indians.[3] This law, borrowed from Virginia, remained on the statute books as long as slavery existed. Kentucky, however, passed no laws forbidding the instruction of slaves. "The duty of providing adequate religious instruction is now generally admitted," said an article in the *African Repository,* a publication issued by the American Colonization Society, in 1854.[4] Inducement for the instruction of slaves was probably brought about through self-interest, "since religion," the *Repository* writer says, "promotes morality, good health and faithful service." In the main, the slaves were instructed orally; and in fewer instances, some were taught to read. The books used were those by evangelical writers such as *Baxter's Call, Allien's Alarm,* Bunyan's *Grace Abounding, Pilgrim's Progress,* and the Bible. The hymnbook was more acceptable than any of the other books available for the instruction of the colored people, for music appealed to them. In the Transylvania Library is a handwritten petition signed by seventeen women of Lexington who pledged to devote a portion of every Sabbath afternoon to the religious instruction of female Africans if the university would permit them to have a room in one of the buildings. "The Petition of Sundry Ladies for a Room in the University for a Female African School" is the title of the document, which is dated March 18, 1816. On the back of the petition is written "Acceded to." Opportunities to learn were largely limited to house slaves, though the churches admitted colored persons to membership,[5] and these, no doubt, received religious instruction and so came into contact with those who were interested in teaching

---

[3] Littell, *Statute Law of Kentucky,* I, 113-123.
[4] *African Repository,* XXX (1854), 322-323.
[5] Names of Colored Members of the Church at Cane Ridge, June 15, 1838, in Transylvania College Library.

them. In the next twenty years, occasional secular schools were set up much after the fashion of the earliest schools for white children in the pioneer settlements. There was a school in Lexington in 1830 attended by thirty Negro children and taught by a white man from Tennessee. Other schools were to be found in Richmond, Danville, Louisville, and Maysville in the 1830's. After 1847 a man by the name of William H. Gibson taught in Louisville a school of one hundred pupils, many of whom were slaves permitted by their masters to attend the school.[6]

The situation was changing: the proportion of Negroes to whites was 34.8 per cent in 1810; and, in addition, the free colored people in the town of Lexington were 24.5 per cent of the slave population in 1840. The problem of education was passing into a much wider phase than that of teaching a few house slaves.[7]

At the end of the eighteenth century, slavery in much of the South was looked upon as a declining institution. The libertarian philosophy of Revolutionary Virginia was carried by many of her sons to the western country, as can be seen in early Kentucky wills that echo the words of the Declaration of Independence and the Virginia Bill of Rights in provisions for the manumission of slaves. But the introduction of power machinery in the English textile mills created a great demand for cotton, and the invention of the cotton gin gave slavery a new lease on life. Cotton lands in the seaboard area were falling off in fertility, but in the years immediately after the War of 1812 there came a great migration to the West and an extension of the cotton plantation system. Southern planters held new hopes for a revival of agriculture, and they needed more slaves. Kentucky was affected by these changes to the southward and by her own agricultural evolution from

[6] Carter G. Woodson, *The Education of the Negro Prior to 1861* (Washington, 1919), 169, 219, 223-224.
[7] W. B. Strother, "Some Aspects of Negro Culture in Lexington, Kentucky" (M.A. thesis, University of Kentucky, 1939), 7.

backwoods clearings to broad acres of hemp and tobacco fields. With these developments and an aggressive crusade against slavery beginning in 1831, a marked modification in the attitude toward the Negro was to be noted. If a slave could learn to read well, it was feared that he might become a victim of the "filthy" abolitionist literature, and so produce great trouble for the slavery system.[8] "The most formidable weapon in the hands of the abolitionist," said the editor of the *Presbyterian Herald,* "is the indifference which he charges to the Christian slaveholder toward the spiritual welfare of the slaves under his control. Disarm him of this weapon, and you have done much to render him powerless."[9] Instruction for people held in bondage was meager indeed. The Presbyterian Synod meeting of 1834 issued an address to the people of Kentucky saying "that throughout the whole State, there is but one school in which the slaves can be taught during the week. On the Sabbath, there are three or four schools whose light is seen glimmering through the darkness that covers the black population of the whole State." For the Negro population of Kentucky there was no provision made of an educational nature with the exception of individual enterprises in which a meager instruction in Christian habits of life was given to household servants. One of the anomalies of the slave regime as compared with present-day attitudes was to be seen in the membership of many slaves in the white churches of that time.[10]

When the general school law was enacted by the legislature in 1837, as a consequence of the distribution of the surplus revenue then in the Federal treasury, the colored children of the state were not even thought of. A census was to be taken under the provisions of the act to ascertain the number of children of school age, but again it was not regarded as

---

[8] Lewis and Milton Clarke, *Narrative of the Sufferings of Lewis and Milton Clarke* ... (Boston, 1846), 17.

[9] *Presbyterian Herald,* April 16, 1846; October 4, 1849.

[10] Ivan E. McDougle, *Slavery in Kentucky, 1792-1865* (Washington, 1918), 79-81.

THE COLOR LINE IN EDUCATION 147

necessary to count the private property in the form of slave children, so no enumeration was made of them. The state constitution of 1850 had something to say about the distribution of school funds among the different counties of the state on the basis of free white children between the ages of six and eighteen years. In 1851 a common school was defined as "one in which a competent teacher was employed for three months in the year, and which received all white children between the ages of six and eighteen, who resided in the district."[11] This law was followed by another one two years later requiring the distribution of the school fund on the same basis, but no mention of colored children appeared in the act.

When the Thirteenth Amendment was ratified in 1865, Kentucky found itself with a recently enslaved people free to leave their masters. The situation was a difficult one and great effort was required in dealing with it. With the right to vote, the colored people might ultimately be a menace to law and order. The public conscience was to some extent aroused and expressed itself in a kind of hoist-yourself-by-your-own-boot-straps act in 1866. This act specified that one half of all the money that accrued from the taxes on property owned by Negroes should be used for the education of colored children, and the other half of such tax moneys should go to take care of the paupers of the Negro race living within the state.[12] Not to be overcome by the failure of the law to provide sufficient funds for these purposes, the next year the legislature levied a poll tax on all Negro males over eighteen years of age, and, in addition, required the county commissioners to pay $2.50 to the colored schools for each child attending for three months.[13] As might have been foreseen, the needs of a people thrown upon their own resources after decades of enslavement were greater than could be met by the funds raised through taxes; so an act of 1871 placed the same rate of tax on the Negroes as that levied upon the

[11] Kentucky *Acts, 1851-52,* 164, 168.
[12] *Ibid., 1866,* ch. 636, p. 51.   [13] *Ibid., 1867,* ch. 1912, p. 957.

whites.[14] "It is worthy of attention," said Superintendent Z. F. Smith in his report for 1870, "that no well matured and satisfactory plan for the education of the colored population has so far been considered or established by legislation." He was quite right, for the social conscience had not responded to any moral or Christian call to help a people so greatly in need.

Public sentiment, however, was changing, but not markedly so, for the people could not see that the Negroes by themselves were unable to support an adequate school system. "A new entirely independent fund and system should be created for the colored people," were the words of Superintendent Henderson in 1873. Not until fifty-six years had passed were equality of instruction and support of colored schools to be established by the decision of the Court of Appeals in the case of *State Board of Education* v. *Brown*.[15] In 1874 "An Act Establishing a Uniform System of Public Schools for the Colored Children of the State" was regarded as an advance over the previous laws to establish schools for the Negro children. To support this uniform system—uniform in that it was a separately organized state system—taxes were levied on all sources of revenue arising from Negro ownership and Negro activities and placed in a separate fund to be kept inviolate for the schools for colored children. In some counties there were attempts to do more than the law required. The support was still inadequate; and, with that in mind, the legislature passed an act in 1882 to provide an additional tax of two cents for general school purposes. The matter was submitted to a vote of the people who endorsed the legislature's action by a majority of nearly seventeen thousand; and, as a result, the distribution of the school funds was thereafter made on a per capita basis without regard to color.

Now and then the courts were called upon to untangle some of the differences raised by a two-system school organi-

[14] *Ibid., 1871*, ch. 1233, p. 18.
[15] 232 *Kentucky Reports* 434.

THE COLOR LINE IN EDUCATION 149

zation that permitted varying local taxes for white and colored schools, different boards of trustees, and great gaps in the quality and character of instruction. In the city of Owensboro, use of taxes paid by whites to support white schools, and of taxes paid by Negroes to support colored schools, resulted in a nine-months term for white pupils and a three-months term for Negroes. A Federal district court held this action a denial of equal protection of the law and ruled that the state law permitting the discrimination was in conflict with the fourteenth amendment.[16] In another case, the Kentucky Court of Appeals decided that the act of 1874 was unconstitutional because it violated the principle of equal taxation, in that all the children of the state are entitled to an equal share of the proceeds of all state taxation for the purposes of education.[17] Other questions arose and finally ended in the Court of Appeals. One such case came out of a controversy in Fleming County over the question whether the county board of education should maintain a school for colored children in a graded school district. Since the white taxpayers had established a school for the benefit of white children, the county board was required to maintain the school for colored children within the graded school district;[18] this was in 1929. The courts had declared repeatedly that so far as state taxes and state school funds were concerned there must be equality of use between white and colored children.

The towns and cities organized as special school districts were not brought under these divisions because the funds for local school purposes were raised locally. The school code of 1934 made great changes in the position held and opportunities offered by the schools for colored children. The former separation of control of the two types of schools was abolished. More important is the requirement of one tax

---

[16] Claybrook *v.* City of Owensboro, 4 *Kentucky Law Reporter* 876; **23 Federal Reporter** 634.
[17] Dawson *v.* Lee; Lee *v.* Hill, 83 *Kentucky Reports* 49.
[18] 232 *Kentucky Reports* 434.

for all school purposes so that the proceeds of the tax are used for all children regardless of color or creed. Voting for school trustees is a privilege now available to every adult citizen. The law which permitted differences in the salaries of white and colored teachers has been repealed. The two State Boards of Trustees for the State Colleges for Negroes no longer exist since the colleges are administered by the State Board of Education, giving them a legal representation before the governor and legislature in the quest for funds.[19] As far back as 1870 the Louisville Board of Education opened schools for colored children on the same basis as those for white children. Lexington and Maysville followed the general movement; Covington, in 1873, established schools for colored children which, in the judgment of the board, could furnish sufficient educational facilities for them. It was not until 1874 that the city of Ashland took control of the colored schools and merged the two systems into one. Little by little, the separate organizations have been united in practically all the cities of all classes. Judged in the broader sense, the education of the colored children of the state has been placed at last on the same foundation as that of the white children. Equal facilities, according to the courts, do not mean the same facilities, but the two systems have been brought slowly to approximate equality.

Most of the progress made in the education of colored children was in the field of elementary education prior to 1908. Up to that date, the establishment of high schools for Negroes was limited to the urban centers. Gradually, under the urging of the State Department of Public Instruction, the county districts have provided high schools for colored children. The first high school for colored boys and girls was opened in Louisville in 1882. Today, that city has two junior high schools and a central high school for Negro children on the three-year senior high school basis. Here

[19] *Report of the Superintendent of Public Instruction* (1937).

and there, some secondary school work was offered in the cities and towns of the state, but the enrollment was small. While the county high school law of 1908 required that each county establish a county high school, it was taken for granted that it would be a school for white children. Reporting on the biennium 1913-1915, Superintendent Hamlett said, "In only three instances, and those by contract, have county high schools for colored children been established."[20] The tendency, in view of the scattered Negro population in some areas, was to pay tuition for the pupils to the school in the adjoining county. It was reported in 1925 that there were as many high schools for colored pupils in the country districts as in the cities. At that date, Superintendent McHenry Rhoads said that the fifty-six public and private high schools available to Negro pupils were located in forty-three counties, where the largest centers of colored population were to be found. In 1930 the State Board of Education declared quite definitely and emphatically that "Every Board of Education is expected to provide eight elementary grades within walking distance of every child's home.... The county is expected to provide four grades of high school within the county or city of the children's residence. Where this is impossible, due to sparse population, the County Board must pay the tuition and board of students away from home." These requirements are clear and obligatory; nevertheless, there are a few districts that do not have free high school advantages for their colored pupils. However, measured through the years, much progress has been made in the effort to establish adequate schooling for the colored children in the state.

The growth of educational facilities for the Negro during the last twenty-five years has rested upon the leaders of the colored people, ably advised by Professor L. N. Taylor. He has kept agencies informed of the needs in Kentucky.

---

[20] *Ibid.* (1915), Pt. I, 21; Pt. II, 16.

Much valuable assistance in money, advice, and constructive planning has been given by several of the national foundations and funds. The Jeanes Fund has provided money for the salaries of supervising teachers employed in any county with the required number of schools for colored children. In order to provide standard high schools in each community, the Slater Fund has appropriated necessary money to bring at least one high school in the county up to standard. In addition to helping the State Department of Education maintain high school supervision, make plans for buildings, and carry on research, the General Education Board has furnished the funds to establish a division of Negro education. From the Rosenwald Fund, large sums have been contributed to aid in the construction of school buildings, shops, and vocational units, to purchase equipment and libraries, and to maintain transportation for the colored children. These contributions have been of the greatest assistance in advancing educational facilities for the colored people. Without such assistance, the development of better education for Negroes would have been far behind that of today. Not the least helpful has been the advice of the experienced officers of out-of-state agencies which has stimulated the interest of many people in the problems of Negro education and brought the colored schools nearer to an equality with those for white children. In addition, the policies of local boards of education are leaning more and more toward equalized service. Old discriminations that created hard feelings and retarded the education of Negroes have been abandoned. Today, the majority of boards of education spend as much money per capita for colored as for white pupils.[21]

During the years prior to 1885 the leaders in Negro education asked for a State Normal School where students might be trained in teaching procedure. In 1886 the legislature

---

[21] *Ibid.* (1939), 31-32, 52-53.

authorized the establishment of a State Normal School for colored persons at Frankfort. The name was changed to Kentucky State Normal and Industrial Institute in 1902; and more recently, by legislative act, it has been designated as the State College for Negroes. In the half century of its history, the college has passed through many vicissitudes due to small income and considerable political interference. Both of these difficulties which hampered the college so long have now been removed for the most part, and the institution has grown in attendance, plant equipment, and particularly in better instruction, more effective management, and improved curriculum. The legislature has recognized the improvements made under the leadership of President Rufus B. Atwood by granting considerable appropriations, which may be substantially increased if the state attempts to meet the requirement of equal educational opportunities set up by the Supreme Court of the United States in the Gaines Case.

The second of the state's educational institutions for Negroes was located at Paducah. It began as a private enterprise under the direction of D. H. Anderson, who afterwards became the president when the state took over the school in 1918. Even then, the control was not fully vested in the state; but in 1939 the institution was made a state school for Negro youth residing in western Kentucky and was given the name Western Kentucky Vocational Training School. Though it was organized as an opportunity school, there were courses that led to a high school diploma. Its purpose was to give the student a chance to find himself and to become skilled in a worth-while vocation. Under the state's maintenance and direction, the school now promises to develop into an important factor in vocational training.

The passage of the Day Act in 1904[22] prohibited the presence of Negro youth in white schools, and thereby affected the plans of Berea College which had been open to both

[22] Kentucky *Acts, 1904*, ch. 85, pp. 181-182.

white and colored students. To meet this situation, Lincoln Institute was established in 1912, near Shelbyville. The Institute was concerned largely with a teacher-training program but also gave considerable emphasis to industrial training. It maintained a high school which was used by counties for the instruction of colored boys and girls who had no schools open to them. The school continued under private management until 1947 when the property, including grounds, buildings, and equipment, was given by the board of the Institute to the state, on the condition that the state would add to the buildings, make repairs, and appropriate funds for the continuance of the Institute as a public high school for colored children. The legislation enacted in 1946 met these requirements, and the school was accepted as a part of the public education system in 1947.

One of the private schools established by the churches for Negro education was Simmons University, chartered in 1873. This institution was located in Louisville and was maintained at first as a Normal School and as an institution where ministers could be trained for religious work among the colored Baptists of the state. The institution had hard going, changing its character and name in 1873, and again in 1884 when the college was called State University for Negroes, only to return to the title of Simmons University in 1918. With the development of the Louisville Municipal College for Negroes, Simmons University withdrew from the college field and confined its offerings to those necessary for the training of ministers and religious workers.

Louisville has taken seriously its obligation to give an education to the ambitious colored student. The city has issued bonds for buildings and has provided library and laboratory equipment with the purpose of affording the Negroes of Louisville the same opportunities for a college education as those furnished to white students by the University of Louisville. The new Municipal College opened its doors in 1930-1931. The institution is operated and maintained by the city, and its direction is carried on under the supervision of the board of trustees and the administrative officers of the University of Louisville.

The provisions for the higher education of Negroes offered by the state, the city of Louisville, and private institutions are not adequate, in the opinion of those interested in equality of opportunities for colored youth. These leaders point out that there are no places in the state where the Negro can get professional education in law, medicine, and engineering, nor can he have the advantages offered to white men and women in the graduate field unless the doors of the University of Kentucky be opened to him. Recent decisions of the Supreme Court of the United States have brought the matter of equal educational opportunities to the front. Lloyd Gaines, a Negro, applied for admission to the University of Missouri in 1938 and was refused entrance. The success of his suit in the Supreme Court posed problems for other states with segregated schools. Similar applications have been made to the authorities of the University of Kentucky, but they have been refused. One of the applicants filed suit in the state court and afterwards transferred the case (*Charles Lamont Eubanks* v. *the University of Kentucky*) to a Federal court. He asked that the court issue a permanent injunction to restrain university officials from enforcing the policy, custom, and usage of refusing the admittance of qualified Negroes into the university solely because of race or color.[23] As in the Gaines case, the issue of the right of a citizen to the opportunities offered by a public institution of higher learning in the United States was maintained, and the case was decided in favor of the plaintiff.

But the law forbidding education of both races in the same institution remained on the statute books of Kentucky. Under such a legal restriction, undoubtedly favored by a majority of citizens, the only procedure open for the time being was to provide equal opportunities either in existing colleges

[23] Lexington *Herald-Leader*, September 19, 1941.

for Negroes or to create a new institution for them. With that in mind, Governor A. B. Chandler appointed an Advisory Committee to review the situation and report their findings. The committee, composed of representatives of the colleges for white and colored, with other members from the state at large, met November 24, 1939, in the Chamber of the House of Representatives at Frankfort. The first meeting of the committee was valuable in setting up the principles under which a subcommittee was to work and to make a report. The whole committee met again on January 30, 1940, and heard the findings of the subcommittee. A final report was prepared and sent in February, 1940, to Governor Keen Johnson who had succeeded Governor Chandler.[24]

In the report of the committee, it was pointed out that there is conflict in the Kentucky law and the principle recognized by the Federal courts; but an examination of the facts indicates that the spirit of the law is not being carried out in Kentucky since there are, in some areas, facilities providing higher education for white persons which are not provided for Negroes. Equalization of educational opportunities does not necessarily imply identical opportunities, but equalization should be a fact. Equalization will be carried out when the state, by specific acts, provides higher educational facilities

---

[24] Members of the Advisory Committee were: F. L. McVey, Chairman, president, University of Kentucky; R. A. Kent, president, University of Louisville; J. A. Thomas, executive secretary, Louisville Urban League; S. L. Barker, president, Kentucky Negro Educational Association; David A. Lane, Jr., dean, Louisville Municipal College; Charles W. Anderson, Jr., member, General Assembly, House of Representatives; W. H. Humphrey, principal, John G. Fee High School, Maysville; R. E. Jaggers, director, Division of Certification, State Department of Education; Paul L. Garrett, president, Western Kentucky State Teachers College; L. N. Taylor, supervisor of Negro schools, State Department of Education; R. B. Atwood, president, Kentucky State College; W. C. Buford, attorney (representing A. E. Mayzook, chairman, Legislative Committee, Kentucky Negro Educational Association); A. E. Evans (visitor), dean, School of Law, University of Kentucky; J. T. Williams (visitor), dean, Kentucky State College. The members of this committee not present were: J. W. Brooker, Superintendent of Public Instruction, State Department of Education; H. L. Donovan, president, Eastern State Teachers College; James H. Richmond, president, Murray State Teachers College; F. D. Peterson, State Comptroller; W. H. Fouse, former principal, Dunbar High School, Lexington.

in accordance with the demonstrated needs of the persons served. Equal rights before the law to pursue those courses in higher education which will meet his individual and social needs should be given to every citizen, irrespective of race. Such were the general principles that were used as the basis of the recommendations of the committee.

The report of the committee held that the needs of the colored college student could be met in the following ways: (1) the program of the Kentucky State College for Negroes could be expanded so that it would provide for a more effective training in agriculture, business administration, industrial arts, teacher education, and the like, at the undergraduate level, and extended so that a year or more of graduate work could be offered in the field of Education, and possibly other areas; (2) through co-operative planning with the Louisville Municipal College, preparation for public health work, training for nursing, and training in social service administration were possible; (3) through exchange of faculty personnel; and (4) pending further development of the state program, those needed areas at the graduate and undergraduate level not provided at Kentucky State College or in the Louisville Municipal College must necessarily be offered the student in other ways, including the possible future modification of the Day Law.

Since the close of the Civil War, some three quarters of a century have passed; and in that time the educational opportunities for Negroes have grown from meager beginnings. Equality, though not identical opportunity, in the field of education now prevails in elementary, secondary, and college education; but in the professional and graduate fields the Negro youth of Kentucky must seek his training in other states. The accomplishment of a full equality remains still to be attained either through the maintenance of a well-equipped graduate and professional school for Negroes or by opening the doors of the State University to the ambitious colored men and women who seek a place in the professions.

The decisions of the United States Supreme Court in recent actions against state-supported universities have changed materially the situation in regard to higher education for Negroes. To meet the new conditions, at least in part, the University of Kentucky in 1948 arranged to offer graduate and professional courses at Kentucky State College for Negroes. One Negro was admitted to legal training, and for a time University instructors traveled to Frankfort to teach him. This arrangement proved impracticable, and Frankfort lawyers were hired as members of the University law faculty for the specific purpose of instructing the Negro student.

Meantime, a Louisville Negro, Lyman T. Johnson, brought suit against the University in the Federal district court at Lexington to gain admission to the graduate school. Judge H. C. Ford ruled that he must be admitted as a qualified graduate student in history because the arrangements for instruction at Kentucky State College by University instructors in compliance with a contract between the University and the State Board of Education did not afford him the equality of educational opportunity required under the Federal Constitution. The University Board of Trustees decided not to appeal from this ruling, and the president of the University announced that qualified Negro applicants would be admitted to the graduate, law, engineering, and pharmacy schools.

Assistant Attorney General M. B. Holifield, however, warned that the Day Law was still in effect and that it required segregation of white and Negro students in the University. This opinion created a serious problem for the University administration. The instruction of a few students in segregated classes hardly seemed to constitute equality of educational opportunity and would be costly and burdensome. An immediate decision had to be made, and in June, 1949, Lyman Johnson and twenty-seven other Negroes entered graduate classes with white students. Insofar as practicable, the University attempted to carry out segregation but at the same time to offer equal facilities. In the final solution of this problem the Day Law must be amended or repealed. When that is done Kentucky can partially remove the color line in education.

CHAPTER X

THE BIRTH, DEMISE, AND RESURRECTION OF THE STATE SCHOOL FUND

IT WAS in the year 1822 that John Adams, the second President of the United States, then eighty-seven years of age, wrote to the chairman of the committee created by the Kentucky legislature to report on a plan of common schools suitable to the condition of the state. The committee, seeking advice on educational procedure, had sent many letters to prominent men of the country. James Madison, Thomas Jefferson, Robert Y. Hayne, and others responded to the committee's inquiry. The old, retired ex-President John Adams replied, more as a politician than as a statesman, that "the wisdom and generosity of your Legislature in making liberal appropriations of money for the benefit of schools, academies, colleges and the university are an equal honor to them and their constituents; a proof of their veneration for literature and science and a portent of great and lasting good to North and South America, and to the World." This was, of course, taking in a lot of territory; for the plan of the school fund had barely got under way before it passed out of existence with little benefit to the schools of the state and with none at all for the areas outside the boundaries of the commonwealth.

The "Act to establish a Literary Fund, and for other Purposes" had been approved December 18, 1821; and, while not having the use of certain funds for the schools, the trustees provided that a committee consisting of William T. Barry, then Lieutenant Governor, John Pope, David R. Murray, John R. Witherspoon, David White, Jr., and William P. Roper should collect information and present a plan for the common schools.[1] This report was an interesting state paper, but the contents, though now regarded as important, had little effect on that legislative body. In those days few men of influence considered a public system of common schools as really necessary; so it is not surprising to find much of the committee's report devoted to the support of a public system of education. It was the contention of the report that tyrants flourished on the ignorance of the people and that such disasters might be averted through mass education. The few legislators who read the report were undoubtedly impressed by the arguments, but it was a long time before the real value of a public system of education and the need for its active support would be fully accepted by the leaders of the state and the people who elected them to office.

Since the acquirement of land was one of man's chief ambitions in that period, it is small wonder that the land was looked upon as a perpetual endowment when given to support schools, churches, and other institutions. That wild land could furnish a sound and large enough basis for endowment had been fully proved to be a fallacy in the experience of the land-grant academies. The Literary Fund was a different scheme of support. A good many states had created banks with legal authority to issue paper money, deal in lands, and carry on a general banking business. Among the state banks was the Bank of Kentucky, chartered December 26, 1806. This bank had a capital of one million dollars, and one half of it was held by the state, but the policy of the directors alienated the radicals of the Relief party when the bank required payments on notes and mortgages given for the purchase of lands. This was in 1821. Meantime, a second bank was chartered under the name of the Bank of the Commonwealth. Within a year the new state bank had issued $2,300,000 in notes and lent nearly two and a half millions on mortgages. Its stocks and notes fell to a fraction of their face

[1] Kentucky *Acts, 1821,* 352; Kentucky, General Assembly, *House Journal, 1822,* 225-283.

value.[2] The earnings of the bank were to be paid to the Literary Fund for the support of the common schools. After a period of more than a hundred years, the whole movement has the appearance of a pious scheme to bolster up public interest in the earnings of the bank. The legislature was quite willing to vote the bank's earnings to the school fund to prevent resort to state taxation for the support of the schools. Thus began the history of the Literary Fund.

The provisions of the act gave one-half of the clear profits or those "that may hereafter arise from the operations of the Bank of the Commonwealth as a fund to be set apart and appropriated which shall be forever maintained for the establishment and support of a system of general education, to be distributed in just proportions to all the counties of the state as the legislature may devise and adopt." Another half from the clear profits of the branches at Lexington, Danville, and Bowling Green was to be donated to the institutions located in those towns. They were Transylvania University, Centre College, recently established in Danville, and Southern College at Bowling Green. Here again, the proposals to favor the institutions located at the seat of the branch banks may have been a shrewd scheme to hold the loyalty of the citizens who dwelt in those communities to the support of the bank. At any rate, the common schools continued to languish.

In his message to the legislature in 1826, Governor Desha said: "One half the profits of the Bank of the Commonwealth were set apart, as a fund for their support; but no other step was taken. Since that period [1821], nothing had been done in furtherance of this important object. Indeed the Legislature had been induced, by the exigencies of the Treasury, to devote the whole profits of the Bank of the Commonwealth, and even the interest of the school fund, to the support of government; so that they have rather retrograded, than ad-

[2] Clark, *History of Kentucky*, 205.

THE STATE SCHOOL FUND

vanced, in relation to this essential concern."[3] The legislature had even before this inaugurated a pernicious policy of making the school fund subservient to every other public interest. At the time, the school fund had an income of about $60,000 per annum; but with the failure of the Bank of the Commonwealth, even this amount dwindled to nothing. The hopes of those who advocated support for the public schools were gone; and during the next fifty years the general school fund would receive many setbacks through diversion to other uses and even by defalcation. In the end, however, the fund was to be established and supplemented by a system of state aid. Before that could come to pass, a great fight had to be made which would establish the obligation of the state to maintain the fund and to pay the interest.

The first attempt to create and maintain a public school fund ended in failure. The second, which was the result of the distribution to the state of surplus funds held in the Federal treasury in 1837, brought on many controversies over payment of interest to the schools and developed a number of dubious financial transactions. It is this part of the story that is taken up in the pages that follow.

The surplus funds in the treasury of the United States resulted in the main from the sale of public lands. The Kentucky legislature, as did the law bodies of all the other states, received the money surplus arising from sales of lands which were part of the public domain. The public domain belonged to the states as members of the Union, and therefore Congress could make provision for the distribution of the surplus. Henry Clay had introduced a bill in Congress in 1832 providing that a tenth part of land sale proceeds be given to the new states, and the remainder be divided among all the states. The Kentucky legislature, as early as 1821, had passed resolutions requesting that the state's senators and representatives urge Congress to give to Kentucky its share of the public

[3] Kentucky, General Assembly, *House Journal, 1826*, 16.

domain held by the general government to be used by the state "for the purpose of education." "They," said the legislature in the resolution, "look to the public lands as a source from which appropriations for the purposes of education may with justice be claimed by those states for which no appropriations have yet been made." The Clay bill when first passed was not signed by President Andrew Jackson, but at length, on June 23, 1836, he did approve an act to distribute to the states $37,000,000. A proviso had been added to the bill that the money could be recalled if needed by the government. Three distributions were made; because of the panic that followed almost immediately, a fourth one was never given to the states. Kentucky received the sum of $1,433,757 and at once began to distribute this very large amount, not to education, as the resolution declared should be done, but to another cause, that of internal improvements. No time was lost in passing an act "to invest in profitable stocks the surplus revenues of the United States." This act dedicated a million dollars, afterward reduced to $850,000, to the founding and sustaining of a general system of education. In one year's time the ardor for the spread of education and the interest in financing such a system were greatly reduced in the face of demands that something be done for internal improvements.

The frontier country into which large numbers of people were moving was in need of roads, bridges, canals, and other means of transportation. Kentucky, cut off from the East by mountain ranges and a long way from the great market of New Orleans, regarded transportation as a first call. It was too much to expect the average man, or the leaders, to overlook the economic and political implications involved in internal improvements. The surplus revenue afforded a means of getting some of those things done, but to turn the whole sum over to a school fund was just too much to be hoped for. The statements of earlier legislatures, the one of 1821 as an example, at least required some adherence to principle. A way out was found by the use of bonds that could be issued to the State Board of Education by the state, and the money represented by the surplus revenue could then be used for internal improvements in its entirety. The state was then bound by a permanent obligation, never to be paid; and the school fund would receive the interest from the bonds provided the state officers paid it.

It was not long before the issue was joined. It appeared, in 1840, that there was insufficient money on hand to meet the interest due to holders of improvement bonds issued by the state in addition to those held by the State Board of Education. The issue was met by the Commissioners of the Sinking Fund by denying the payment due on the bonds in the hands of the State Board of Education. The friends of the common schools protested vigorously against such treatment of the sacred promise to maintain the fund. The governor of the state, William Owsley, went much further in saying that "the course could be pursued without the slightest detriment to the credit of the state, since it was not imperative to borrow money at six per cent to pay the state a debt it owed itself." This was a type of political juggling that completely ignored the principle of segregated funds, specifically set aside for a definite purpose. In other words, it was not the intention of the legislation, so the officers held, that either the principal or the interest of the common school fund should be regarded as a legitimate debt of the state.

In 1843 only $2,504 had been paid into the fund, whereas unpaid interest amounted to a considerable sum. The real attitude toward the state's obligation to the school fund was brought clearly to the fore when the legislature, by an act approved February 10, 1845, required all bonds held by the Board of Education to be delivered to the governor of the commonwealth and to be burned by him in the presence of the auditor and treasurer of the state. Duplicate lists were to be made and held by the State Board of Education to refresh their memories, presumably on the ground that the state might someday do something about the bonds.

Perhaps the matter can better be put in this way: The State of Kentucky was engaged in rather extensive internal improvements, including expenditures on roads, canals, and banking schemes; bonds had been issued and sold; scrip money, too, was used to pay contractors and others, so it was incumbent upon the authorities to pay the interest upon such debts, if the credit of the state was to be maintained. The evidence points to the notion that the diversion of the surplus to the school fund was regarded merely as a gesture which could be passed over with little noise or conflict. To reduce the debt of the state by approximately a million dollars might help the state's financial situation. The legislature, agreeable to this kind of chicanery, passed the act; and the governor burned the bonds. Thus one branch of the government despoiled another and precipitated a conflict that was to last a full fifteen years, when by the determined fight of Dr. Robert J. Breckinridge, then Superintendent of Public Instruction, the state school fund was restored as a perpetual debt of the state and the unpaid interest incorporated in the principal sum.

The burning of the bonds was a highhanded act, hardly understandable unless explained by the statement above; but even that is an insufficient reason for failure to comply faithfully with the laws creating a fund for the common schools. "The bonds were sacred enough to be burnt, whenever the exigencies of the public credit might seem to render such a proceeding desirable against defenseless creditors." The juggling of the law, supported by Governor Owsley, and the practical repudiation of the obligation of the state to maintain a school fund stimulated repercussions that were bound to arise in the state. Rather apprehensive over the possible effects of the bond-burning episode on their political fitness, and undoubtedly because the people were aroused on the issue, the legislature in the session of 1847-1848 passed an act to remedy the situation. This act did two things: first, it directed the governor to issue a new bond for all the arrears of interest due the school fund; and second, it authorized the taking of a vote on the question of charging a tax of two cents on each one hundred dollars worth of taxable property to be used to aid the schools. The governor, John J. Crittenden, issued the bond to the State Board of Education for the sum of $308,268.42 on which 5 per cent interest was to be paid from January 1, 1848. The people, by a majority of 36,882, voted the two-cent tax law.

For over fifty years the people of Kentucky conducted their government on the basis of the constitution of 1799. It was a simple but inadequate instrument made in a time of simple social organization. By 1850 a vast change had taken place, disturbing procedures, conditions, and methods of doing business and carrying on government. It was quite evident the state needed a new constitution; yet two votes were required before the constitutional convention of 1849 could be called and begin its work. To J. D. Taylor of Mason County, who was appointed chairman of the Committee on Education, should go a great deal of the credit for the section devoted to education. Through his courage, good sense, and courtesy, Section 1 of the eleventh article was adopted, though not as he had hoped.[4] Taylor expected to restore the lands to the school funds, but so large did this loom before the convention as a proposal for greatly increased taxes that the members compromised by making the school fund a perpetual and inviolate obligation of the state.

Article eleven of the constitution declared: "The capital of the fund called and known as the 'Common School Fund,' consisting of one million two hundred and twenty five thousand seven hundred and sixty eight dollars and forty two cents, for which bonds have been executed by the State to the Board of Education, and seventy three thousand five hundred dollars of stock in the Bank of Kentucky; also the sum of fifty one thousand two hundred and twenty three dollars

[4] *Report of the Debates and Proceedings of the Convention for the Revision of the Constitution of the State of Kentucky, 1849* (Frankfort, 1849), 880-901.

and twenty nine cents, balance of interest on the School Fund for the year 1848, unexpended, together with any sum which may be hereafter raised in the State by taxation or otherwise, for purposes of education, shall be held inviolate, for the purpose of sustaining a system of Common Schools. The interest and dividends of said funds, together with any sum which may be produced for that purpose by taxation or otherwise, may be appropriated in aid of Common Schools, but for no other purpose." The article also authorized the legislature to provide by law for the distribution of the income to the counties of the state where the money could be used for common school purposes. On January 12, 1844, Superintendent Ryland T. Dillard had reported the school fund as amounting to $1,258,368.66. The amount over the $850,000 set aside in 1837 for the fund was the unpaid interest accruing during the years of the fund's existence. The constitution adopted in 1850 was the law of the land by the following year; and, supposedly, the state, by adopting the eleventh article, had done at least two things: established the amount in the fund and taken the power away from the legislature to dissipate the obligation of the state to the fund.

Hardly had Governor Helm been in office a sufficient time to warm the gubernatorial chair when he sent a special message to the legislature on the subject of the school fund. The impact of the message must have been startling to the people of the state who thought the question had been taken care of in the new constitution. Now the governor was raising the issue anew in his statement that the constitution of 1850 did not and ought not make the Sinking Fund responsible for the interest, much less the principal, of the state bonds held by the Board of Education.[5] On January 21, 1857, a Senate resolution called upon the Superintendent of Public Instruction to lay before that body all the statistics and facts, as well as any argument he might see proper to present in

[a] Kentucky, General Assembly, *House Journal, 1850,* 40.

relation to the governor's late message to the House of Representatives, on whether or not the Sinking Fund was responsible for the interest on the bonds of the state held by the Board of Education. The resolution was directed to Robert J. Breckinridge, who had been made superintendent by appointment in 1847. The task of stating the tangled facts was no easy one, requiring the courage to confront a governor whose hostility to the school fund was well known. In a long and able report Dr. Breckinridge successfully refuted the governor's contention that the bonds of the school fund did not constitute a state debt. Quoting from the report of the Sinking Fund Commissioners, the Superintendent showed again and again that from 1837 on to the meeting of the constitutional convention the bonds had been accepted as a debt, not a duty, a legal obligation to pay the interest upon the amount which had reached, in 1850, the sum of $1,299,268.42. The state debt was reported to be $7,210,157.50, the whole amount having been spent for internal improvements and the interest on bonds issued by the state.

A part of the debt to the school fund had been used to forward various internal improvement schemes, although the acceptance of the money from the Federal government had been accompanied by resolutions devoting such sums to education. The legislature was evidently impressed by the arguments of the Superintendent, for it passed an act directing the Commissioners of the Sinking Fund to pay, out of any money in their possession, the interest due to the school fund on the bonds issued to the Board of Education. Still recalcitrant, Governor Helm vetoed the bill; the legislature passed it over his veto, but even then he refused to obey the law. His successor, Governor Lazarus Powell, in his message to the legislature on November 4, 1851, said that the auditor had been instructed to issue his warrant upon the treasury in favor of the Board of Education. The obligation of the state had been proved and accepted, but there were other questions involving the administration of the school fund.

How the fund was to be distributed became an important question. The law of 1852 had changed the procedure from a distribution based on the number of children in the schools to a per capita basis of children between the ages of six and eighteen. Such moneys as were not used went back to the commissioners of the school fund to increase the principal. The new law changed this procedure: first, by placing the distribution on the basis of a census of children of school age regardless of whether there were schools in a county or not; and second, by crediting the apportionments to the county to be used where and how the county school commissioners might decide to use it. Thus, accumulation of the general school fund was no longer possible. Against this type of procedure, Superintendent Breckinridge protested vigorously. "Such a principle of distribution is evil and wrong." "It is idle to ask how many children are there. The true question is, how many children are there who can be induced to acquire an education?" Nevertheless, the act became a law and made the common school one that was to be open for at least three months. On the per capita basis of allotting the school fund receipts, no distinction was made between one school and another. They were all alike under the law. As late as 1880, Joseph Desha Pickett, at the time Superintendent of Public Instruction, was saying in his report: "The law, as it now stands, does not require a single common school to be taught in the whole state, although the state makes annual provision to pay a teacher for every district school. If a school is not taught, its district loses its proportion of the State per capita and of the interest on its County Bond for the surplus, but the county reclaims it the following year. In fact, the people are taxed at large to support the schools; and if a school is not taught and its apportionment not called for, it is added to its bond against the State, and then commands interest from the tax payers." At the time of the Pickett report, there were 114 counties holding bonds against the state for surpluses. "The result," Pickett reported, "is a premium on neglected schools."

The establishment of a state school fund created the impression in the county districts that the state, providing as it did a per capita payment, assumed that the maintenance of better schools by the local communities was not required by law. Nevertheless, the people in many areas were beginning to see the necessity of supplementing the public fund by district taxation. During the history of the state school fund, additional sources of money had been acquired through a tax which finally reached fifty cents on the dollar of levies on personal and real property. There were many abuses in making the census for the per capita division, but the law of 1912 placed the fund belonging to a county in the hands of the County Board of Education to be distributed on the basis of teacher qualification and relative attendance in a school. The old district unit was no longer the agency for distributing state funds.

The only productive school fund that the state possessed consisted of 798 shares of stock in the Bank of Kentucky which yielded $8,000 annually. When that bank went into liquidation in 1931, however, the state became liable as a stockholder for a proportionate amount of the money owed to depositors. The so-called school fund, whose history is traced in this chapter, was supplemented by a second bond of $606,941.03, derived from the return of direct taxes by the Federal government in 1892. This sum, following the example of the use of the surplus revenue receipts in 1837, was devoted to the erection of the new capitol building, built in Frankfort during Governor J. C. W. Beckham's term of office. Outside of the shares of the Bank of Kentucky stock there was in reality no common school fund. It is true the state has obligated itself to pay on the accumulated debt of $1,933,641.03 an annual interest of $116,000. The people do not have the benefit of an endowment of nearly two million dollars which would exist if the funds set aside for the purpose had been properly safeguarded. On the contrary, they must raise the interest and all state support by taxation. Thus, the purpose of a school fund to aid the schools never operated in the state, for the state must raise annually by taxes the amount of interest on the debt in addition to the per capita appropriated by the legislature as state aid to the schools.

The constitution of 1891 included a section dealing with the distribution of the school fund and the state support of the common schools. This method gave the funds to the counties on a schoolchild basis; and, in turn, each school district was to receive its state support in the same way. The inequalities of such a method were first to be seen in the districts, owing to the great differences between them. It was impossible to have a uniform number of children in each district, but the system continued until 1893, when the State Superintendent was required to set up an arbitrary number of forty-five pupils, so that each district had the per capita on that number; and, in addition, the remainder over the forty-five pupil districts was distributed on the basis of school population. An act of 1912, when the district and school population basis had been dropped, provided a new method within the county for distributing both the state and county funds. After this date the districts shared in the funds available according to need. By this means, the length of term within the counties was fixed; and the salaries of teachers were paid on a common basis.[6] But the inequalities as between one county and another were not remedied by the improved system of per capita distribution of state support. The vast differences in the ability of counties to support education by local taxation were not considered by the law and the constitution as they stood at the time. Much was said in the gatherings of educators about the great disparity in educational results in different parts of the state. The State Superintendents commented upon the inequalities and the

[6] Kentucky Educational Commission, *Public Education in Kentucky*, 139.

hardships of maintaining a decent standard of education in many of the counties. The average amount of taxable property behind each child in the state was $2,452, whereas some of the counties had as little as a fifth of that amount.[7] For the next twenty years the debate and discussion about equality of educational opportunities went on. Public opinion slowly formed into a definite attitude on this need for help in raising the general average of public school education in the state. In the 1940 session of the legislature, a bill was introduced to propose a change in the constitution so that 10 per cent of the per capita school aid could be distributed on the basis of need rather than by the school census procedure. Such an amendment was proposed in 1942 and was adopted.

Little by little the per capita distribution increased. The school tax levied by the state for school support disappeared with the reduction of the real estate tax from thirty to five cents on assessed value. Now, the state no longer lays a tax on tangible personal property, with the result that the school aid is appropriated by the legislature for each biennium.

In 1876 the school apportionment was $1.90 for each pupil child; by 1895 the per capita had grown but little, reaching the sum of $2.15. Reporting in 1915, Superintendent Hamlett stated that the per capita was $5.25; twenty-five years later the amount had doubled; and in 1938 the distribution was $11 for each school-aged child. Though the per capita later grew to a considerable amount, bringing the state's contribution to $13, the schoolteachers and administrators felt that better schools required a still larger state contribution to public education. They asked for $15 per capita. To this Governor Chandler replied in his message to the legislature of 1938: "Some so-called leaders of our school people have recently made demands upon the Governor and the Legislature that they furnish, during the next biennium, a sum equal to $15.00 per capita for the main-

[7] *Ibid.*, 139-140.

tenance of the public schools. This demand, in my judgment, is an unjust one. It should not have been made; but, having been made, it should be promptly rejected by the Legislature."[8] The per capita was not increased to the amount asked for. Nevertheless, there continues to be a growing demand for a larger per capita apportionment which, declare the advocates for state aid, should be as high as $25 per capita.

A century and a quarter may well be regarded as a substantial span of time. In fact, the century and a quarter of the school fund cover most of the history of the state whose sesquicentennial was celebrated in 1942. Slowly the state had grown into a larger conception of its obligation to support public education. Serious mistakes had been made, and indifference, even hostility, had checked the growth and support of the common schools during this period; but Kentuckians can take some pride in the progress the state has made, and its citizens can feel that the public schools have steadily advanced in accomplishment. The lessons of the past are plainly to be seen, and the opportunity to profit by them is now facing the people. Vigilance, vision, careful planning, and understanding will contribute immeasurably to the building of a strong school system. The trying history of the common school fund cannot be repeated without disaster to the whole public school structure. Happily, the hostile attitude shown in the long contest over the school fund has at least been held in check.

[8] Kentucky, General Assembly, *House Journal, 1938*, 22.

CHAPTER XI

TEACHER TRAINING BEGINS AND REACHES A PROFESSIONAL STATUS

TODAY there are four state teachers' colleges in Kentucky. Two of them, Eastern and Western, were established in 1906, at Richmond and Bowling Green; the remaining two were located at Morehead and Murray in 1922. These institutions were called Normal Schools when first authorized by legislative act; later they were designated as Teachers Colleges, and finally called State Colleges. Looked at from the professional point of view, the difference in name is an important matter, since the change from Normal School to Teachers College shows clearly a new emphasis placed upon teacher training and the arrival of institutions which are engaged in professionalizing the calling of teaching within the gates of the academic world. This was the goal long sought by the advocates of better teacher preparation. The teachers themselves were told that they held the destinies of the republic in their hands and should not only be given an opportunity to prepare for their great task, but, if the public interest required it, be compelled by law to meet high standards of training. A great wave of pedagogy, followed by a flood of educational philosophies, flowed across the land. Much of it was crude, some of it unwise; but there was underneath it all the sound principle that teaching could be bettered materially by adequate preparation.

Prophets, here and there, had raised their voices in vain throughout the hundred years that were required to soften the attitude toward professional training and to give the state special institutions for the education of teachers. Now and then a governor would write a sentence, or at most form a brief paragraph, on the subject in his message to the legislature. While the state remained indifferent, a host of private institutions arose to meet the need, mainly for the profit that was in it. Some flourished, but many fell by the wayside. Gradually the needs of education made some impression upon the people; and at the beginning of this century money was appropriated by the state for the establishment and support of teachers' colleges.

The name for the schools engaged in preparing teachers was borrowed from the French *ecole normale*. In 1794 the National Convention, meeting in Paris, decided to create an *Ecole Normale* in which citizens of the republic already instructed in the useful sciences should be trained to teach. The course was a short one of five months, and the students who attended it were to return to their own districts and there start other normal schools. The first normal school was opened in France on January 20, 1795. Efforts were made forty years later to establish such a school in England; but the scheme, for the time being, failed to receive Parliament's support. In this country, various academies gave a few courses in teaching methods around the beginning of the nineteenth century. All of this instruction was incidental and could not be regarded as professional. The distinctive term, normal school, came into use when a translation of a *Report on the State of Public Education in Prussia* by Victor Cousin was published in 1834. Three years later, Calvin E. Stowe brought to the attention of educators in this country the Prussian report. This interest bore fruit in the work of the legislative committee of Massachusetts, in 1838, by the establishment of the first American normal school at Lexington, Massachusetts, the following year. A little later institutions were opened at Barre and Bridgewater. A school was established at Philadelphia in 1848; another, at New Britain, Connecticut, the following year; and one at Ypsilanti, Michigan, in 1850.[1] The pro-

---

[1] "Normal School," in *Cyclopedia of Education*, ed. by Paul Monroe, IV, 481.

fessional development of teaching was on its way, but many years were to pass before the training of teachers would be recognized and accepted as an important part of an educational system in Kentucky.

A committee which was appointed by the Kentucky legislature in 1821 to investigate educational procedure elsewhere made a brief statement about teachers. "The teachers," said the report, "should be men of good moral character, capable of teaching manners as well as letters; and none should be employed unless he could procure a certificate of qualification from two or more inspectors living within the county." To get such a result, the supposition was that the inspectors would select the best of those who applied for positions. Another legislative report, presented by William T. Barry in 1822, gave some attention to teachers and their qualifications and recommended that the law provide for the examination and certification of those persons who proposed to teach. No action was taken by the lawmaking body.

A different turn in the recommendations for the preparation of teachers came from the trustees of Transylvania University in their appeal to the legislature following the investigation of that institution by a legislative committee in 1827. A plan was presented in 1828 by the Board of Trustees to extend the functions of the university to include the training of teachers. To encourage prospective teachers to take the courses offered, it was proposed to give them free tuition. Having reached the conclusion that the plan was feasible and would meet a great need in the state, the trustees petitioned the legislature for a subsidy to aid in the training of teachers. What might have been done to help the plan along is a matter of conjecture, but aid for the plan became impossible when the university building was burned and such funds as might have been used for teacher training were diverted to the rebuilding of the destroyed structure. The Peers report referred to at length in Chapter IV contained much that was pertinent to the training of teachers. A small number of promising students were to be trained in Transylvania University, and the work of those persons in their schools was to be compared with that of teachers without the training. Out of the plan would come a complete demonstration of the value of teacher preparation which would impress the public with the results of the experiment. There was another side to the plan, one which provided for aid to the teachers already serving the public. Professor Peers was not successful in his efforts to persuade the legislature to do something about teacher training, but he was determined to do his best. Some months after the publication of his report of 1829, the Lexington *Reporter* published an item from Peers informing the public that his school would be opened on December 28.[2] This school was "to combine the excellencies of the different literary institutions of Philadelphia, New York, Boston and New England which were visited by me during an absence of three months." Peers generously offered the privileges of his institution without tuition to five young gentlemen who could follow a course in "School Keeping and the Sciences of Intellectual Philosophy as applicable to mental culture."

Hard times had fallen on Transylvania University after the departure of President Holley. In 1830 President Alva Woods resigned; and for three years the university got along as best it could without definite guidance. At the end of that time, Peers was named president. An impressive inaugural ceremony inducted him into office. His incumbency was accompanied by the dedication of Morrison College, the celebration of the anniversary of the battle of the Thames, and the meeting of a convention of teachers, something quite new in Kentucky. President Peers, in his inaugural, urged the establishment of a school for the training of teachers; but the proposal lay dormant, to be used later as a means of interesting the legislature in the fortunes of the university and at the same time of meeting teacher training problems. President

[2] Lexington *Kentucky Reporter*, December 16, 1829.

Peers soon resigned to take the pastorate of a church of his denomination in Louisville. Discouraged as he undoubtedly was by the failure of his plan to reach official ears, he may have been gratified when his successor, the Rev. Thomas W. Coit, made an attempt in 1836 to place the Peers plan on a working basis. The legislature was asked to contribute $5,000 and to convert the university into a state normal school. For this subsidy, the institution agreed to give free tuition to one hundred state students. Important as it was that some definite plan be provided, the legislature thought otherwise, and the bill failed. The idea of a subsidy from the state for the preparation of teachers remained untouched for the next twenty years. Then the legislature made an appropriation for two years to be used by Transylvania University but refused to renew the grant at the expiration of the biennium.

By 1838 the state had proceeded in its consideration of schools as a part of the duty of the commonwealth to enact a bill to establish a system of common schools. The system, then only a nucleus, provided for the selection of a Superintendent of Public Instruction to administer it. Governor James Clark appointed to the new office the Rev. Joseph Bullock, who accepted, combining the office of Superintendent with the duties of pastor of the Presbyterian Church in Frankfort. Superintendent Bullock had had no teaching experience, but filled his office effectively. His first comment did not disclose a large conception of teacher training, for he said, "The founding of one or more normal schools for the purpose of training the sons of the soil for teaching is a favorite measure with many of the friends of education." This was hardly to be regarded as a battle cry, but he supplemented the remark by saying, "It is the view of reason and experience that normal schools must exist before education can be performed in the best possible manner and with the greatest possible success." The men who followed him in the office for seventy years continued to urge the establishment of schools for the training of teachers. Some were mild in their urgency; others were persistent and forceful. Dr. Hubbard H. Kavanaugh, afterwards a Methodist bishop, in his report said, "It is a system that needs a school of superior grade exclusively devoted to the instruction of teachers."[3] The next Superintendent of Public Instruction was Benjamin Bosworth Smith, who was quite definite in his recommendations urging the establishment of four normal schools, two for men and two for women, in the central part of the state and in the Green River area. In a second report, his first suggestions having come to naught, he urged that a normal school be established at Bowling Green at least. Throughout the years, the Superintendents kept expounding the need for normal schools, with some results as leaders in the political field began to hear what to them was the faint whispering of the pedagogues calling for the recognition of their profession.

The year after the constitution of 1850 was adopted, the method of selecting the Superintendent of Public Instruction was changed from appointment by the governor to choice by ballot. Dr. Robert J. Breckinridge was the last one to be appointed to the office and the first to be elected under the provisions of the new constitution. He made the definite proposal that $8,000 of the school fund income be used to maintain a school for teachers. He did not favor the establishment of a special school, but the bill which accompanied his report urged that provisions be made for the reorganization of Transylvania University and the establishment there of a school for teachers. The successor of Dr. Breckinridge was John D. Matthews, who directed attention to the bill prepared by his predecessor. The governor, Charles S. Morehead, pressed the proposal upon the attention of the legislature. The trustees of Transylvania University offered the college building and the services of the faculty to the state for the purposes of a normal school. The property and funds of the university, valued at more than a hundred thousand

[3] *Annual Report of the Superintendent of Public Instruction* (1840), 34.

dollars, were made available immediately. The act accepting the proposal was approved by the governor, March 10, 1856. Matters moved rapidly, for the new board of trustees met on June 10 and consented to all the changes to be made in the university's organization; they elected a president and five professors and agreed that the courses of study should cover all branches then taught in the common schools, together with the theory and practice of teaching. So that no time should be lost, the new normal school opened its doors in Lexington the first Monday of September, 1856, with eighty students enrolled. In the course of the first year, the Superintendent of Public Instruction reported, the county school commissioners sent 119 students to the new school. Said he, "The state has every reason to be proud of her school for teachers, and to cherish it as the apple of her eye."[4]

The new project for teacher training was hardly under way when the legislature refused to renew the $12,000 annual appropriation on the ground that the money was taken from the common school fund and could not be used for the support of a college. The legislature went through the process of unscrambling what it had done two years previously by passing an act to repeal the law of 1856 creating the school. It returned the property and gave up all claim upon the university. "This act has given a retrograde movement to state education which cannot be retraced at least for a quarter of a century," declared the indignant Dr. Matthews. And he was correct, but too optimistic in his estimate of the time required to right the mistake made by those ignorant and scheming men.

The need for teacher training, however, was insistent, and the efforts made to meet these needs were encouraged and abetted by the Superintendents of Public Instruction. Failing to get a normal school from the legislature, the friends of the movement resorted to other devices. A course of study was set up which the teachers were required by law to follow,

[4] *Ibid.* (1857).

and county institutes for teachers were provided and financed by a two-dollar fee. County institutes, which began in the early 1870's, were evidently not satisfactory teaching devices. Later, certain towns in the different congressional districts were designated as places where district institutes would be held. Superintendent Henderson hoped for an appropriation of $1,000 to carry the expense of district institutes and to give teachers the benefit of the presence of experienced persons on the programs. He saw clearly enough that the institute was not a substitute for a normal school in the preparation and training of teachers. Henderson succeeded in getting the legislature to pass a bill authorizing the holding of a normal institute for ten weeks in the buildings belonging to the Kentucky Military Institute at Farmdale. The plan was experimental and continued for the two summers of 1878 and 1879. The small grant was not renewed, however, partly because of the meager attendance of students.[5]

In 1880 the reorganization of the Agricultural and Mechanical College at Lexington gave an opportunity to place and maintain a Normal Department in the State College. The new charter of the institution provided what some thought was an answer to the long agitation for a normal school—"a normal department which was designated particularly, but not exclusively, to qualifying teachers for the common schools." The arrangement was not a real solution to the problem of state support for teacher training, because of the indifference on the part of the administration and the attitude of the college staff to the procedure of training teachers. The department went along as best it could under the circumstances until the state established two normal schools, one at Richmond and another at Bowling Green.[6] It was a year later when the Agricultural and Mechanical College, having been

---

[5] Travis E. Smith, *The Rise of Teacher Training in Kentucky* (Nashville, 1932), 127-134, 135-136; Hamlett, *History of Education in Kentucky*, 123.

[6] H. L. Donovan, *A State's Elementary Teacher-Training Problem* (Nashville, 1925), 17.

expanded into a State University (1907), discontinued the Normal Department and created the much more comprehensive and inclusive Department of Education. This department continued as a division of the College of Arts and Sciences in the university until 1922, when it was given a college status with a training school well organized and equipped. Through a gift of $150,000 from the General Education Board, supplemented by a similar sum appropriated by the state, the College of Education obtained a large building well adapted to its own work and that of the associated schools.

Many private schools also undertook to meet the needs of the state for teacher training. In *The Rise of Teacher Training in Kentucky,* Dr. Travis E. Smith presents a list of thirty-four such schools that received legislative charters between 1868 and 1905.[7] In Ohio, the Lebanon National Normal School drew from Kentucky many teachers seeking training in their profession. The example of this institution and its success, together with the lack of high schools and the possible opportunity for profit, may account for the many institutions that then made their appearance. One of the staff of the Lebanon Normal School had come to Glasgow, Kentucky, in 1875 and had started a school under the title of the Glasgow Normal School and Business College. The legislature granted a charter to the institution, authorizing it to hold annual commencements, public examinations, and to confer honorary degrees. The graduates received diplomas which entitled them to the rights of a first-class teacher's certificate.

In the meantime, buildings of the Bowling Green Female College were unoccupied due to failure in the operation of that institution. In 1884 the citizens of Bowling Green, recognizing that the buildings should be put to some good use, invited Professor Mell to come to their city and to

[7] Smith, *Rise of Teacher Training in Kentucky,* 161-162.

establish a school on the location of the defunct college. The founder of the Glasgow school accepted the invitation and began a successful history that was to culminate in the founding of the Western State Teachers College in 1906. Among the varied list of normal schools was one at Morehead, which the state was to acquire in 1922 for a Teachers College. Also, Mrs. Phoebe Button and her son, Frank C. Button, founded a school in what was referred to as the mountain area. This institution, sponsored by the Kentucky Christian Missionary Society, had begun its work in 1887. Many other institutions were started. Some of them did fine work, others were indifferently conducted, but all filled a place in preparing teachers while the people became accustomed to the idea that teacher training was fundamental to the success of a public school system.

After the adoption of the constitution of 1850, the legislature passed special acts permitting cities to maintain independent school systems. The city of Louisville, availing itself of this right in the city charter of 1851, was able to establish an independent school system. After twenty years of operation, the State Board of Education found the certificate and examining method of selecting teachers to be far from satisfactory. This situation led to the establishment of a city normal school in 1871. On the supposition that only women were needed in the system, the school's attendance was limited to girls. The annual demand for new teachers was thirty-six; of this number, thirty were selected from the Girls' High School and six at large. The school did a good service for Louisville and continued until 1935, when it was closed and the control and direction of teacher training in the city educational system were assumed by the University of Louisville.[8] By this arrangement, the City Board of Education was assured of a well-trained supply of teachers; and the university fostered an important service for the municipality.

[8] *Centennial History of the University of Louisville,* 221-222.

Evidently the legislature was able to see the need of better trained teachers in the schools for colored children, and a greater need than that of a common school education for those teaching in the schools for white children. The treatment accorded the schools for colored children was far from satisfactory, but in an act of 1886 the legislature established the Kentucky Normal and Industrial Institute for Negroes at Frankfort. The appropriation provided $7,000 for buildings and $3,000 annually for maintenance. Those sums were small indeed, but they did represent a principle, in that the state's obligation to provide such training was recognized. As already commented upon, the state had established a Normal Department in 1880 in the State Agricultural and Mechanical College at Lexington; but that provision did not satisfy the teachers of the state so far as they had any opinion at all about the raising of the standard of instruction in the schools. One turns in vain the pages of Superintendent Hamlett's *History of Education in Kentucky* to find in the administrations of State Superintendents from 1880 to 1907 any comments on the Kentucky Normal and Industrial Institute for colored persons. That institution, however, struggled along, receiving small grants for buildings and repairs and little sums for annual support. After 1907 the school grew considerably, due to an increasing recognition of its importance; and after a third of the new century had passed, the state materially increased the support given this school. Assisted by funds from the state, the Rosenwald Foundation, and the General Education Board, the training of colored teachers greatly improved.

In 1906 the legislature passed an act authorizing the establishment of normal schools at Richmond and Bowling Green. The following legislature, sometimes called the Educational Legislature, enacted laws which not only appropriated considerable money for the state's educational institutions, but changed the name of the State College to the State University of Kentucky and required that there should be a high school in every county. This was not all, for the legislature also enacted a county school district law, established a state educational commission to study the school system, and passed a compulsory school law which applied to cities of all four classes. These were notable accomplishments not to be explained by a change from indifference to interest in educational needs on the part of the legislature, but by the expression and influence of public opinion. James H. Fuqua, then Superintendent of Public Instruction, called a gathering of citizens in Frankfort in April, 1905. There was a large attendance at the meeting which authorized the appointment of committees that were told to proceed with vigor. At a conference in June, 1905, the committee, meeting with the Kentucky Education Association, formed the Educational Improvement Commission. The Education Association was asked to appoint a state campaign committee consisting of three members from each congressional district. Money was raised, speakers were appointed, and meetings were held in every county. The press ably supported the campaign. When the legislative committee appeared before the General Assembly, it was able to speak with authority backed by an aroused state public opinion. When the bill was presented to the law body, there was no opposition, and it passed without a single negative vote. The people interested in education had learned how to convince the legislature, and the aroused and organized feeling in favor of education was to be used many times in forcing favorable legislation.

The bill which was introduced in the General Assembly in 1906 by Richard W. Miller of Madison County provided for three normal schools. Each institution was to receive $50,000 for grounds, buildings, and equipment, and $25,000 annually to meet operating costs. To encourage teachers and also to increase good will toward the institutions, six students from each county were to be admitted without tuition charges. There were objections to the cost of so many new schools to which was added the demand for $50,000 for the purpose of enlarging the Normal Department of the University. To meet the situation, a new bill was introduced and substituted for the first one. By March 8, the General Assembly had passed the amended bill which was promptly signed by Governor Beckham. This legislation provided for a school in both districts one and two. There was a board of regents for each institution, the Superintendent of Public Instruction sitting on both boards. The city of Bowling Green and the owners of the Southern Normal School and Bowling Green Business University assisted in making buildings possible for the use of the new institution. Dr. Henry H. Cherry, one of the owners, gave to the state the good will of the institution. In Richmond, arrangements were made to present to the state the buildings of the old Central University.

The two institutions, however, began their history with plants hardly adequate for their activities. On the financial side, each institution was to have $5,000 with which to buy equipment and $20,000 to be used to defray the annual expenses of operation. When the boards of regents, through Superintendent Fuqua, applied for the appropriation of $5,-000, an injunction was filed against the auditor by the attorneys of N. A. Marsee, a property holder in Bell County. Judge R. L. Stout refused to grant the injunction. This was on July 20, 1906, and the case was appealed, with the result that the Court of Appeals, on April 24, 1907, affirmed the opinion of the Circuit Court.[9] Anticipating that the decision would be favorable to the contention of the schools, those interested borrowed money from local banks and opened the institutions in January, 1907. It was apparent to those who had charge of the new normal schools that buildings, equipment, and support were inadequate; so under the enthusiasm created by two "Whirl Wind Educational Campaigns" in 1907, the legislature opened the purse of the state and gave the State University $200,000 for new buildings, and each normal school $150,000. Under the able leadership of R. N. Roark,

---

[9] Marsee v. Hager, State Auditor, 125 *Kentucky Reports* 445.

at the Eastern Normal School, and Henry H. Cherry, as the president of the Western Normal School, these institutions began their interesting and useful history. President Roark, who had been the head of the Normal Department of the State University, died in 1909; he was succeeded by J. G. Crabbe, who at the time of his election to the presidency was State Superintendent of Public Instruction. Other presidents followed at Eastern Normal School in the persons of T. J. Coates, who died in 1928; Dr. H. L. Donovan; and later Richmond City Superintendent W. F. O'Donnell, who took office when Dr. Donovan became president of the University of Kentucky in 1941. At the Western Normal School, President Cherry continued in office from 1907 until his death in 1938, when he was succeeded by Paul Garrett, Superintendent of Schools in Versailles.

Two more normal schools were added to Kentucky's teacher training provisions in 1922. The incentive for these additions to the state's educational facilities came largely from the report of the Educational Commission, created by the legislature in 1920. In this report, the shortage of trained teachers was strongly emphasized by the statement that 1,450 elementary teachers were needed annually to take the places of those who were leaving the profession each year. The two schools already established could not graduate more than 400 well-trained teachers in a year.[10] So it appeared that there was an annual need for 1,000 new teachers, a need that could not be supplied by existing colleges, public and private. To meet this demand, five new normal schools would be required. The commission said, "To create that many at one stroke would be ill advised, but the next General Assembly should make a beginning by establishing at least one, preferably two." The commission recommended that one school be located in the Big Sandy Valley and the other west of the Tennessee River. The next legislature, in 1922, promptly took up the question of providing two more normal schools to

---

[10] *Public Education in Kentucky*, 181-183.

train white teachers. "Whereas, the state normal schools already established can neither reach nor train all the elementary teachers needed for the common schools; therefore, be it enacted by the Commonwealth of Kentucky," was the way the bill began. Toward the end of the session, Governor Edwin P. Morrow signed a bill which provided that lands and buildings amounting in value to at least $100,000 must be given by the communities where the schools were to be established. When this was done, $30,000 would be available for annual support.[11] Here was a scheme to get something for their towns, thought many citizens residing in communities within the areas or near them. Ardent campaigns supporting the claims of contending locations began at once.

The legislature did not leave the problem in the lap of a Republican governor, but provided that the Speaker of the House should name five members and the Lieutenant Governor, as presiding officer of the Senate, should name three members of the commission. When this was done, the locating commission consisted of Edward C. O'Rear, Earl W. Senff, W. S. Wallen, Thomas A. Combs, W. Goodpastor, J. L. Harmon, Alexander G. Barrett, and A. Potter. The commission then traveled over the state looking at sites and buildings, inquiring about water supplies, and hearing all and sundry who had anything to say about the location of the new schools. The selection of Morehead and Murray as the two favored towns was finally made, with considerable grumbling and opposition coming from the defeated town contestants.[12] The two new institutions were well treated by the legislature, which rapidly built large plants for the use of the schools. The first president of the Murray Normal School was John W. Carr, who was followed by Rainey T. Wells, who resigned to accept a more remunerative office on the legal staff of a fraternal order. He was succeeded by James H. Richmond,

---

[11] Kentucky, General Assembly, *Senate Journal, 1922*, 679-680.

[12] Unpublished Minutes of State Normal School Commission, November 21, 1922, May 21, 23, 29, July 18, August 6, 1923.

who was, at the time of his appointment, Superintendent of Public Instruction. Dr. Richmond died while in office in 1945. He was succeeded by Dr. Ralph H. Woods. At Morehead, Frank C. Button was asked to continue on where he and his mother had started many years before when the new normal school was located. When Dr. Button resigned he was succeeded by John H. Payne, who in turn resigned and was succeeded by Harvey Babb, former Superintendent of Schools at Mt. Sterling. Internal dissensions, which had disturbed the institution since the end of the Button administration, resulted in the withdrawal of Babb, who was followed by Dr. W. H. Vaughn and later by Dr. William Jesse Baird in 1946.

In 1922 the Normal Schools, by the recognition of the legislature, became Teachers Colleges with the right to grant certificates upon credentials and to confer degrees. The law set forth very definite requirements in hours and credits for the attainment of a degree or a certificate to teach. It was apparent by this time that normal schools must broaden their curricula to a four-year college course, not only to meet requirements for teacher training, but to give opportunity for majors in all fields of knowledge needed by the elementary and secondary schoolteachers of the state. Another act followed in 1930 which authorized the colleges to extend their curricula whenever the needs of the commonwealth should require it. Soon a year of graduate study was added; and with this action, the normal schools became Teachers Colleges, then State Colleges, with quite as much emphasis being laid upon the general college course as upon that of teacher training. In fact, the state now has four colleges of Arts and Sciences in addition to the one within the organization of the State University.

CHAPTER XII

A KENTUCKY EDUCATION ASSOCIATION

FROM small beginnings dating as far back as 1829, a large and powerful Kentucky Education Association at last emerged. With the growth in membership, professional standing, and influence, the association has accomplished many important things which have advanced the interest and welfare of public education in Kentucky. Seldom has its purpose been deterred or influenced by personal interest. The public schools, while having friends in the association, also possessed the advantage of an increasing number of wise advisers. These men and women looked to public education as a great agency through which the state might confidently expect a growing number of young citizens to take their place in the development of the commonwealth of Kentucky. In 1945 the association had a membership of eighteen thousand, with every school in the state not yet represented on the roster of its membership. Such figures stand out in marked contrast to the small groups who attended the meetings in the last century. Teaching has gradually reached a professional status; although not yet fully recognized, it has made great gains, largely through the efforts of the association to raise the standards of instruction, to better the curricula, to increase the pay, and to insure the tenure of the public school teachers and administrators. Without the Kentucky Education Association, the purpose and effectiveness of public education in the state would have bogged down to the despair of such friends as it had. Nor is this too large a claim to make when the whole story of education in Kentucky is fully understood.

The material on which a history of the Kentucky Education Association might rest still remains scattered and somewhat difficult to find, though Superintendent J. O. Lewis has gathered much of it. He opens his history of the association with the call issued by Dr. R. J. Breckinridge, State Superintendent of Public Instruction, to the friends of education to meet in conference at Frankfort, November 12, 1851, to consider the entire subject of public education in the state. The meeting was a lively one, if the resolutions and the minutes of the meeting are evidence of the variety of topics considered and the time taken for discussion. This meeting resulted in the organization of an association called the "Friends of Education."[1]

In the newspapers of the day there are to be found accounts of teachers' meetings as early as 1829. "Pursuant to public notice," says the Lexington *Kentucky Reporter* in a brief article, "a considerable number of teachers of Fayette and the adjoining counties assembled at the Courthouse in Lexington, April 18, 1829."[2] Among those present was the Rev. Alva Woods, president of Transylvania University. It was resolved at this meeting "that in order to remedy as far as possible, all such inconsequences and impediments in the business of teaching and for any mutual improvement and advantage by a free interchange of views and opinions on the subject of education, we shall at the next meeting constitute ourselves a Society or Association, to be designated by an appropriate name to be agreed upon." The Teachers' Association met on July 18. In printing the notice of the meeting, the editor said in his paper that "we consider such efforts as it is now making as intimately connected with the future moral and intellectual well being of the people of this country."[3] B. O. Peers, Beverly Hicks, and Professor Matthews were appointed at the meeting of April 18, 1829, to draw up

---

[1] James O. Lewis, "A History of the Kentucky Educational Association" (M.A. thesis, University of Chicago, 1927), 1-4.

[2] Lexington *Kentucky Reporter*, April 22, 1829.

[3] *Ibid.*, July 8, 1829.

a constitution and bylaws. The next meeting was fixed for May 3, 1829. To this meeting and the others that followed, not only were teachers invited but the school trustees as well.[4] The next news item about the early teachers' organization is to be found in the Frankfort *Commonwealth,* in which it appears that the annual Convention of Professional Teachers met in Frankfort, August 27, 1834. The convention, evidently desiring inspiration and somewhat tired of talks and debates, instructed the Executive Committee to secure for the next meeting addresses from distinguished and talented gentlemen on the subject of education. The resolutions laid on the minds of the members of the Executive Committee the need to consider and adopt the best means of raising the business of education to the standing of a profession.[5] Both admonitions to the Executive Committee still remain on the agenda of subjects yet to be considered in its solemn meetings of today, after more than a century of talk.

In the year in which the foregoing activities were taking place, there appears an interesting item in the same paper, a notice that the first annual meeting of the Kentucky Common School Society would be held in Frankfort, January 14, 1835. Evidently the high-sounding name of "Professional Teachers," adopted by the organization formed at an earlier date, had created some umbrage and perhaps sounded a note of snobbishness. A state convention of teachers, held in Frankfort in the summer of 1834, resolved to hold future meetings in Lexington. The first week in November was selected as the date of the convention. This time was referred to as the anniversary of the State Society of Education. The Executive Committee extended an invitation to all professional teachers and friends of education to convene in Lexington during November, 1835. The invitation was signed by members of the committee who evidently wished to emphasize their professional status by the manner in which they designated them-

[4] *Ibid.,* April 22, 1829.
[5] Frankfort *Commonwealth,* September 2, 1834.

selves. A line was drawn between the professional and common school teachers in the organization.[6] And again the following year, reference to the annual meeting of the professional teachers appeared in the *Kentucky Gazette* of September 1, 1836. This meeting was held in Cincinnati to consider the chief interests of an institution referred to as a college. The notice does not state what college. Several years later, a short article appeared over the signature of Noble Butler, as secretary, under the title of "College of Teachers." "The meeting," writes Butler, "will be devoted to the discussion of school laws; how the good may be retained and the evil removed; can able and efficient teachers be provided for the whole country; what measure can be taken to reform our colleges and schools and cause them to be properly appreciated and sustained?" The appeal to the readers is in the following sentence: "Shall we feel more zeal in matters of temporary importance than in the great and lasting interest of education?"[7] That all should come and lend their aid in stimulating public intelligence and virtue was the call to teachers and citizens.

Teachers had been meeting together more or less regularly for at least twenty years before Dr. Beckinridge made his call for a convention of the Friends of Education in 1851. The purpose of these earlier meetings was largely to provide for better acquaintance among the teachers and to discuss the means by which the status of the teacher might be improved. The addresses on the programs were largely devoted to moral and ethical questions, for professional requirements and pedagogical methods were not so far to the fore then as today. The call for the convention stated that the entire subject of public education in the state would be considered. To stimulate discussion, eight special topics were submitted as desirable subjects for consideration: (1) the length of the school term; (2) the particular course of studies in the district schools;

---

[6] Lexington *Intelligencer*, September 29, 1835.
[7] Frankfort *Protestant and Herald*, July 20, 1839.

(3) the particular textbooks in each branch of study; (4) the best modes of conducting courses; (5) the general use of the Scriptures as a class book; (6) the establishment of normal schools for teachers; (7) the increase of, and the best mode for distributing, the school funds; (8) school architecture. All of these subjects were decidedly pertinent and practical.

Before the convention adjourned, resolutions were adopted which followed the outline in the call. It was the sense of the convention that the school quarter should consist of twelve weeks, and a daily session of six or seven hours. The course of study should include, said the resolutions, a thorough knowledge of spelling, reading, writing, geography with maps, arithmetic, the history of the United States, English grammar, and the elements of general history. The convention set up a committee of five to examine and recommend textbooks and to report at the next annual meeting. The resolutions were concerned with schoolhouses and their equipment, the length of the school term, and the need for one association in every county. Attention was called to the need for high schools and for the training of teachers for the common schools of the state. The declaration ended with the request that the Bible be used in all the schools and that the commonwealth provide more money for the complete establishment and support of the schools.[8] The Friends of Education had their feet on the ground, for the program they set up in their resolutions was a practical one. It was, in fact, a program that the state might well have adopted; and if the plan laid out at the time had only been followed, the state would have materially aided the growth of the public school system and would have stayed the enervating forces at work during the next twenty years.

The Friends of Education met in Louisville the following year, but enthusiasm had died down considerably, due no doubt to the retirement of Dr. Breckinridge from the

[8] *Annual Report of State Superintendent of Public Instruction* (1851), 201-205.

office of State Superintendent; for he had furnished most of the leadership and had given a crusader spirit to the Friends of Education. For five years, no state meeting was held so far as can be ascertained from the records of the time. Then in 1857 a convention met in December during the Christmas holidays. Evidently no organization existed, for the convention appointed a committee on constitution which was to serve as a basis of a permanent organization. On the last day of the session, the constitution was adopted and the title of "Kentucky Association of Teachers" was accepted as the name of the new organization.[9] By an act of the General Assembly in 1858, the new association was granted a charter which provided for a president, two vice-presidents, and a secretary-treasurer, all of whom constituted a board of directors authorized to fill vacancies and name their successors.[10] Meetings were held in 1858 and 1859, and then for the next five years the association did not meet. The state had declared its neutrality in the war; and when invaded by both armies, the people were in great confusion over the political and economic issues involved, while Kentucky came more and more under the control of Federal sympathizers. In 1865 there was a note in the proceedings of the association indicating that a three-day session had been held, beginning August 1, which was attended by nearly one hundred persons. Again reference was made to an association showing that the war years had left no successor to the earlier organization. Shelbyville was the scene of the meeting in 1866, and in 1867 the association gathered in the darkness of the Gothic chapel of Mammoth Cave. The president was the Superintendent of Public Instruction, Daniel Stevenson, who spoke upon the larger school unit, recommending the county as a better form of organization for the conduct of the public schools than the district. He also discussed the distribution of the school funds on something more than a per capita basis. The number of

---

[9] Lewis, "A History of the Kentucky Educational Association," 4-5.
[10] Kentucky *Acts, 1858*, 174.

days taught as well as the number of pupils should be considered in the distribution of the school fund.[11]

From time to time, the early meetings of the association were enlivened by demands for constructive legislation and for more money with which to support the schools of the state. These demands were coolly received by the legislature. In 1868 the General Assembly had by law made the Superintendent of Public Instruction ex officio president of the association. This caused much dissatisfaction among the members, who wanted to elect their own president. The first Superintendent to serve ex officio was Dr. Z. F. Smith, and the second, H. A. M. Henderson. The legislature heeded the protests of the association and rescinded the act of 1868, but in a new law placed the association under the direction and control of the State Board of Education. It is doubtful if a similar example of such procedure can be found in the annals of education. "The Board shall have power to organize and keep in existence a State Teachers' Association, to be composed of the members of the board, all the officers and teachers connected with the common schools throughout the State, all officers and teachers connected with public free schools in any city or town in the Commonwealth, together with such other teachers and friends of popular education as the board of education may invite to become members of such organization, for the purpose of promoting the cause of common schools in the State." The law permitted the members of the association to elect their own officers and to adopt by-laws and rules for the government of the organization.[12] It does not appear that the Board of Education tried to influence the action of the association, but the very fact that the organization could charge no fees left it without much to go on. Little by little attendance fell off, and the recorded membership was listed as fourteen in 1884. When the Board of Education in 1868 tried to fix the time and place of meeting,

[11] Lewis, "A History of the Kentucky Educational Association," 7-8.
[12] Ibid., 10.

there had been a vigorous protest. The ends of the organization, declared Captain Gaines, could not be accomplished with the association "under a half control" of the State Board and the State Superintendent of Public Instruction. It was the view of many members that "From their arbitrary control as a body, we must free ourselves. . . . only as an independent organization can we work out the great end in view." The debate was a heated one, interrupted by Dr. Poynter, who took the opportunity to introduce a resolution calling upon the organization to appoint a committee to confer with the State Board of Education to make an adjustment that would resolve the difficulties and prevent the creation of a short-lived organization.[18] The records do not show any committee report, nor is there evidence that the controversy was continued.

The members of the association, however, were far from satisfied with its accomplishments. The meeting in Paducah, 1892, adopted a third constitution; although the purpose of the organization was fairly well known, the membership found it difficult to get much done. The offering of motions in open meeting followed by discussion developed big talk but little action. By 1895 the association felt the need of permanent committees, and at the meeting of that year it created the Committee of Ten. The yeast of a better organization was working among the members as shown in the constitution of 1907 and by the incorporation of the association in the same year. The constitution of 1907 provided for an executive committee, an elected secretary for a term of three years on a salary, and the establishment of departments to encourage the discussion of the problems of special groups. From one year to another the constitution was amended; but the instrument was not satisfactory, though the organization continued to function under it for nearly twenty years. A new constitution, the work of a committee appointed in 1925, was adopted

---

[18] *Ibid.*, 11-12.

the following year. When the incorporation period of twenty-five years ended in 1932, the association took the opportunity offered by the need of reincorporation entirely to reorganize the association and its working procedures. The purpose activating the association continued to be much the same, although more definitely stated. In brief, it was to form a closer union of the teachers of the state, to advance the ideals and standards of the teaching profession, and to promote educational welfare within the borders of Kentucky. Membership was extended to all persons engaged in educational work and to those interested in education. With better transportation facilities and increased interest, the district associations, based upon the eleven congressional districts, were given an important place in the new organization. Representatives of these district groups were to form the delegate assembly, on the basis of one delegate for each one hundred members, thus making a body of nearly two hundred. The delegate assembly was to elect the officers of the association and to advise the board of directors as well as recommend and adopt educational policies and activities to be pursued by the association.[14]

In addition to sending delegates to the assembly, the district associations could elect one member each on the board of directors. This body was the advisory board of the association. The duties of the board were set forth in section four, of article four, of the constitution. The board appointed the executive secretary for a four-year period; it also made arrangements for meetings and performed such other duties as were prescribed by the constitution.

At the meeting of the assembly in 1934, the board of directors was instructed to establish a planning board composed of nine members representing county and city superintendents, the State Department of Education, the University of Kentucky, the teachers colleges, private colleges, and the laity. Upon this board was laid the duty of instigating legis-

---

[14] Constitution of the Kentucky Education Association, Article VIII.

lation, of studying and evaluating it, of assisting in the promotion of favorable laws, and of opposing detrimental lawmaking. The history of educational legislation since 1934 justifies—in fact, shows—the able work of the planning board in the advancement of education in Kentucky. In 1935 the Kentucky Education Association supplied the major portion of the funds required to finance the state-wide survey of education in Kentucky; and the following year it appropriated the funds necessary for placing the survey report before the people of the state. As a result, a new code was written which has proved to be a real help to educational progress.

For some time, discussion continued on the problem of teacher retirement, though it was not until 1937 that the association started a real campaign for a law to legalize and to create a retiring system. Two years later the legislature appropriated a half million dollars to finance the plan authorized in 1938. Another matter that interested the educational groups in the state centered about the amendment of the constitution so that a better and more equitable distribution of public school funds might be authorized. The fixed system of distribution on a per capita basis left much to be desired. In the less populated and poorer counties of the state, the funds for the support of schools were wholly inadequate; and these schools were unable to meet the higher standards of instruction and school maintenance desired by the State Department and required by law. The amendment to distribute 10 per cent of the school fund to assist county schools passed by a vote of the people and became a law in 1942. Prior to 1933 the association had advocated vocational education in the schools, sponsored consolidation of schools, and insisted upon a seven-month term. All of these important steps were enacted. A minimum salary for county superintendents, better salaries for teachers, and uniform certification were urged by the organization; and the provisions for such action became part of the law of the state. The need for rural high schools received the attention of the association, and in 1918 every county in Kentucky was required to have at least one high school. Free textbooks had been a matter of concern among the people for some time; but the appropriation of money for textbooks was delayed from session to session, until finally provision was made for free books in the first six grades. All these accomplishments cover but a portion of the activities of the association for the past three decades. When added together its activities show an increasing amount of valuable work and achievement.

In the early history of the educational associations, there was no official publication, although their doings are to be found in fragmentary reports printed in the local press where the associations met. As early as 1851, the Friends of Education discussed the establishment of an official journal, but the cost was too much for the limited number of members to undertake; however, they did approve the use of a periodical called *Home and School,* published in Louisville, as their medium of publicity. Nothing more was done about their own publication for some time. There is a brief comment in the report of the State Superintendent in 1859 that the *Educational Monthly* was published under the auspices of the association.[15] A *Kentucky Journal of Education* is reported as the semiofficial publication of 1869. Fifteen years later, the *Educational Courant,* edited by R. H. Cand of Louisville, was made the official organ of the association, and the editor served as secretary, a policy now in effect, though assistant editors have been employed now and then to help the secretary in preparing material for publication. In 1901 the *Southern School Journal,* edited by Rice Eubanks, was made the official journal. In 1921 the *Association Bulletin* was issued as a quarterly, and became the first publication owned and edited under the auspices of the Kentucky Education Association. Thus a long time had passed before the association was able to express its ideas through its own journal. The

[15] *Annual Report of State Superintendent of Public Instruction* (1859), 6.

Bulletin became the *Journal* two years later; and in 1925 the quarterly publication was extended to one issued each month of the school year. In addition, the secretary's office now issues a gossipy sheet called *Flashes* in which the activities of members and meetings of educational organizations are reported.

Now for a considerable period, the Kentucky Education Association has advanced in power, financial stability, and leadership. The annual election of a secretary has been discontinued, and a permanent officer is appointed by the board of directors. The first salaried and continuously employed secretary of the association was R. E. Williams, who served from 1916 to 1933. He was succeeded by W. P. King, who has continued in office since the death of Williams. Other men had served as secretaries previously; the first was E. A. Holyoke, and the first permanent part-time secretary was R. H. Carothers, who held the office from 1884 to 1894. T. W. Vinson gave part-time service from 1906 to 1916.

The position of president has been held from 1851 to 1945 by sixty-five different persons. Of this number, ten were in office for two or more years. With the exception of McHenry Rhoads, no president has filled the position for more than one term since 1894. In the early days, the State Superintendent became president by virtue of his position as head of the Department of Education. Thus Daniel Stevenson, Zachary F. Smith, and H. A. M. Henderson, by law, were presidents of the association from 1865 to 1878. The other presidents who headed the association for more than one term are: R. D. Allen, 1883 to 1886; R. R. Roark, 1886 to 1888; J. J. Glenn, for two years; and C. H. Dietrich, the last of the double termers, 1890 to 1892. The main business of the president, aside from that of presiding over meetings, is to prepare the general programs. On the whole, these programs have been maintained at a high level, though the tendency is to fill the time allotted with entertainment and information on current questions. Many persons of distinction have addressed the association from time to time. The growth in members and the attendance at the annual meeting have reached such numbers that Louisville has been the only city in the state capable of entertaining the convention. Even in that city the auditorium is not large enough to seat more than half of those who wish to attend the general meetings. The association and the city of Louisville hope that this situation may be improved upon in the not distant future.

With such a large membership in the Kentucky Education Association, the board of directors is constantly being asked to find places on the program for the special interests of different groups. The emphasis upon technique and subject matter places a mandate, so many think, to provide time in which special and detailed matters may be discussed. The constitution of the association sets up six departments: superintendents, elementary education, secondary education, vocational education, higher education, and fine arts. These, in turn, include from two to seven sections each; but that is not all, for there are no less than fourteen associated groups. Without doubt these multiplied activities have greatly impaired the departmental meetings, even in the face of the effort to hold one general program for each department. And in some cases a sectional meeting has overshadowed not only the department, but drawn to it the members belonging to other sections. The association now faces a serious problem of co-ordination to clarify the minds of the association membership on the purpose, philosophy, and guidance of public education in Kentucky. No doubt, as in other times, the directors and leaders will meet this issue so important to the welfare of the organization.

The Kentucky Negro Education Association had its beginnings in a call to a number of Negro teachers to meet with the Superintendent of Public Instruction to consider a legislative proposal to establish a normal school for Negro teachers. This was in 1877; the Superintendent was H. A. M. Henderson. At this meeting, sufficient leadership and enthusiasm were manifested to give an incentive to the organization of the present association, which held in 1945 its sixty-eighth annual convention.[16] The membership now numbers 1,700. During its history, this association has sponsored legislation to improve the educational facilities for Negroes and to secure the participation of colored citizens in state and federal activities. Perhaps the most important legislation sponsored by the association has been that relating to the establishment of dual boards of education and the removal of the bar to participation in the general tax funds raised for the support of education. When the survey of 1933 was authorized by the legislature, the Kentucky Negro Education Association gave $500 to help finance the work done by the survey commission. The association publishes a journal which now appears four times a year. In 1942, at the annual convention, a new constitution was adopted. The purpose stated in Article II in forming the now incorporated organization was "to elevate the teaching profession and to advance the cause of education among all the people of Kentucky, especially the Negro population." Any person who paid the annual fee of one dollar could become an associate member, but the active membership was limited to persons engaged in educational work. The usual officers were provided for, with the addition of a historian. The business of the association was placed in the hands of a board of directors composed of the presidents of the district teachers' associations. With the approval of the board, twenty or more persons were permitted to organize a department or conference which would have full autonomy to elect officers and conduct meetings. In the main, the constitution, while providing for the work of the association, placed a number of restrictions on membership and the holding of office. The programs of the conventions give a great deal of time to music; about a third is taken

[16] *KNEA Journal*, XII, No. 2 (1942), 5-6.

up with general addresses, and the remaining portion with sectional meetings.

At the University of Kentucky, a state conference on education has been held since 1927. At the beginning, the time of the conference was devoted to educational questions of general interest, in which opportunity was offered to everyone for questions or comments. In the past decade other organizations have joined in the meetings until the original purpose has been considerably modified. In fact, the program today is very extensive, including what might be called the full meeting of many sections of the Kentucky Education Association. There are no fees and no memberships required of those who attend. The programs have been of a high order in which notable figures in the field of education have taken part. The proceedings of the conferences have been published by the University of Kentucky, and in them are to be found many significant papers. Meeting at the same time and place, the Kentucky Association of Schools and Colleges holds its annual convention to consider matters of classification and standardization in which both colleges and high schools are concerned.

The private colleges of the state organized an association in 1929, which is now called the Kentucky Association of Church-Affiliated Colleges. This association meets annually and uses the time to consider matters of special interest to its members.[17] There are other teachers' organizations, but this chapter has endeavored to tell the story of the larger groups because of their achievements during a history of nearly one hundred years.

[17] A. B. Crawford, "The History of State Educational Associations," (M.A. thesis, University of Kentucky, 1932).

CHAPTER XIII

EDUCATIONAL CAMPAIGNS AND SURVEYS

IN THE first three decades of this century much attention was given to surveys and studies dealing with the organization and management of public school systems. Cities here and there sought to find out what the school facts were and how to meet the problems arising from those facts. Colleges and universities also began to look at their interior mechanisms; and a few of the states, stimulated by interested and sometimes irate citizens, undertook to examine the whole educational system within their boundaries. These activities produced a great mass of material in the form of reports and recommendations which in many instances proved to be of real value. There arose, too, a gifted group of surveyors and survey experts who were asked to guide these studies. Sometimes the reports of the commissions were so drastic that the public, especially those interests, individuals, and communities whose affairs would be disturbed if certain recommendations were carried out, raised strong protests with the result that the reports were laid aside to gather dust in the pigeonholes of time. Still it can be said that even these reports when published produced some effect, which, though not apparent at the time, nevertheless made a contribution and caused a turn for the better in the public's opinion of education. Some of the investigations cost a great deal of money which was raised by private individuals, appropriated by legislatures and school boards, or taken from college budgets. In not a few instances the funds provided were supplemented by gifts from the educational foundations such as the General Education Board and the Carnegie Foundation for the Advancement of Teaching.

In the survey of a state, the United States Bureau of Education, now the United State Office of Education, would offer the services of the staff, assisted by invited experts, in making the study of a state's educational system. When the work was completed, the state so surveyed had a great deal of information for future guidance toward bettering its system of education. The fact that outside experts had come into a state or institution to make a study of its needs did not always mean that they were able to sense the whole situation. Such failure, or partial failure, often resulted in the states and cities using their own people to make what are sometimes called self-surveys. The work of the Kentucky Educational Commission of 1933 was one such survey, the results from which were decidedly satisfactory.

A Kentucky "whirlwind campaign" for education took place in 1908 and 1909. Its purpose was to arouse the people to the difficulties confronting public education in the state and to make them conscious not only of the lack of funds but of the need for specific legislation. Another campaign, called the Bond Issue Campaign, was carried on in 1924 for the purpose of securing the consent of the people to an issue of $75,000,000 in bonds necessary for the improvement of the state's institutions of higher learning, for the construction and the repair of roads, and for the remodeling and extending of state penal and charitable institutions. It was an interesting campaign, but the bond issue failed to pass, by a vote of 275,873 for the proposal as opposed to 374,319 against. The surveys undertaken from 1916 on have been of the study type made by the Illiteracy Commission concerning work done by that body to advance the cause of literacy during the years 1916-1920. The report of the Commission of 1921 on the elementary and secondary schools of the state was an extended survey of the state's educational system. In 1933 another study was made which included finance, consideration of curricula, administration, teacher training, tenure of teachers, and, in fact, the whole organization of public education in Kentucky.

"I opened the campaign for better education in Kentucky, November 28, 1908," says State Superintendent J. G. Crabbe in his report of that year. "The campaign was a continuous cyclone bombardment against illiteracy and ignorance, for a period of nine days." A staff of twenty-nine speakers addressed audiences aggregating sixty thousand; and in their travels the speakers, one or more, visited every county in the state. Considerable interest was aroused in Kentucky by this campaign; and as a consequence the people were brought to a real enthusiasm for an adequate system of public education. The energetic Dr. Crabbe followed his first campaign with a second which was better planned and more extensively advertised than the first had been. In addition, the operations of the campaign were extended into the rural districts in an effort "to put new life and vigor in the country schools." Much of the paraphernalia of the modern campaign was used. There were special programs, bands, parades, and rallies in every county of the state. The barbecues and noonday meals brought thousands of people to these meetings. The speakers were primed with materials prepared by the Department of Education. Facts and figures were supplied to the one hundred speakers so that they might be well informed about education or the lack of it in the state. A roster of the men and women who made the speeches is an honor roll that included the best the state could produce. "Much has been accomplished," said the Superintendent, "but the work is not complete. It is merely in its infancy and we propose 'to fight it out on this line.'"[1]

No doubt the campaign did much to arouse a genuine interest in public education among the people. The second "whirlwind campaign" demonstrated that under the leadership of interested and devoted men and women, supported by

---

[1] Hamlett, *History of Education in Kentucky*, 200-202.

the press, pulpit, and public-spirited organizations, the people could be aroused and their interest sustained for the vital thing called public education. The State Federation of Women's Clubs for years prior to the campaign had labored in behalf of educational interests in the state, and the support of that great organization added much to the effectiveness of the campaign. In January of 1908 the so-called Educational Legislature began its work; and from this session came many important laws. The new normal schools were granted money and the State University, given that status by legislative act, also received funds for buildings and support. Other legislation provided for an educational commission, established county boards of education, helped the normal school for colored persons, passed laws regulating school attendance, and required by law that every county should provide a high school within two years. Thus the ideals set forth in the whirlwind campaigns came to maturity in the Sullivan Bill.

While there was an advance in the establishment of colleges for teacher preparation and some forward steps were taken toward a better high school system, further progress was retarded by lack of sufficient funds. The report of the Commission of 1921 emphasized all those needs and thereby provided a real basis for a bond issue necessary to obtain funds to meet the educational requirements of the state. Money was needed not only for education, but for roads and charitable and penal institutions. North Carolina had voted $76,000,000 for road construction alone, of which $50,000,000 was provided by the issue of bonds. By the time Kentucky had begun to think in the same terms, North Carolina had built main highways throughout the state which were in marked contrast to the narrow, black-topped roads in Kentucky.[2] What had been started so doubtfully now had resulted in modern highways which filled the citizens of North Carolina with pride and satisfaction. On the contrary, in Kentucky

[2] *Manufacturers Record*, LXXXV, No. 21 (May 22, 1924), 76-82.

there was resentment about the inadequate roads. Among the more thoughtful people, deep concern was felt about the condition of the University and the colleges of higher learning, the charitable and penal institutions, and the backwardness of the rural schools. Out of this situation came the conviction that Kentucky could better the unsatisfactory conditions existing in her institutions and on her highways by borrowing money and pledging the state's credit for thirty years. When lumped together, the proposed bond issue amounted to $75,000,000. The educational institutions of the state were to receive $8,250,000 for buildings and equipment; $5,000,000 for the rejuvenation of public schools; $6,000,000 for debt refunding; $5,000,000 was to be appropriated for charitable and penal institutions; $350,000 for the State Board of Health; $400,000 for the Geological Survey to map the state; $350,000 for the tuberculosis sanatorium; and $50,000,000 for roads.[3] It was a sizable sum, from any point of view, to be submitted to the people for their approval. In the whole previous history of the state no bond issue had ever been approved by popular vote. Was there enough interest among the people of the state and was there enough concern about education, or the care of the state's wards, or the need for modern roads to break down this long-time tradition? This fear of defeat of a bond issue was based upon a constitutional debt limit of a half-million dollars which could not be increased except through the consent of the people at the polls.

After much discussion, the legislature passed the act proposing a constitutional amendment; it was approved by the governor on March 7, 1924. A good deal of criticism was directed against the bill in the assembly and in the press on the number of beneficiaries appearing in the bond issue proposal. It was said that the numerous purposes recorded in the act were an attempt to line up as many interests in behalf of the bill as possible so as to secure a large support for

[3] Kentucky *Acts, 1924*, 436-452.

its adoption by the people. The campaign that followed was a vigorous one in which both sides, by speeches, huge posters, letters, and advertisements, endeavored to influence the voters. There were also caustic editorials and comments in the press that reflected upon the honesty of politicians and the disinterestedness of educators. The main burden of support was carried by the institutions concerned, the highway department, and such citizens as were interested in the adoption of the bond issue. On the other side, those who feared the financial structure of the bond scheme and who always opposed expenditures of money for public purposes fought as vigorously as they could any increase in the public debt. In addition, the opponents of the measure pointed to the inadequacy of support for the payment of interest and declared the sinking fund plan would result in the depletion of other funds and thus increase taxes. The history of the state's finances since that date might justify this position for part of the period, especially during the depression of 1929-1938. Looking back on this campaign from the vantage point of nearly twenty years, it appears that Kentucky would have found the debt a difficult burden to carry. It waited a long time for help from Federal funds, in the form of the WPA and the PWA, and for the betterment of state revenue through the passage of an income tax and a sales tax. Nevertheless, the state continued to get along with its narrow, old-fashioned roads for another ten years, and was compelled to endure depreciating and devastating criticism of its institutions by experts from outside and from the grand juries of the counties in which the institutions were located. What the state lost in self-respect, what damage was done to the inmates of her institutions, and how the children attending the public schools suffered are things that will forever remain unknown. It might have been well had Kentucky been lifted to a higher level of attainment even if it had to be by her own boot straps.

In 1911 the United States Census Bureau issued a report on illiteracy in this country. According to that report there were 5,516,163 men and women in the United States who could neither read nor write. Of this number, 208,084 lived in Kentucky. The report was a great shock to the people of the country, and much was said about the illiterates and the danger from such a large number of persons who could not be reached by the written or printed word. The fact that such a large proportion of the illiterates was to be found in Kentucky, almost one-tenth of the population in the state, raised much criticism about the accuracy of the report. So great was the resentment that the Census Bureau was finally persuaded to allow the names and addresses of illiterates to be listed. Here was proof positive that the facts gathered by the census takers were unfortunately true.

Shortly after the appearance of the census figures, an able and energetic woman, Cora Wilson Stewart, began a literacy campaign in Rowan County, in 1911. After three years of such work in some twenty-five counties, the legislature created the Kentucky Illiteracy Commission with authority to gather data and organize schools; but in the traditional legislative manner, it failed to appropriate the money to carry on this work. Appeals were made to clubs, federations, and other interested groups with the result that considerable funds were raised. In 1916 the legislature, impressed by the interest of the people in the movement, provided an appropriation to assist in financing it. The procedure followed was that of using rural schoolhouses at night, hence the romantic name of "Moonlight Schools." Teachers volunteered or were paid modest compensation to carry on and to give instruction to those who came. When the commission got under way, district agents were employed to hold meetings and to urge people who could not read or write to attend the schools. The campaign continued for four years, supported by state appropriations and contributions made by many people and organizations. During the period December 1, 1915, to July 1, 1920, the commission received funds amounting to $103,706.63. Of this amount, the state gave $85,000; a Committee of One Hundred, $4,410; the Thirty Thousand Campaign raised $10,938.19; and the Federation of Women's Clubs contributed $11,255.61.[4] The state was congratulated upon all sides, for Kentucky was the first to inaugurate a movement to reduce the number of adult illiterates. "It marks," said a writer in a bulletin of the United States Bureau of Education, "a new era in Kentucky and for all the country, for the idea will be taken up by other states and the march will go on until the curse and shame of illiteracy have been lifted from every state in the Union." Before the commission had finished its work, a final report was published in which five recommendations were made. These were as follows: to establish a state department of night schools, to pay teachers in such schools reasonable salaries, to appoint a commissioner of adult education, to establish a state school for adults, and to provide for an adequate teaching staff in the state's penal institutions.[5]

By 1920 the movement had spent itself; the results of the four years' campaign were analyzed, and the idea that illiteracy is not a matter of reading and writing but a state of mind had taken hold of the school people of the state. Of the five recommendations presented in the report, one only found a place in the educational program of the state when the Department of Education created a Bureau of Adult Education. The commission claimed that 130,000 of Kentucky's illiterates had been redeemed by the work which it had done. The state school census, taken in 1918, placed the number of illiterates in the state as 90,000. Two years later, the 1920 Census stated that the percentage of illiteracy had dropped to 8.4 per cent. A decade later, the same authority placed the illiterates in Kentucky at 131,545 or 6.6 per cent of the population. To complete the facts about illiteracy, attention is called at this point to the change in method in enumerating illiterates adopted by the Bureau of the Census

[4] *Kentucky Illiteracy Commission Report, 1916-1920*, 122.
[5] *Ibid.*, 9.

in 1940. It now asks the question: How many persons of twenty-five years of age or more are there in a state who have had less than a year of schooling? In 1940 there were 58,533 persons in that classification in Kentucky. However, the revelation brought to the people of the state by the census of 1920, as well as the feeling prevailing among the leading men and women engaged in teaching and administering the public schools, led to the passage of an act of 1920 which provided for an educational survey. Prior to that time, Dr. Leonard P. Ayres had been engaged in studying the comparative standing of the state school systems. According to his figures, Kentucky had dropped from thirty-fifth in 1890 to forty-fifth in 1918. This information, spread over the state and the nation, added materially to the demand that the people of Kentucky should at least know what the situation was. So the bill to create an investigating commission passed, and the state appropriated $10,000 to assist in its work. The General Education Board contributed $15,000 and provided a small staff directed by Dr. Frank Bachman. The governor appointed on the commission Dr. W. A. Ganfield, of Centre College; A. G. Barret, of the Louisville Board of Education; J. L. Harman, president of Bowling Green Business University; C. J. Haydon, of the Springfield Board of Education; and Miss Katie McDaniel, of Hopkinsville. On May 11, 1920, the commission was organized and set to work to study the elementary and secondary schools of the state. For fifteen months the investigations set up by the survey continued. The director visited sixty-six counties and studied carefully the conditions in thirty-three. By the use of tests, thousands of pupils in nine counties and in fifteen cities were given examinations, and data on pupil progress were collected on 136,828 pupils. Information about the training of teachers was gathered by the survey staff, covering the records and training of 86 per cent of the total number of teachers. The study was a sample procedure but was widely enough distributed to give a clear picture of the Kentucky educational system and its efficiency in training the boys and girls of the commonwealth. "It must be apparent," said the commission in its report, "that the improvement of the schools of Kentucky requires better organization and administration, better trained teachers, larger schools, a longer school term, and more liberal financial support."[6] The facts collected by the commission supported in every particular this diplomatic statement of the situation, for a far more severe denunciation of the backwardness of the school system might reasonably have been made. On the principle that molasses catches more flies than vinegar, the commission made a statesmanlike summary of its findings and refrained from caustic criticism that would have irritated the people and retarded the cause which the commission was advocating. As it was, the survey and the report of the commission marked a renewal of interest in public education and a forward step in accomplishing results. The report was both an impetus and a challenge which resulted in marked educational progress during the next twenty years.

At the head of the public schools in Kentucky, as elsewhere, is a department of education with a policy-determining board called the State Board of Education. Under the Kentucky constitution, the Superintendent of Public Instruction is elected by the people. The Survey Report of 1921 points out that "this provision in the constitution is a hindrance to the progress of good administration." "If Kentucky should obtain a non-partisan board of education, composed of men and women who are profoundly interested in popular education and keenly aware of existing defects; if the state superintendent were aided by an adequate force of active, well-trained assistants, working uninterruptedly to enlighten the people and to assist local officers—if these simple steps should be now taken, the educational millennium would not at once dawn, but every year would see the state creep a notch higher in the scale of relative educational efficiency."[7] But the time

[6] *Public Education in Kentucky,* v-ix, 149.
[7] *Ibid.,* 155.

had not yet arrived when Kentucky would create a non-partisan board and appoint a permanent Superintendent of Public Instruction, though the department of education has measurably improved during the years since the publication of that report. The commission stressed the need of better local organization and administration, greater financial support of public education, and additional provision for the training of teachers. The financial support for larger state maintenance of schools, especially in remote rural counties, was urged. These are but the high lights in a report which concluded with an admonition to the people on the relation of educational opportunities to the progress of a state. What was said at the close of the report has been said before, but it may well be repeated: "The tide of prosperity does not rise in countries that pay little for education, it rises in those that pay much. A vigorous and industrious population does not seek a state which has poor schools; it seeks a state which has good schools. Having so far done less than it should, and less than it could afford, let Kentucky by a supreme effort now do at least what it can afford."[8]

Twelve years after the Survey of 1921, a second and more comprehensive study of the educational system in Kentucky was undertaken; the second survey was limited to the schools of the first twelve grades and devoted most of the report, issued in 1933, to the standards of instruction, teacher preparation, and administration. In the 140 years of the state's history, many laws had been enacted dealing with various phases of the educational structure. So many laws were on the statute books that the courts and administrative officers were often confused by conflicts in the laws, by omissions, and by the duplications of acts. As the state moved on to a better administration of the schools, many laws stood in the way of the advancement which the school officers had expected to make. The hope for a thorough codification of

[8] *Ibid.*, 202.

school laws in the decade following the earlier survey became a demand as the decade ended. The Superintendent of Public Instruction listened with a sympathetic ear to the growing insistence that something be done. Dr. James H. Richmond was State Superintendent at the time; and, recognizing the need for codifying the school law, he pushed the matter vigorously. Codification, however, involved more than systematizing the laws; for there were many omissions in the legal statements as well as need for new statutes in order to legalize the various changes then taking place in school organization. The consolidation of schools and the transportation of pupils were two of the numerous additional functions and organizations of the schools requiring a clear presentation of the law that would enable county school systems to meet the problems facing them. There were other matters requiring careful consideration by the codifiers when they should begin their work. Since there were also implications and conflicts, the codification of school laws involved too many questions beyond and above their mere collection into one volume. It was thought by many that there should be a complete inventory of the whole school system, including the public institutions of higher education, and the entire tax support of the schools. By the time the legislature had met in 1932, the proposed bill authorizing the study of Kentucky's educational system was comprehensive enough to give the commission all the powers necessary to carry on its work. The study was to be a Kentucky study conducted by selected educators in the state and financed by the Kentucky Education Association, the Kentucky Negro Education Association, and the General Education Board. The contributions were $7,500 from the first organization, $500 from the second, and a grant of $5,000 from the General Education Board.

Immediately after the passage of the act creating the commission, Governor Ruby Laffoon appointed the following persons to serve on the commission: James H. Richmond, Frank L. McVey, H. H. Cherry, J. W. Bradner, H. W.

Peters, W. J. Webb, Yancey Altsheler, Mrs. James G. Sheehan, and Ben Williamson. The members of the commission represented the Department of Education, higher education, the public schools, local boards of education, the Parent-Teacher Association, rural schools, and business. A month later, the members held the first meeting in Frankfort, May 16, 1932. The chairman, Dr. Richmond, presided and James W. Cammack, Jr., was selected as secretary. At this meeting a plan of work, broad and comprehensive, was adopted after discussion. As the commission had in mind both an extensive and thorough study of education in the state, the general divisions of the survey were established as:

1. Aims and functions of the public schools.
2. The organization and control of public education.
3. The financing of public education.
4. The codification of the laws in light of the recommendations of the commission.

In order to do the work required by so broad a study, seventeen committees were named and given definite tasks. In the furtherance of the program, eighty-five laymen and school men who were residents of the state were selected to serve without pay. The need for co-ordinating the work of so many committees was recognized as fundamental to the success of the survey; to do this effectually, a co-ordinating body of six under the chairmanship of Dr. Herman L. Donovan was appointed by the commission. When the report appeared in 1933, the contents made a deep impression upon the people of the state as well as upon professional educators who lived in other parts of the country; for it contained not only definite recommendations on administration, finance, and instruction, but it dealt with the aims and functions of the public schools, not commonly set out in such reports. In fact, the Commission of 1933 endeavored to give the people of Kentucky a seasoned and carefully planned system based upon a philosophical background of public education.[9]

In the last three pages of the survey report, the commission reduced its conclusions to a few recommendations which stated clearly the findings of the seventeen committees. The first objective called for the revision and the simplification of the school laws. Complete codification resulting in the new school code was presented at the meeting of the legislature in 1934 and enacted into law with few changes. The report called for the reorganization of the Board of Education to be composed of the State Superintendent of Public Instruction and seven lay members appointed by the governor. The purpose in changing the make-up of the ex officio board was to provide a continuous and progressive operation of the elementary and secondary schools. Too many one-room schools had been a cause for concern to the State Department of Education in the past, a situation the report hoped might be remedied by encouraging the consolidated type of school. For years the school trustees and the district schools had raised the questions of nepotism, sale of school positions, and favoritism in securing teachers. These problems could be solved by requiring county organization of schools and the election of trustees at large. "The schools," said the report, "are for the children of the commonwealth." The qualifications of teachers should not remain in the hands of district officers, but rather should be made state-wide with the minimum requirement of two years of special college training.

The concern of the commission, and particularly of the committee on the financial support of education, resulted in three chapters, or more than half of the report.[10] In 150 pages of these chapters, the reader will find an extensive discussion of school costs, the financial support of education, and financial administration. On the points raised by this ade-

[9] *Report of the Kentucky Educational Commission* (1933), Division I, 3-33.
[10] *Ibid.*, Chaps. IX, X, XI.

quate study, the conclusion of the survey emphasizes specifically the importance of a modernized state budget which would enable school support to receive the consideration it deserves as an important phase of the whole structure of government. In many districts, the floating school debt is a serious problem that calls for the protection of school funds and their careful handling. The commission was positive in its recommendations for a larger common school fund which should be supplemented by an equalization fund to remove the inequalities in district support.

One of the important parts of the public educational system in Kentucky is that of higher education, consisting of the university and the several state colleges. Considerable competition for students, state support, and leadership in the presentation and offering of courses had gone on for years. There was not much thought given to the common problems of curricula and financial support, for each institution sought aid from the state regardless of the needs of the others. In the hope that something might be done to remedy the situation, the recommendations of the commission included the proposal to create a council of higher education composed of representatives of the University of Kentucky, the four teachers' colleges, and the State Board of Education. After an existence of fifteen years, the council can now report some accomplishments; but the all-important one of curricular adjustments as between institutions remains yet almost untouched.

When the work of the Educational Commission of 1933 is examined as a whole, the consensus is that it did an excellent piece of work. Many results followed the enactment of the laws recommended by the commission, and many more will come into practice as the years go on; for the educational interests of the state now have a program, a philosophy, the means, and the organization of administrative procedure with which to open the way for the advancement of public education in Kentucky.

CHAPTER XIV

"THE TUMULT AND THE SHOUTING DIES"

IN THESE days of world upheaval and of difficulties involved in the reconversion from a war to a peacetime economy, it seems incredible that anxiety over the theory of evolution could have brought on such a flood of speeches, letters, pamphlets, and legislative bills as occurred throughout the country in the period 1921-1929. A quarter of a century has passed since the tumult began when fifteen legislatures were asked to pass bills making it a penalty to teach evolution, Darwinism, and atheism in the public schools of these states. The penalties for such teaching ranged from $50 to $5,000 in fines and/or imprisonment for ten days to a year in county jails or state penitentiaries. The conflict lasted eight long years. Gradually, the tumult and the shouting died when legislature after legislature, with the exception of two states, Mississippi and Tennessee, refused to enact the laws demanded by the opponents of evolution.

The captains and the kings departed to seek new causes to engage their abilities and energies. The Great Commoner and generalissimo of the fight against evolution, William Jennings Bryan, died in the midst of the Scopes trial held in Dayton, Tennessee, in the summer of 1925. In the course of a quarter of a century, other leaders in the anti-evolution cause have been gathered to their fathers, leaving the thinning lines of protagonists without the vehement leadership that had headed the movement in the days of the conflict, and the nation has grown weary of the controversy or forgotten about it. Since then people nearly everywhere have been told about the amazing conclusions of the scientists concerning the age of the earth, the changing character of its surface, the extent of the universe, the influences of environment and heredity upon the inhabitants of the globe, and the revelations brought to light by microscope, laboratory research, and observation and study of carefully gathered facts. The people are now familiar with the story of mankind on the earth. They have been informed about the different ages through which the planet has passed, and the slow progress of man as he struggled upward on his way to a more complicated civilization. The school children have learned many things relating to the flora and fauna of the earth; they have heard much of tides, winds, floods, heat and cold; and they have seen under the microscope and in film pictures the amazing wonders of nature. It is doubtful, in view of all that has developed in the last twenty-five years, that another period of such conflict compounded of mingled truth and fallacy could occur—certainly not over the same cause which engaged the people's attention from 1921 to 1929 when so much stress was placed upon the origin of man as set forth in the Book of Genesis and interpreted by the literal minded. The dissemination of information by radio, book, magazine, newspaper, and lecture has changed the whole aspect of the controversy of the past and brought into the field of the people's attention today new problems and new concepts of government, social economy, racial relations, world peace, and religion.

But this interesting conflict of years ago was something more than the mere airing of opinions and an effort to invoke the American procedure clearly stated in the phrase "there ought to be a law." May it not have been the impact of pioneer ideas and folkways upon the onward swing of a civilization that had emerged through three centuries of white Anglo-Saxon history on the North American continent? The frontier had ceased to exist, according to the United States Census Bureau, by 1890; but that was a geographical concept, one that did not include the remnants where the earlier social and thought standards of pioneer days still continued. A recent writer says: "The social characteristics of the frontier mind have appeared not only in the political and economic movements of the agrarian West, but in the multiplication of religious sects, and in periodic waves of revivalism. The experience of the frontier has thus transferred to American democracy certain of the traits of evangelical protestantism—a fervor of collective conviction, a crusading spirit, utopian enthusiasm, and emotional instability."[1] The very experiences of men on the frontier under what they regarded as the special will of God had confirmed their faith in a divine providence; this belief had not been worn down and diluted among many who had been touched by the spirit of revivalism, so it was natural that this spirit should reassert itself now and then. The anti-evolution controversy of the twenties was the clash between the earlier frontier idea of man's place in the universe and the later view of religious opinion as based upon the findings of scholars. The anti-evolution side reduced the essence of the discussions and debates to the simple question: Did man descend from the ape? This, they felt, was the issue involved. It was easy for the man in the street to make a decision about so simple a question as that. Some there were who did not care, but others were shocked at the suggestion, and thus the issue was joined. Name calling, giving the lie, and even fisticuffs were not unusual. To settle the matter the protagonists sought remedy in legislation—"there ought to be a law."

Under the federal system of government in these United States, the legislatures of the different states convene, with one or two exceptions, every two years. Nearly all of these bodies meet in the odd year; only six come together in the even years. Of the six states that had legislative sessions in the even years, Kentucky was one; the others were Louisiana, Mississippi, New Jersey, Rhode Island, and Virginia. For strategic purposes, Kentucky was chosen as the initial battle-

[1] Ralph Barton Perry, *Puritanism and Democracy* (Vanguard Press, New York, 1944), 212.

ground. The reason for this choice may be accounted for in the number of Protestant adherents in the state and particularly in the fact that many of these were believers in the fundamentalist concept of religious theology. Some preliminary skirmishes had been under way in the state during the fall of 1921, so it was a foregone conclusion that bills would be introduced by selected members when the state legislature should meet in January, 1922. Brief articles and long letters appeared in some of the city newspapers and in many of the weekly publications; these contributions, some sensible, some vitriolic, and some foolish, form an interesting collection of literature that will be enlightening to the future historian when he tries to make an interpretation of the social forces then at work in the Commonwealth. An editorial writer in the Louisville *Courier-Journal* in December, 1921, calls the movement the "Baptist campaign to prevent the teaching of Darwinism at the University of Kentucky." Such a movement is "contrary to a fundamental principle of the American Commonwealth: that which separates Church and State."[2] Nevertheless, mighty forces were brought to the line of battle to create by law the regulation of teaching, of speaking, and perhaps of thinking in the public schools of the state. As the conflict went on, the attack of the forces supporting the action was centered upon the University of Kentucky.

Early in the session of the 1922 legislature, G. W. Ellis of Barren County introduced a bill in the House making it unlawful to teach evolution, Darwinism, atheism, or agnosticism in the schools of the state. The bill provided a fine of $50 to $5,000 or a jail sentence of ten days to a year, with the provision that both fines and jail sentence might be laid on the culprit convicted of a violation of the law. If the institution in which the offense was committed were found to be guilty of a violation of the law, its charter was to be forfeited. About the same time, another bill was offered in

[2] Louisville *Courier-Journal*, December 8, 1921.

the Senate by J. R. Rash, a member from Hopkinsville.[3] With the introduction of the anti-evolution bills, a great resurgence of opinion and belief soon brought forth much talk and writing about the bills and freedom of thought. William Jennings Bryan appeared in the state, speaking in Lexington, Danville, and before the combined House and Senate of the legislative session.[4] Great crowds came to hear him, some to support the movements against the teaching of evolution and others just to see and hear the famous orator. The meeting in Lexington was held in the Woodland Auditorium, January 19, 1922. Colonel George Bain introduced the speaker, and the Rev. J. W. Porter presided over the meeting. Bryan delivered his Chautauqua lecture entitled "The Enemies of the Bible." Following the address, which was received with great applause, the Rev. Walter L. Brock of the Immanuel Baptist Church came to the platform and read a set of resolutions which he asked to be presented for the General Assembly of Kentucky. These resolutions petitioned for legislation which would prohibit the teaching of evolution in state schools and would aid in the elimination of Darwinism and similar evolution theories. A motion was made and the resolutions carried without a dissenting vote.[5]

The Great Commoner made a long speech on that evening, twenty-five years ago. He defended the Bible and God's work on scriptural authority, and hurled a challenge for those who rejected the Bible and accepted Darwinism to put their theory to a test. He warned students that the professor who taught the Darwinian theory of evolution was the most dangerous man that could be met and likened him to an adder. "The greatest of man's three obligations is his relation to God. Words of uncertainty fill Darwin's work and make his hypothesis groundless. It is groundless because there is not a single fact in the universe that man is descended from the

[3] House Bill No. 191; Senate Bill No. 136; *Scientific Monthly*, XXIV (May, 1927), 473-474.
[4] Lexington *Herald*, January 23, 1922.
[5] *Ibid.*, January 20, 1922.

lower animals. Darwin does not use facts; he uses conclusions drawn from similarities. . . . There are myriads of living creatures about us . . . and yet not one is in transition from one species to another; every one is perfect. . . . The remains of nearly one-hundred species of vertebrate life have been found in the rocks, of which more than one-half are found living today, and none of the survivors shows material change."

Bryan's speech contained many illustrations such as a black cow eating green grass gives white milk from which yellow butter is made. He heaped ridicule upon the scientists and their followers. But what worried Bryan were the questions: "How could the males strengthen their minds by fighting for the females if at the same time the females were breeding the hair off by selecting the males? Or did the males select for three years and then allow the females to do the selecting during leap year?" He flayed the theories of the "guessers" and added that "if the Bible said anything so idiotic as those evolutionists put forth in the name of science, scientists would have a great time in ridiculing the sacred pages."[6]

In an article appearing in *Science,* Professor Arthur M. Miller wrote: "In their spoken and written attacks on evolution these advocates of suppressive measures quote largely from two publications issued by the Bible Institute Colportage Association, Chicago, Illinois. One of these is a booklet . . . by Alex. Patterson entitled 'The Other Side of Evolution' and the other is a pamphlet . . . by W. A. Griffith Thomas entitled 'What about Evolution?' In these publications the attempt is made to refute evolution mainly by the citation of authority. With respect to well known advocates of evolution, such as Tyndall, Haeckel, Huxley, Spencer, and even Darwin himself, commendably cautious statements, particularly with reference to the *causes* of evolution, are twisted and

[6] *Ibid.,* January 21, 1922.

construed into 'fatal admissions' affecting their belief in the *fact* of evolution.

"For expressions of positive opposition to the theory, recourse is had mainly to men of science long since dead. . . . It is from the book by Patterson that Mr. Bryan gets his leg-from-wart, eye-from-freckle, joke which he is so fond of retailing from the Chautauqua platform."[7]

Before Bryan came to Kentucky on his brief campaign in the state, he had written a letter to Dr. J. W. Porter of the First Baptist Church in Lexington, which that pastor read to his congregation. After expressing his gratification at what had been done in Kentucky, the Commoner wrote, "The movement will sweep the country and will drive Darwinism from our schools. The enemy is already fighting. The agnostics who are undermining the faith of our students will be glad enough to teach anything the people want taught when the people speak with emphasis."[8] After reading the letter from Bryan, the pastor declared that Darwinism would be run out of Kentucky if it took every cent the Baptist people of the Commonwealth had. "Only those who believe they are made in the image of God will die for truth. We have all the Elijahs on our side. Strength to our arms!"[9]

The fight over evolution had become a matter of such public interest that the editor of the New York *Times* asked Dr. Harry Emerson Fosdick to comment on Bryan's position in the controversy. Dr. Fosdick began by saying: "I do so, if only to voice the sentiments of a large number of Christian people who in the name of religion are quite as shocked as any scientist could be in the name of science at Mr. Bryan's sincere but appalling obscurantism. . . . Suffice it to say that when Mr. Bryan reduces evolution to a hypothesis and then identifies a hypothesis with a 'guess' he is guilty of a sophistry so shallow and palpable that one wonders at his hardihood

[7] *Science,* LV (February 17, 1922), 178-179.
[8] *Ibid.,* 178; Lexington *Herald,* December 26, 1921.
[9] Lexington *Herald,* December 26, 1921.

in risking it. . . . Today, the evolutionary hypothesis, after many years of pitiless attack and searching investigation, is, as a whole, the most adequate explanation of the facts with regard to the origin of species that we have yet attained, and it was never so solidly grounded as it is today. . . . Mr. Bryan is regalvanizing into life that same outmoded idea of what the Bible is and proposes in the twentieth century that we shall use Genesis which reflects the pre-scientific view of the Hebrew people centuries before Christ as an authoritative textbook in science, beyond whose conclusions we dare not go.

"Why, then, should Mr. Bryan complain because his attitude toward evolution is compared repeatedly, as he says it is, with the attitude of the theological opponents of Copernicus and Galileo? On his own statement the parallelism is complete."

Dr. Fosdick selected passages from the Bible to the effect that the earth is flat (Psalm 136:6), the heavens are like an upturned bowl (Job 37:18), and that "beneath the earth was mysterious Sheol where dwelt the shadowy dead" (Isaiah 14:9-11). These, with other similar selections, brought the writer of the article in the *Times* to ask: "Are we to understand that this is Mr. Bryan's science, that we must teach this science in our schools, that we are estopped by divine revelations from ever going beyond this science? . . . One who is a teacher and preacher of religion raises his protest against all this just because it does such gross injustice to the Bible. . . . If one could appeal directly to Mr. Bryan he would wish to say: let the scientists thrash out the problems of man's biological origin, but in the meantime do not teach men that if God did not make us by fiat then we have nothing but a bestial heritage. That is a lie which once believed will have a terrific harvest. It is regrettable business that a prominent Christian should be teaching that."[10]

The purpose in quoting from the speech of Bryan and from the article by Fosdick in the New York *Times* is to

---

[10] New York *Times*, March 12, 1922.

"THE TUMULT AND THE SHOUTING DIES" 229

give the reader an appreciation of the views expressed during the contest in Kentucky. The many protests and arguments that were offered by the numerous writers and speakers who proposed to be heard cannot be covered within the limits of a chapter. Earnest men wrote and spoke, but there were also those who hurried to the scene of action "to champion any cause for the purpose of showing off." As an instance of the propaganda methods, Edward Y. Clark who had been active in the Ku Klux Klan proposed to operate through small local organizations by which the "Supreme Kingdom" would prevent employment of teachers suspected of evolutionary beliefs.[11] Other organizations sprang into existence in 1922-1925 such as the "Bible Crusaders," "Fundamentalists, Bryan League," "World Christian," and the "Christian Fundamentalist Association." The secretary of this last organization prophesied that within twelve months every state in the United States would be organized.[12] The opposition, organized in educational associations and scientific societies, was not idle;[13] and it, too, protested vigorously against the views and purposes of the anti-evolution forces.

To strengthen the cause of the opposition to the bills in the legislature, President McVey of the University of Kentucky sent telegrams to fifty leading educators, ministers, and journalists. Replies were received from forty-seven persons and were given to the press late in January, 1922. The telegram which Dr. McVey sent read as follows: "Bill has been introduced in Kentucky legislature with heavy penalty to prohibit teaching of evolution, or use of books favoring evolution in all schools supported by public funds. Wire collect your opinion to be used in opposing the bill." Nicholas Murray Butler replied sarcastically in characteristic fashion: "It [the bill] should, I think, be amended before passage to

---

[11] *Scientific Monthly,* XXIV (May, 1927), 477.
[12] *Current History,* XXIV, 893.
[13] National Education Association meeting in Chicago, reported in *Lexington Herald,* March 2, 1922.

include in its prohibitions the use of any book in which the word evolution is defined, used, or referred to in any way. It might be desirable to include a prohibition of books that use any of the letters by which the word evolution could be spelled, since in this way some unscrupulous person might, by ingenious effort, evade the salutary provisions of the law. I take it for granted that the introducer of the bill is in close communion with the Soviet Russia, since he is faithfully reproducing one of their fundamental policies. Truly we are getting on."[14]

The former United States Commissioner of Education, Dr. P. P. Claxton, wired: "The bill is unwise, absurd, ridiculous." Dr. Henry S. Pritchett declared: "A bill to prohibit teaching of evolution would be a great disservice, both to religion and science." The Rev. E. D. Jones of Central Christian Church, Detroit, Michigan, telegraphed: "Such a bill as you describe is a relic of the Dark Ages." Dr. Lyman Abbott said in his message, "Evolution is God's way of doing things." The other replies made equally strong objections to the bill before the General Assembly.

A letter to the people of Kentucky was released for publication on Sunday, February 12, 1922, by the University of Kentucky, for the purpose of clearing up "the confusion and misunderstandings which have arisen relative to the bills introduced in the Legislature providing for the prohibition of the teaching of evolution" in tax-supported schools. *(See Appendix C.)* The letter appealed to the good sense and fairness of the people of the state, pointing out, however, that the attack was concentrating more and more upon the university. The writer went on to tell why evolution was taught and what it means. Reference was made to Section 5 of the Bill of Rights in the state constitution and its stern command against preference by law to any religious creed or denomination. What influence the two press releases had on the views

---

[14] From files of the President of the University of Kentucky, in Bureau of Source Materials on Higher Education, University of Kentucky Library.

of the members of the legislature is difficult to measure; but the contents did define the issue and made the position of the university clear, giving the supporters of that institution an understanding of the conflict as it stood by the middle of February, 1922.[15]

Meantime, January of the year 1922 had passed, and February had entered upon its briefer span. The bills on the teaching of evolution in tax-supported schools and institutions of higher learning were in the committee stage. In the Legislative Digest of the General Assembly of 1922 the comment on the history of the Ellis bill, House Bill 191, reads like a railroad timetable: "January 23, referred to Kentucky statutes; February 7, reported favorably and placed in the calendar; March 3, placed in the Orders of the Day; March 9, called out by the Rules, read a third time and defeated, 42 to 41."

Before that desirable end had been reached, many interesting developments occurred. The following statement from an article in *Science,* March 24, 1922, presents the legislative procedures on the anti-evolution bill:

"The Kentucky House of Representatives spent five hours to-day [March 9] in discussing and hearing discussions of the 'monkey bill' of Representative G. W. Ellis of Barren County, forbidding the teaching of evolution in public schools and universities. The measure was defeated by a vote of 42 to 41, after a recapitulation of the vote during which members were dragged into the chamber from other parts of the capital.

"Dr. F. L. McVey, president of the state university, and the Rev. Dr. E. L. Powell, pastor of the First Christian Church, Louisville, discussed the bill by invitation. The former declared that the legislature is not within its rights in passing such a law as that proposed, and urged the members not to base the inspiration of the Bible on matters not essential, but to heed teachings of the Book. He asserted that the

[15] *Ibid.;* Lexington *Leader,* March 2, 1922; Louisville *Post,* February 4, 1922.

Bible is not an authority on science, legislation, chemistry, or any of one thousand other subjects, but on moral, spiritual and religious matters. Dr. McVey went into the subject of evolution, pointing out that many accept the teachings as not in contradiction to the Bible, and insisted that the university makes no attempt to interfere with the religion of its students. He told of the various religious activities of the university, and warned the House that it would set a dangerous precedent in the passage of the Ellis bill. He recalled fights on scientific theories in the past based on the ground that they are opposing the Bible, and reviewed briefly the manner in which various scientific subjects are taught.

"Mr. Ellis brought forward Noel W. Gaines of Frankfort, formerly an army officer, who has been in the limelight several times in his career, most recently when he was involved in the 'ground glass' controversy in a Southern camp, to speak for the bill. Mr. Gaines put William Jennings Bryan to shame in his denunciation of those who believe evolution, directing many of his remarks directly at Dr. Powell and Mr. McVey. He talked for nearly an hour and was frequently applauded and cheered, while spectators in the gallery and around the walls of the chamber roared with laughter. One of his 'stunts' was a division of the sheep and goats, placing Dr. McVey, Dr. Powell, and various zoology text books on one side and the Bible, the Declaration of Independence, and himself on the other. He had the books before him as he ran up and down behind the clerk's desk, scattering them about as he waved his arms in emphatic gestures. Finally he threw one of the textbooks to the floor and trampled it under foot.

" 'I am ashamed of this day in the Kentucky legislature,' said Representative G. C. Waggoner of Scott County, a minister and veteran legislator, toward the close of the debate.

" 'This bill smacks of intolerance and the shadows of the Dark Ages are settling about us.' Mr. Waggoner opposed the bill on the ground that in passing it the legislature would exceed its functions as a law-making body and would set a

"THE TUMULT AND THE SHOUTING DIES" 233

dangerous precedent. 'There have been times here to-day when those on both sides of this discussion were about ready to place their opponents on the rack and torture them,' continued Mr. Waggoner. 'I don't know anything about evolution and from what I've heard I don't believe there are others here who do. We have set up a straw man and have been boxing industriously at him all day.'

"In his final appeal for the passage of his bill, Mr. Ellis said he had sent his son to the University of Kentucky and that he returned with his faith destroyed and argued religion against his father and mother. The voice of the aged representative was broken with emotion as he told of this experience.

"When the roll was called the vote stood 38 to 36 for the bill, which meant its defeat, as 40 votes are required for passage. As Mr. Meyers was about to announce this the proponents demanded that the absentees be called. Then the vote was 40 to 39 for the bill. The opponents demanded a recapitulation. During that they dragged in two more members and the proponents one, making it 41 to 41. Representative Bryce Cundiff, who had declined to vote on the ground that he 'was a hard-shell Baptist and believed what was would be anyhow,' said he would have to discard his religion and vote 'No.' Then the bill was declared to be defeated" by a vote of 42 to 41.

The history of the Rash bill in the Senate did not parallel that of the Ellis bill in the House. After a speech by the author, February 15, before the committee of the whole, Senator Frank Daugherty moved to table the bill. The motion was lost by 22 to 11. Substitute bills were introduced at the instance of Frank L. McVey, Dr. E. L. Powell, and Dr. E. Y. Mullins in collaboration with some Baptist ministers. Both groups declared that they were against any legislation whatever but offered the proposals as the best way out. The speaking went on for an hour or more; Dr. J. W. Porter repeated many of the ideas brought out by Bryan that he did not want his children taught that brute blood was flowing through their veins. The next day the bill came up again, but action was postponed until February 21, when the "Committee on Rules took charge of all bills still remaining in the legislative hopper. The bill had been made a special order on that day. On the vote the next day, the Committee-of-the-Whole refused to take up the bill but left it on the Orders of the Day where it remained when the Senate adjourned 'sine die' on March 16, 1922."[16] Thus Kentucky escaped the aspersions and embarrassment which followed her sister state, Tennessee, for a quarter of a century. Two years later when the legislature met in Frankfort, no bills against evolution were offered, but in 1926 two bills were presented to the Assembly, which were milder in penalties than those of 1922. No action was taken on the bills of 1926, and the fight was over in Kentucky, but it continued in other states for several years.

An editorial in the Lexington *Herald* written by the editor, Desha Breckinridge, after the legislative battle was over, raised the question: "Is it true that a scant majority of the most intelligent, best informed and progressive citizens of the state believe it advisable to permit free intellectual investigation and full information as to scientific thought in the schools of Kentucky?

"The scant vote arouses most serious consideration for the state of public sentiment in Kentucky.

"The vote in the House indicates an emphatic need for general education in the state."[17]

During the long conflict, it was charged that "there was a million-dollar fund behind a National movement akin to the bill. Publicity and advertisements appearing locally have been traced to Chicago."[18] There may have been more than a shadow of truth in the above statement, for the movement spread from state to state in a uniform manner. Then "a

---

[16] *Science,* LV (March 24, 1922), 316-317, 318-319; Louisville *Courier-Journal,* March 10, 1922.

[17] Lexington *Herald,* March 13, 1922.   [18] New York *Times,* March 10, 1922.

veritable whirlwind to quarantine the dangerous infection of Darwinism" was referred to many times in the publications of various organizations sponsoring the movement for the expulsion of the teachings of evolution from the schools.

Although the fight to stop the teaching of evolution in the public schools in Kentucky came to an end in 1926 by the failure of the bills to pass, the conflict spread to other states of the Union. "It has become a matter of greatest importance to thinking citizens in every section of the United States," said the editor of the *Independent* in an article entitled "A Year of the Monkey War."[19] Thirteen states had had bills under consideration; this meant that the fight had spread widely. The only state that had passed restrictive legislation was Tennessee, in 1925; the next year, Mississippi placed a like bill in its statute book. In the other states where bills were introduced, in every instance the legislature refused to let them come out of the committees to which they had been referred, or defeated them on the floor when brought to a vote. As early as 1923 Oklahoma had passed a law prohibiting the use of textbooks which contained any materialistic concept of history in the elementary grades; the law was repealed in 1925. In Florida, a resolution was adopted in 1923 deploring the teaching of evolution; a similar resolution offered in the West Virginia legislature the same year failed to pass. The Georgia legislature defeated an anti-evolution bill by a large majority in the same year. Since 1926 was an off year for most of the legislatures, the real flood of bills came in the following year. The list is quite impressive as evidence of the purpose, strategy, and strength of the anti-evolution group. Arkansas, February 8, defeated a bill in the Senate; Delaware, February 8, referred a bill to the Committee on Fish, Game, and Oysters, where it died. In Maine on February 17, in New Hampshire on February 9, in North Dakota on February 7, and in North Carolina on February 15, bills

[19] *Independent,* CXIX (Oct. 1, 1927), 326.

were considered. Bills were introduced also in the legislatures of Alabama, New York, Texas, and Minnesota. In all these states, the bills either did not reach the legislative floor or were defeated when the roll call was taken for the vote. Skirmishes continued on into 1929, but the ridicule of the anti-evolutionists arising from the Scopes trial in 1925 and the continued opposition of most of the public to the whole movement brought the conflict to an end by 1929.

The trial of John T. Scopes in Dayton, Tennessee, in the summer of 1925 occupied the attention of the whole nation. This young teacher was indicted for violation of the then recent law passed by the Tennessee legislature. Well-known persons took part in the trial, with Clarence Darrow heading the legal staff defending Scopes and William Jennings Bryan upholding the prosecuting attorney who led the attack. The trial went on for weeks in the crowded town of Dayton. It was there that Bryan died on one very hot summer day. The jury found Scopes guilty, and the case went to the State Supreme Court on appeal. In its opinion, the court seemed to be undecided and used vague language. A writer commenting on the decision said that the ruling seemed "to mean that one can teach about anything he pleases in Tennessee so long as he does not come out flat-footed for atheism or philosophic materialism."[20] To judge by the attitude taken by many citizens in Tennessee, the whole procedure was regarded as a good deal of a joke. In Kentucky, the fight from beginning to end was taken seriously, since the outcome involved principles of great importance such as freedom of speech and thought and the right of teaching in the public school.

Thus Kentucky barely escaped a situation dangerous to the cause of education. Another day might find it unprepared unless illiteracy and prejudice have been eradicated to a far greater extent than our present progress indicates.

[20] *Scientific Monthly*, XXIV (May, 1927), 473, 477.

CHAPTER XV

THE PUBLIC SCHOOLS MOVE FORWARD

DURING successive administrations, the State Superintendents of Public Instruction in Kentucky have shown considerable zeal for and loyalty to the ideals inherent in a public system of education. Under the latest constitution, 1891, these officers are limited to a tenure of four years. Regardless of how well they serve the state, when their four years of official service are over, they return to subordinate positions in the public schools or enter other occupations. Thus such knowledge and experience in administration as these men gain in office are lost to public education when newly elected and inexperienced officers take up the task where their predecessors lay it down.

Before 1850 the State Superintendent was appointed by the governor, who usually selected a clergyman to guide the school system. Most of these appointees continued to preach in their pulpits as formerly, and some attempted to keep their flocks together and guide sinners in the path of righteousness while holding the important office of State Superintendent. Although handicapped by the restriction of tenure, the superintendents, early and late, left a record which showed interest and zeal on their part and, in some instances, considerable statesmanship. They called attention to the shortcomings in the public school system, and, by cajoling the governors, urged them to the point of taking an effective stand on public education in their biennial messages to the Assembly. In turn, the Superintendents besieged the legislative body for funds to help the cause, asked for laws that would provide an adequate organization of the schools, and pointed out again and again the need for better trained teachers. Yet these reforms were slow in coming, for the people clung to the "destrect school" and the three-man board of control. Uniformity of textbooks was almost unheard of since the books belonging to the families and handmade arithmetics were used as late as 1890. The maintenance of the schools had rested upon a meager state school fund, a small county tax, and a voluntary tax until 1850.

Superintendent Robert Richardson reported in 1860 that a majority of the counties were relying upon the state school fund for the entire support of their school systems, and he urged that local districts contribute at least as much as did the state. Such progress as was under way at the time was seriously interrupted by the Civil War. The number of children reported to the Superintendent was 230,466 in 1859, with less than a hundred thousand in attendance. Seven years later the figure for school children was 334,566, and of these but 104,481 were reported in attendance. By 1870 the tide had begun to turn; the war was over, and the people showed a growing interest in the education of their children. For the first time the school fund reached nearly a million dollars, making a possible per capita distribution of two dollars. As the per capita was so small, the Superintendent of Public Instruction complained because the local school boards failed to levy taxes for the support of schools.

Laws were passed in 1864, 1871, and 1893 authorizing trustees to levy taxes as high as twenty-five cents on each one hundred dollars of taxable property. In 1894 Superintendent E. P. Thompson declared in his report for that year, "Local taxation by districts, subject to the will of the people, is a failure."[1]

To correct this situation, James H. Fuqua, State Superintendent in 1906, advocated that the distribution of the state school fund be dependent in some measure upon what

---

[1] *Report of the Superintendent of Public Instruction* (1894).

the counties did for themselves in regard to local taxation.[2] In 1908 the legislature was so convinced of the need for change that it enacted a highly important law modifying the educational system of the state. By this law, known as the Sullivan Act, the county became the school unit; and in consequence, the county unit of administration was established. The districts in the county were determined by the number of children, while the subdistrict trustees formed an admission board for each district, and the chairmen of those boards comprised the county board of education. Although this organization was by no means ideal, it was a great improvement over the scattered system that had prevailed heretofore. Most important of all the provisions in the law was the requirement that the counties must levy a tax of twenty cents on each one hundred dollars worth of taxable property. No longer would the school districts depend upon the voluntary voting of taxes, for now the tax must be levied. In the field of secondary education, the law required each county to maintain a high school at public expense.[3]

In those days children could be found on the early morning trains journeying to the county seat or some larger town for their schooling. The roads were far from good; bus service and school transportation systems did not yet exist. There were district schools for the grade children, but the facilities for high school instruction were located largely in the towns and cities. The law requiring each county to maintain a high school was not carried out as promptly as its sponsors had hoped, yet some progress had been made not only in the creation of high schools but in the grading of instruction through the consolidation of the rural schools at strategic points. Prior to 1908 there were fewer than fifty public high schools in the state, enrolling in all less than five thousand pupils. The rural children were without secondary educational opportunities except where there were private schools, and these

[2] *Ibid.* (1906), 21.
[3] Kentucky *Acts, 1908*, 133.

were not numerous. The legislature had suggested without result that the counties provide high school education. It therefore passed an act in the session of 1914 requiring the counties to maintain such schools.

At the time of the passage of this legislation, there were 15,574 pupils enrolled in high schools. By 1941 the attendance was nearly ten times as many, or 144,447. In the days of small enrollments, the number of high schools had been 316, with an average of barely fifty children to a school. In 1941 the public white high schools numbered 592; the colored, 74; private high schools, 72; a total of 738, with an average of about 200 pupils to the school. It is interesting to note that the number of high schools, which reached 848 in 1935, had dropped to 738 in 1941, a reduction of 110 within six years. The cause for the drop in the number of high schools as well as for the increased enrollments may be found in the merger of existing schools into larger county school centers. Private high schools numbered 98 in 1928, and 72 in the last reported census. Larger schools, extended transportation, better instruction, and well-prepared teachers account for the very rapid change that has taken place in the high school situation in the past twenty-five years.

To complete the picture of the attendance in the school system of Kentucky, further figures from the report of the Superintendent of Public Instruction in 1941 may well be brought in at this point. The school census of that year showed that there were 763,379 children in the state between the ages of six and seventeen years. Of this number, 599,467 were enrolled in the county and independent district schools. The number of those promoted and retained was placed at 553,923. These are impressive facts from the report of the schools of the state, but they are not such as to give the citizen of the state all the comfort he might hope for. If what is shown above was true, there were approximately 210,000 children of school age who were not in school, and 45,000 children who were enrolled but did not finish the year for one or more reasons. What these reasons were the report does not say, but that they included illness, lack of clothes, distance from school, and indifference of parents may be accepted as explanations. Great as the progress in public education has been in the Commonwealth, there are yet many threads and strands to be woven into the fabric before it will be completed.

Considerable advancement can be seen during the past thirty years in the development of a better school administration. The district system hung on long after the county had become a unit for taxation, legal procedure, administration of justice, and the execution of the law. Nevertheless, the maintenance and direction of the schools remained within the small district. The law made the county the unit and left to the trustee of a district the power to nominate the teacher of his district. This arrangement was far from a desirable one. The whittling down of school districts went on until the legislature, in 1920, created a county school board of five members elected by the people from the county at large. Nominations were made by petition, and the county superintendent was selected by the board; more important still, the teachers were nominated by the county superintendent and elected by the county board.

The enemies of the new law were able to secure modifications in 1922; after amendment in that year, the county was divided into five districts with one member elected from a district area every five years. Again, two years later, the power of nominating and of placing teachers was taken from the county superintendent and given to the district trustees. Attempts were made in 1926 to return the election of the county superintendents to the people, but the bill, after passing both houses, was vetoed by Governor William J. Fields. Those opposing the election of a county educational officer by the board re-entered the fray in 1928 and in 1932. The outcome of the last battle resulted in the return of the election of the superintendent to the people of the rural areas, but the citizens in the independent districts were not allowed to have a voice in the election of town and city superintendents.[4] Such an arrangement in the opinion of the Court of Appeals, where suit was brought, was discriminatory and violated Section VI of the constitution. The matter of selecting a county superintendent of schools now rested with the county board of education which might choose that official if it had the courage to do so. The majority of these superintendents throughout the state are now appointed by the county boards.

One of the accomplishments of the school code of 1933 was the reduction of the mass of school legislation within the compass of a usable book. That in itself was well worth doing, but a more important contribution was the simplification of the educational organization. In the law existing before 1933, there were three types of school districts—county, independent, and city districts which were organized in the first, second, third, and fourth class cities. Only two types of districts have been recognized since the code was adopted by the legislature. In cases where the independent graded districts are continued, they must have at least 250 children of school age in the district according to the school census. The purpose of the law is to draw into the county unit all independent graded districts as rapidly as possible. That this process is going on is shown in the report of Superintendent Harry W. Peters which declared that in 1939 there were 262 local school administrative districts, of which 120 were county and 142 independent districts. The change in four years indicates a contrast of 305 districts in 1935 against the 262 existing in 1939 and 256 in 1941.

Much has been said about the one-teacher schools in the county system. There were more than five thousand such schools in the state in 1936. By 1939 the number of such schools was 4,383. This reduction was brought about by the

[4] *Ibid., 1932,* 357.

consolidation of schools and the supplementary agency of transportation facilities.[5]

Time has been a factor in the development of the Kentucky educational system as it now stands, for an individualistic people were not to be easily deprived of the district, one-teacher, one-room school. The politicians were not particularly keen about a consolidated system, and those who trafficked in teacher placement were even less pleased. New expense would be incurred for the added buildings, and the bus operation required by any consolidation plan would increase the cost of common schooling. Although at first the consolidated school idea moved slowly, in the last ten years it has gained ground rapidly. One reason for this change has been the help given by the Federal government to school building projects through the WPA and PWA. Those who remember the school structures in 1930 have been amazed at the progress in architecture, construction, and equipment of school buildings to be found all over the state today. In the period 1930-1939, there were 1,758 school projects undertaken in Kentucky, which cost $24,708,627; of this sum the Federal government contributed $9,708,921. The new buildings have attracted much attention and have affected the status of the one-room school. Much more important than the material schoolhouse has been the realization on the part of many parents with no education themselves that school training for their children is a necessity. The admission of pupils into high school without payment of tuition removed an obstacle that had existed in Kentucky from early days. Certainly the rapid growth in the number of children enrolled in schools indicates that when opportunities and facilities are available, attendance increases. The State Department of Education rejoiced, as did the people, in the advancement of the school system; but an orderly and wise development of consolidated

---

[5] "History of Education in Kentucky, 1915-1940," *Commonwealth of Kentucky Educational Bulletin*, VII, No. 10 (December, 1939), 130; *Biennial Report of Superintendent of Public Instruction* (June, 1939), 9-14, 16-17, 21-25.

schools was not always possible. School boards wanted school buildings located on main highways without regard to centers of population. In consequence, too many such schools appeared at relatively short distances from each other. As roads have improved, the location of school buildings has become a matter not merely of paved highways but of educational purpose based on the needs of communities served by the schools. Sometimes the location of a school building has been decided upon by the ownership of real estate; but as a professional view of education comes to dominate the county units, these problems are determined more and more upon their merits.

The story of the householder who bought an impressive pair of andirons and was then forced to redecorate and refurnish a large part of his house applies to the problem of transporting school children from homes to schools. The county districts range from 250 to 500 square miles in area. What was regarded as an incidental problem has grown into a major one. The movement of busses, their operation and maintenance, may actually hamper the continuance, and certainly the enlargement, of educational programs in county units. Growing by leaps and bounds, the costs of transportation threaten to swamp the budgets now prevailing in many of the counties. There is but one answer to such expenditures which were nonexistent twenty-five years ago, and that is to provide more money through taxation with which to meet these costs. How far will this service be allowed to cut into the instruction budgets which now are by no means all that they should be? The rural schools need new equipment, better paid teachers, and more of them, if they are to provide the instruction children in this day must have. It is interesting to note how much advance has been made in the operation of school busses. Many of the counties have found that the ownership of the busses by the county leads to better operation at a lower cost, as well as more supervision over the children in the busses for protection of youthful passengers than that afforded by the contract system.

Naturally enough, the whole school transport system in Kentucky, as well as everywhere else in the nation, was threatened by World War II. Restrictions of tires, gasoline, and repairs and the purchase of new motor units checked the growth of consolidation and forced some county units to return to the one-room schools in areas off main highways. Such a situation is to be regretted, but the conditions were unavoidable. Further consolidation of schools was brought to an end temporarily; and even in schools where consolidation already existed, it was found difficult to continue the system in full force. The prospect throughout the war for the extension of the consolidation movement was viewed with much anxiety by administrators of county units.

Another and far-reaching phase of the transportation question was brought into the list of problems when the legislature in 1940 passed an act permitting the transportation in public school busses of children attending private and parochial schools.[6] The Attorney General declined to give an opinion, stating that the matter was before the Court of Appeals. A test case had been brought in the Circuit Court of Jefferson County. The lower court ruled that the act was constitutional, and the case was sent to the Court of Appeals.[7] The constitution of the state in quite emphatic language declared that funds produced for the purpose of common school education "shall be appropriated to the common schools and for no other purpose." In another place, the instrument states: "No portion of any fund or tax now existing, or that may hereafter be raised or levied for educational purposes, shall be appropriated to or be used by any church, sectarian, or denominational school." The language is clear, but an argument can be made that the benefit is personal and is not

---

[6] Kentucky *Acts, 1940*, chap. 66.
[7] Lexington *Herald*, May 13, 1942.

for the gain of the private or parochial school. The higher court rendered a decision that the state could not transport the pupils of such schools. The decision upon the principles involved will determine not only the matter of the transportation of the children attending private and parochial schools, but also the provision of free textbooks, health service, and even instruction. In the decision of the Court of Appeals, the old controversy of church and state was involved. This problem, which had produced so many disastrous results in the early days of the state's educational history, seemed to have been clearly met by the upholding of the constitutional provisions for the separation of church and state.[8]

But the problem which faced public school boards throughout the nation in providing bus transportation for school children was accentuated in 1946 by a decision of the Supreme Court of the United States on a case originating in New Jersey. This had to do with the provision of transportation for children who were required to attend school under the state law. Since the educational requirements were met by accredited parochial schools, the court held that transportation was a general program for the purpose of helping parents get their children to school safely and expediently, regardless of their religious creed. The particular school district in this instance did not maintain busses, but paid the fares of the children to and from school. The court held that the provision for transportation was a safety measure and did not violate the constitutional provision for the separation of church and state.

Traditionally, the program of public education in the elementary and secondary fields has been devoted to the three R's, with an increasing stress upon literature and the natural and social sciences. In Kentucky, this program was not extended to vocational education except in a few places, notably

[8] 294 *Kentucky Reports* 469.

in Louisville where the Ahrens Trade School and the du-Pont Manual High School gave instruction in the vocational subjects. The Smith-Hughes Act, passed by Congress in 1917, changed the situation immeasurably. This act provided funds for instruction in agriculture, home economics, trades, and industry on the secondary level and made grants for the training of teachers in these subjects. According to the vocational education division of the State Department of Education, "the purpose of public education is to aid people in solving real life problems and to provide them the opportunities to develop the abilities and attitudes needed for proficiency and happiness in desirable life activities." So the conclusion is that vocational education should become a part of the total program of education. With the Federal funds amounting to $468,888 in 1941, and with a similar amount provided by local school boards, the program has been expanded to the impressive figures of 673 departments with 40,654 pupils enrolled, or approximately 30 per cent of the high school enrollment of the state. From the inauguration of the Smith-Hughes system, teacher training for the positions open under the act has been conducted at the public institutions of higher education. In the single instance of teacher training, the legislature appropriated funds to match the Federal grants provided by the Smith-Hughes Act. The state grant amounted to $40,000 in 1941.

In the fields of agriculture and home economics, the county high schools have maintained courses and departments for teaching those subjects ever since Federal funds were first made available. The development in trade and industrial training, however, has been much slower. In some industrial communities such courses were opened in the city and town high schools, but the progress elsewhere has been slow. With better programs, the activities in trades and industrial education have been stimulated. Thus part-time and night courses found a place in the high school. In 1941, the report shows 7,161 enrollments in courses in trades and industries. The long and patient labors of A. N. May, supervisor of this work, now began to show results. The war affected many of the functions and activities of communities. The schools were not exempt from this upheaval, for they were called upon to provide workers for places in the war industries. Supplementary and refresher courses were attended by 14,646 persons, and 12,032 of the youth were enrolled in defense training programs.

In the depression years of the 1930's, the National Youth Administration undertook the employment and instruction of boys and girls who were out of work or who were without funds with which to meet even the low costs required for school attendance. A program was sponsored by local boards of education which employed teachers and enrolled the more than six thousand persons who attended the classes. Girls employed on National Youth Administration projects were given training in the improvement of homemaking while working on these projects. While this vocational instruction was going on, the state conducted two training schools, one in the Purchase area, located at Paducah, for Negro youth and one for white boys and girls at Paintsville, in the mountain region of eastern Kentucky. In addition to mathematics, science, and what is called "shop English," the school at Paducah developed departments of cabinetmaking, carpentry, brick masonry, auto mechanics, garment servicing, janitor service, home service occupations, cosmetology, and barbering. For the support of the school, the legislature appropriated $40,000. At the other end of the state, the Mayo State Vocational School began its career in 1939, offering courses in mining, mechanics, carpentry, electricity, and retail selling. Since then other courses in auto mechanics and commercial subjects have been added. The program later included national defense training, co-operative part-time instruction and evening classes, in addition to the daytime courses maintained for the 175 regularly enrolled students. The school has an annual income of $62,857 from the state appropriation and vocational funds.[9]

On numerous occasions, the orator on an educational program has declared in stentorian tones that the key to the successful education of the children of the state is the teacher. This statement is not made now as frequently as formerly because there has been considerable advancement in the securing and selection of teachers; the teacher has reached a recognized status, and it is no longer necessary to urge the acceptance of the slogan. The state now acts as the agency and director of the certification of teachers. Up to 1870 the county boards and examiners gave oral examinations to the candidates for certificates. In the 1870's written examinations in the common school branches were often required. In 1880 the state examiners became supervisors of the examinations held by the county board of examiners. The subjects were the common school branches, and, in addition, advanced standing was open to the candidates if they answered correctly the questions on algebra and literature. In case the candidate had college credits, he was given advanced standing. By 1920 the law providing for the certification of teachers eliminated the county boards and placed the authority to hold written examinations in the hands of the State Board of Examiners. The power to issue certificates for teaching continued to be held by the city school boards until 1924, when the state became the certifying agency, though that authority was shared by the public institutions of higher education.[10]

To put the problem of certification in the words of the director of teacher training and certification, J. E. Jaggers, "Kentucky has accepted and has taken steps to implement a sound philosophy of education based upon the principles of democracy." Under this philosophy, trained teachers should have a broad general education, intensive and extensive prep-

[9] *Report of Superintendent of Public Instruction* (December, 1941), 637-38.
[10] Warren Peyton, "Certification of Teachers, Superintendents, and Supervisors in Kentucky" (M.A. thesis, University of Kentucky, 1931).

aration on the school levels where they are to teach, and also should gain such experience and training as may help them in understanding children and in meeting their learning needs.[11] With these objectives in mind, the Council on Public Higher Education, after asking the advice of five hundred instructors and staffs, prepared a curriculum for the training of teachers within this philosophy. The plan was broad enough to allow the colleges freedom to experiment in developing their courses of instruction. Objection to a restricted plan of instruction was voiced by many, but the facts were against them. In Kentucky there were six public teachers' colleges, five for white persons and one for Negroes. In addition, there were twelve four-year private colleges and twelve more colleges offering only two years of instruction. Some of these possessed training schools; others were forced to rely upon elementary schools, public or private, for the observation and teacher training necessary to meet requirements for the certification of their students. In consequence, a good deal of confusion existed in the work of preparing teachers which the council plan hoped to eliminate. A common program was quite necessary in view of the requirements set up in the school code of 1934. Under that law, the issuance of elementary certificates upon training of less than two years of college work was ended; and the teacher in the secondary schools was required to have four years of college training. To encourage more extended education, certificates were based upon the extent of the college training. Almost at once the new plan began to bear fruit, for in 1940-1941 nearly 40 per cent of those who were certified for teaching positions held master's or bachelor's degrees. A further effect of the law passed by the legislature in 1934 is shown by the figures of the three-year period 1938-1941; out of 1,969 certificates issued, there were but five hundred based on less than two years of college training.

[11] *Report of Superintendent of Public Instruction* (December, 1941), 610-11.

The states surrounding Kentucky in the southern area had their own laws and requirements regulating the employment of teachers. These laws and regulations were often in conflict with those of Kentucky, bringing a sense of confusion and discrimination that disheartened the teacher who wished to work in states other than the one in which he had received his education. This situation was recognized as unfortunate by the State Departments of Education and by leaders in teacher training. It was agreed that a study should be made of the situation and a program formulated which could be used as the basis of reciprocal relations in teacher certification. Accordingly, Dr. J. E. Jaggers started the study in 1938 which he finished in 1941. His research was so well done that twelve states agreed on a unified program as the basis for accepting the training of teachers from states other than their own. Thus a great step forward had been made, not only in the relations of the states, but in the organization of the courses of study and methods to be used in training teachers.

When the nation became involved in World War II, a great demand for workers opened new jobs and higher pay for many people. The schools were drained of teachers, and many administrators were called to new duties at greatly increased salaries. The schools suffered as the shortage of teachers grew, forcing the authorities to lower the standards of certification. Again, teacher positions were filled by persons unable to meet the requirements. The certification of the better qualified teachers was slowed down, and the good accomplished through long and careful planning based upon an increased respect of the public for the office of teacher was lost for the war's duration and longer. Thus public schools have borne a heavy burden as their share of the war's disasters. So much has this been the case that pessimistic observers of the scene have said that as a result of the war the public schools are back where they were a quarter of a century ago. This may be an overstatement, though the war continued for nearly four years and the school system was seriously affected from 1942 when there were nearly four thousand new teachers brought into the schools. Many of these were without teaching experience and could not meet the certification laws. A continuance of such infiltration of raw recruits endangered standards of instruction and left the school system at a low ebb when the war was over and the rebuilding of staffs began.

One might say that real equalization of educational opportunities can never be attained in the larger sense because some schools will always have better staffs, equipment, and administration than others. Nevertheless, much criticism has been directed against the state system of public education in Kentucky because of the variation and wide differences existing between the school opportunities in many parts of the state. One way to meet this situation was to authorize the distribution of at least part of the general school fund on the basis of need. The legislature of 1930 enacted a law appropriating a million and a quarter dollars for equalization purposes.[12] The basis of distribution for the school fund ignored the differences in financial resources, grade, and quality of the schools. Nor did the law pretend to equalize the sacrifices made by taxpayers to support their schools. To meet these differences in the school situation, the legislature passed an act placing the emphasis upon the salaries of teachers. When a county was not paying seventy-five dollars per month for seven months and that county was using all the state per capita and one-half of the local tax for teachers' salaries, then the State Board of Education could prorate from the fund appropriation an amount sufficient to meet the minimum salary requirement. One distribution of the fund had been made when the act was attacked in the courts as unconstitutional.[13] Under the constitutional provisions, the Court of Appeals had no option in the matter since the document

[12] Kentucky *Acts, 1930*, 98.
[13] 244 *Kentucky Reports* 826.

especially specified but one way of distributing the school fund. Other attempts were made to find more revenue by increasing the tax levy in counties to seventy-five cents on each $100 of taxable property. The independent districts were allowed to levy a tax as high as $1.50 on every $100 of taxable property. Such was the situation when the legislature authorized the submission of a constitutional amendment empowering the state board to use 10 per cent of the school fund according to need. The amendment was voted by the people in the election of 1941, and the legislature passed an act incorporating into law the provisions for the distribution of a part of the school fund on the basis of need. The hard-and-fast per capita basis of spreading the school fund had come to an end with the recognition of need as a criterion for the use of a part of the school fund.

The public schools of Kentucky were steadily improving up to the time of World War II. Support of the schools had been measurably increased. The old district system had been superseded by the county unit with an option to select the teachers in the county system. Consolidation of county schools had advanced rapidly when the counties were compelled by law to maintain at least one high school in each county area. There followed a transportation system which had grown to major proportions through laying a heavy burden upon the county's educational budget. School offerings were greatly expanded and provisions set up for the training of teachers. The schools and colleges engaged in teacher training had moved toward better educational programs. Along with this advance, the certification of teachers was transferred from county units and independent districts to the State Department of Education. Under the provisions of the Smith-Hughes Act, the State Department of Education, through the use of Federal and state funds, was able to provide a program for pre-school children, the handicapped, and adults. The old problem of equalization of educational opportunities was at last broken down so that some advance could be made in the better distribution of the school fund which had grown by legislative act to an annual payment of fifteen million dollars. Another advance was seen in the professional growth of the State Department of Education and in the enlargement of a professionally trained staff. Progress had indeed been made, and the schools were steadily moving forward when World War II, like a Cyclops of old, barred the way.

CHAPTER XVI

INDEPENDENT DISTRICTS IN TOWNS AND CITIES ESTABLISH SCHOOLS

EVEN today, after a century of painful effort, the public school system has not more than two county units in which plant, staff, and equipment are equal to those of the best public schools in the larger cities of the state. Progress has been made in the rural parts of Kentucky, but the difference in wealth and interest has placed the public schools in the cities on a higher plane of instruction and administration than those of the county and rural districts. From the first, the independent districts were separated from the rural units; and under the law, these districts had special power to levy taxes for school purposes. As centers of population grew through the distribution, sale, and manufacture of products, the people in these centers were able to establish good schools and, what is more important, to maintain them. To the centers came merchants, bankers, professional men and women, artisans, and manufacturers attracted by the opportunities offered there. In the earlier days, many of these newcomers were young and in the process of establishing their families; as a consequence, there arose a public demand for schools. This explains in part the advance of the independent district public school over the rural school. The concentration of population within the confines of a city offered the advantage not only in larger school buildings, but also in an orderly grading and instruction of pupils.

In regard to the teachers themselves, the towns provided better living conditions and higher pay. Perhaps, too, the people living in the cities were more aware of their children's educational needs; and, as a result, the town authorities were obliged to provide adequate schools. In many cases the independent school district fell heir to the plant belonging to some defunct private academy. The trustees of such an academy were generally anxious to turn over their responsibilities to a public school board. Here and there, however, attempts were made to establish a real public school system supported by the state school fund and local taxes. Such sources of support were inadequate, and so the early public schools required pupils to pay attendance fees. The fees were small, but, small as they were, the children of poor persons could not pay them. In some cases the tuition was omitted; but in thus requiring fees, the schools were not in reality public schools.

Before a public school could be established in a town, there was much to be done in finding support, buildings, teachers, and equipment. All this development came slowly, being held up by the Civil War, depressions, and the lack of a strong public opinion favoring a public system of education. While it is not possible to trace the story in every independent district, the general trends formed in some of the larger towns were followed closely by the independent districts throughout the state. With the development of the county unit, the independent districts have declined in number but increased in size, and the importance of these city districts has grown with the enlargement of the urban population in the state.

The city of Louisville is the only metropolitan area in the state and the largest municipality in Kentucky. The paper plan of a public school system, inaugurated by the legislature in 1838, exempted the cities of Louisville, Lexington, and Maysville from the provisions of the act and permitted them to organize and maintain separate systems. From time to time, other towns were allowed to work out their own educational salvation free from the restrictions of the state law. The result was a variety in educational procedure until the code of 1934 created two types of school districts, the independent and the county unit.

The story of education in Louisville begins in the traditional manner as follows: "By an act of February 10, 1798, the legislature donated six thousand acres of land to the trustees of Jefferson Seminary to be located in Louisville. Later in the same year, the trustees were authorized to raise $5,000 by a lottery for the benefit of the Seminary." The Seminary is really part of the history of the University of Louisville. The elementary phases of education included in the Seminary had been taught in log schoolhouses conducted by early schoolmasters for the fees received from the pupils. One of these schools stood on the corner of Seventh and Market streets; another, a block away on Sixth Street; and a third, on Sixth between Market and Jefferson. Elementary education drifted along until 1828 when the city was granted its first charter. Under this charter, the mayor and councilmen were authorized to establish one or more free schools in each ward and to levy taxes for the support of the schools. It is said that the gentlemen of the mayor's office and the council had read Professor B. O. Peers' report on education made to the legislature in 1828. Under the authority of the charter, the council resolved on April 14, 1829, to establish a school free to all white children between the ages of six and fourteen.

Professor Mann Butler, the head of Jefferson Seminary, was chosen agent of the public schools. Much was said and written in those days about the Lancasterian or monitorial system, a plan that offered a cheap way of instructing children in school. Mr. Butler went to Boston and New York to investigate and report on the desirability of the Lancaster method. He came back an enthusiast and recommended the adoption of the monitorial system by which a few skilled teachers with the assistance of monitors might instruct as many as a thousand pupils. The first free school was opened in the upper story of the Old Baptist Church, August 17, 1829. In this inadequate space, 250 children were crowded while instructors heard recitations. Pandemonium may not be too strong a word to describe the confusion that existed in the crowded quarters of that Baptist church. The following year, a new three-story building was erected on Fifth and Walnut streets at a cost of $10,000. The first story was used for a boys' elementary school, the second, for girls, and the third housed the grammar departments. Free instruction was lost, and the free school ceased to exist when the council established fees at one dollar per quarter for the primary school and one dollar and a half for the other departments.

Nowadays children go to school approximately six hours per day for nine months; but in 1830 the youngsters in Louisville attended school eight hours a day in the spring and fall months, seven hours during the winter months, for eleven months in the year. There was no homework required, for the children were expected to get their lessons as they bent over the improvised desks in the meager light of the late afternoon. After twelve years of work and planning, the city had fourteen schools with a total attendance of about a thousand pupils. Principals received $750 a year; assistants, $400; and the school agent, $800. To the council and the mayor much credit is due for their decision to abolish the monitorial method and once again to make the system free by omitting all fees for tuition. This bold stand was taken on May 25, 1840.

A second city charter was adopted in 1851, based on the new state constitution, and through it a greater emphasis was placed upon the principle of the free school. Curiously enough the new charter provided for a board of trustees in each ward, probably to encourage the establishment of a school housed in a decent building in all wards of the city. All white children in the city were to be admitted to the schools on an equal basis. Nor were the council and mayor blind to the need of instruction for girls, since the charter directed that a female high school should be established, a provision that related to the education of the daughters of the city and not to the gender of the building that housed the school.

The important financial aspect was not neglected in the new charter, as provision was made for levying a tax of twelve and a half to twenty-five cents on each hundred dollars of assessed valuation and placing in the city school fund the receipts from the state school fund, the fines and forfeitures resulting from the operation of the city court, and the values received from escheated property in the city. And finally, the city council was given authority to issue bonds to the amount of $75,000 to be used in the erection of school buildings. All of this activity indicated that the city was quite in earnest about its school problem. The war of 1861-1865, as wars always do, bore heavily upon the schools, first by causing the buildings to be used for hospitals, and second by reducing the support for the educational program. By 1871 the effects of the war upon the city were offset, for the agent of schools could report seventeen buildings erected, the tax for school purposes raised to thirty cents, an annual income of $151,539.20, a much increased pupil attendance, and a staff of 267 members. Such was the statement of effort that spelled progress for a city which had a population of 43,154 in 1850 and 100,573 in 1870.

Instruction in the secondary field was limited to the Collegiate Institute and a few private schools up to 1855, when the council resolved to provide a high school for girls, which was started in 1856. Eight years later, a new building on First Street between Walnut and Chestnut was dedicated with much ceremony.[1] The old doubts about a free system of education were somewhat allayed by the statement of a new writer who said "the system inaugurated placed [the school] above the standards of respectability that it was hoped a school established under our free system of education could attain." The year 1856 was notable also for the founding

[1] Louisville *Journal*, January 22, 1864.

of a boys' high school under the name of "Male High School" on the corner of Ninth and Chestnut streets.

A new charter for the city was enacted in 1870. The corporate title of the governing body was designated as the Board of Trustees of the Male High School, the Female High School, and the Public Schools of Louisville, a title much too long, but one that maintained the specific identity of the two high schools; for the law gave these schools the status of a college and the right to confer any degree recognized by the colleges and the university in the commonwealth of Kentucky.[2]

Fourteen years later, an amendment to the charter changed the name to the Louisville School Board, though the board remained subordinate to the city council, a situation that continued until 1890 when the board was given full power and control over the schools except in the matter of raising money for them. Representatives from each of the twelve wards made the board membership a body of twenty-four. A law of 1910 created a board of education elected at large from the city with full powers to direct and control the management of the schools. The plan of management separated the functions of the superintendent from the maintenance of plant, grounds, and equipment. As a consequence of the change in the law, the board entered upon a period of activity involving the erection of new buildings, rejuvenation of the teaching staff, and the acquirement of additional property for school purposes. In the meantime, the city council increased the rate of taxation, and the legislature fixed a maximum limit of bonded indebtedness at a million dollars, and also authorized the board to provide for a teachers' pension system. Gradually these educational functions have been separated from the political activities of city government. Under the leadership of able superintendents, the schools have advanced, but there remain problems facing the board that go back to the days of council control.

[2] Kentucky *Acts, 1869-70,* 30.

INDEPENDENT DISTRICTS

In the city of Lexington, one of the second-class municipalities, the schools remained under the immediate direction or the partial control of the mayor and council from the incorporation of the town in 1831 to 1922, when the board of education was fully emancipated from the city council. Almost a century passed before Lexington could free her schools from a control that had long ago been relinquished in the more forward-looking cities. Part of this situation can be attributed to the legislatures which were reluctant to set the schools free from political agencies. In a notice appearing in the Lexington *Reporter* in 1812, reference is made to a free school.[3] The promoter of the plan, Joseph Chambers, stated that he wished to receive subscriptions for the support of the school and invited all and sundry to send in their contributions. He hoped that enough support would be forthcoming to keep the school going so that children could be admitted without the payment of tuition, but Chambers was unable to attain his objective.

In 1833 the city of Lexington was scourged by cholera, leaving a great number of children without parents. The problem of educating the orphans was a highly important one. A great meeting, called together in Morrison Hall, resolved to make provisions for a public school and, before adjourning, appointed a committee to find a place for a city school.[4] The committee ascertained that the Rankin meetinghouse on the corner of Short and Market streets could be secured; the building was repaired, and the school opened in March, 1834, with Joseph Gayle and his daughter Isabelle as teachers. In the report, it is said that 107 pupils attended. At the end of the year the expenses came to $660, and the amount received from tuition was $227.55, leaving a balance against the school of $432.45. By 1852 it was possible for the school authorities to declare that education should be free. Progress was slow, for it was not until 1887 that graded

---

[3] Lexington *Reporter*, October 28, 1812.
[4] J. S. Chambers, *The Conquest of Cholera* (New York, 1938), Chap. V.

schools were authorized and the term extended to five months. In 1890 the term was lengthened to seven months. Lexington, however, did somewhat better than the state requirement. As an adjunct to the schools, a kindergarten was established in 1890; in the next four years four more kindergartens were added to the school system. The slow development of high schools in the city may be due to the presence of a number of private schools and the maintenance of academies at Kentucky University and the State College. Some high school instruction was given beyond the eighth grade at the Johnson and Dudley schools; and at the Morton School a more extensive course was offered. Lexington's first high school became a fact in 1904, with Colonel John Graves as principal, a staff of ten teachers, and an enrollment of 220 pupils.[5] Five years later the board of education erected a sizable building known as the Morton High School in honor of William Morton who contributed $12,000. Two other buildings, one in 1916 and another in 1928, were built to house the growing high school. In 1917 the superintendent reported eight public schools for white children and four for colored pupils. The growth in buildings and equipment came largely through the passage of a bond issue of $400,000 in 1917. With the help of such funds, the schools of Lexington were housed in modern buildings after a long struggle with old and inadequate ones. Progress, too, had been made in the curricula offered in the schools. From a two-year course beyond the eighth grade prior to 1904, the high schools were expanded to include four years of instruction. The so-called eight-four plan was reorganized in 1917 on the six-three-three basis, with junior and senior high schools. In the development of the courses, manual training, commercial subjects, domestic science, music, art, and automotive mechanics had been added. By 1942 the system included 8,039 pupils and twelve buildings.[6]

[5] Letter from Miss Masie Wolverton, April 18, 1937.
[6] *Report of Superintendent of Lexington Schools* (1942).

In the second largest city of Kentucky, Covington's first school was a private one open only to those who could pay tuition. Mr. and Mrs. Gist stated in an advertisement that they would receive in their home boys and girls, between the ages of five and fourteen, for instruction in the rudiments of knowledge upon the payment of two dollars per quarter of eleven weeks.[7] Five years later a subscription school was started to teach children whose parents could not pay for their schooling. This arrangement continued until 1830, when the city council set aside all of one hundred dollars to help maintain a free school. A log cabin was purchased, located on the banks of the Ohio where the children would not be exposed to prowling Indians.[8] Only forty-five pupils were reported as attending the free school in 1836. In 1846 and in 1849 two private high schools were organized, the first by W. S. Mead and the second by A. Drury. The courses embraced history, natural and moral philosophy, rhetoric, logic, algebra, geometry, trigonometry, and surveying. The beginning of public secondary education in Covington, says Howard H. Mills, goes back to 1853, in the district school at Eleventh and Scott streets. By 1869 the Covington High School was offering a four-year course to 121 pupils. A school for Negro children was provided in 1873. The support of such a school rested upon taxes paid by Negro property holders, which included forfeitures and a poll tax. In Covington, as elsewhere, this financial support was insufficient to pay for a good school.

The account of the secondary schools in the three larger cities of the state parallels the educational development in other towns and cities. That record differs in detail and in time, but in most respects the educational program followed the same lines. By and large the growth was slow, hindered by lack of funds and real incentive to meet the needs for instruction of the youth who had reached the end of the grade schools. As late as 1908-1909 there were but sixteen high

---

[7] Cincinnati *Daily Gazette*, August 21, 1820.
[8] Howard H. Mills, "A History of Education of Covington, Kentucky" (M.A. thesis, University of Kentucky, 1929).

schools supported in districts where special charters had been granted to the towns. In the graded districts there were 100 high schools organized under the law of 1888. A scant two-thirds of those maintained four-year high schools.[9] Compared with the figures for this earlier date, the statistics for 1940-1941 show a remarkable growth. In 1915 the State Superintendent of Public Instruction reported 15,547 white children enrolled in the public high schools. No figures are given at that date for the attendance of colored pupils or for those in private high schools. In 1940-1941, the reports show a total enrollment of 144,447 in all classes of high schools. Of this number there were 123,822 in the schools for white children, 10,440 in the schools for colored children, and 10,185 in private high schools. In twenty-five years the number of secondary schools had more than doubled; and the enrollment had increased more than nine times. Some of the high schools reported did not maintain work up to the twelfth grade. The number that did so, including both public and private schools, was 649 in 1940. Despite the growth in enrollment, the number of public high schools has declined due to consolidation and the development of larger high schools. Most of this decline resulted from the merger of one-room schools into large county school centers. This development has brought high school advantages to the youth in the rural areas. There are, however, parts of the state where high school opportunities are not fully developed.

The number of private high schools has remained fairly constant in the last five years. While there is a slow decline in numbers of such schools, the enrollment has increased about 1,000 in the past five years.[10] The continued growth in attendance at such schools is to be found in the increase in number and attendance of parochial schools located in the larger cities. The Southern Association of Schools and Colleges

---

[9] Carl H. Kardatzke, "The Origin and Development of the Public High School System in Kentucky" (Ph.D. thesis, University of Kentucky, 1933).

[10] *Report of Superintendent of Public Instruction* (December, 1941), 599-604.

has admitted a number of Kentucky high schools to full recognition. The number, though small, is steadily increasing as standards of the association are approximated.

A great deal of criticism has been directed against the high school courses of study. That the curriculum is too literary and not practical enough to meet the needs of the average student is the main contention of the critics, and yet many people still cling to the ideals of a liberal education. This latter opinion is based partly on the requirements for college entrance and partly on the hope of a broader concept of life for those who attain a liberal education.

A look at the course of study followed in the Cynthiana High School seventy years ago shows that the young people who went to school in that pleasant city studied reading, spelling, arithmetic, grammar, history, natural philosophy, algebra, and a subject or two from a miscellaneous group such as botany, physiology, and geography. In the second semester the pace was stepped up, and the pupil was brought to the more erudite topics such as algebra to logarithms, geometry, natural philosophy, Latin, German or French, and high-toned spelling called orthography. In the second year, Greek, geometry, and chemistry were added, and in the third year, surveying, mental philosophy, and history swelled the requirements. When the youngster had reached his fourth year in high school he came in contact with logic, mental and moral philosophy, English literature, and composition.[11] Twenty years before the Cynthiana High School curriculum was in use, the Louisville Male High School had offered subjects that remind one of the college course of the 1790's, for in it were Greek, Latin up to Horace, moral philosophy, Butler's *Analogy*, trigonometry, surveying and navigation, ancient history, Goethe's *Faust*, and the works of Schiller.[12] These courses, later designated as classical, scientific, and

[11] *Ibid.* (1873).
[12] *Louisville School Board Report* (1858), 2.

commercial, when completed qualified the graduates for the A.B. or B.S. degree; a commercial diploma was given also until 1912.

When listed, the subjects offered are formidable, showing the influence of the colleges upon the high schools of those times, but perhaps more than that, indicating teacher preparation, such as there was, and the domination of the upper-class ideas of education. Since 1885, reading, spelling, natural philosophy, rhetoric, Greek, moral science, astronomy, mental philosophy, surveying, geology, logic, Greek Testament, moral philosophy, and Xenophon's *Anabasis* have been dropped from high school courses of study.[13] Later, when the State Department of Public Instruction was able to classify high schools and to set up courses of studies, some order was introduced into the curricula. In place of those subjects eliminated, agriculture, household arts, manual training and shop work, physical education, art, music, public speaking, and the social studies came into the curricula of the high schools with some loss in the rigor of subjects and some gain in the increase of community interest in secondary education.

While the spirit of doing things in public education gripped their minds and stirred the educational leaders to action, a state curriculum committee was formed by Superintendent J. H. Richmond in 1934 to study the offerings in the elementary and secondary schools.[14] The objectives of this large and able committee were to construct new courses of study and to stimulate inquiry in the problems of the curriculum. State and regional committees and thirty-two subcommittees were appointed to study the programs in various grades and phases of public education as carried on in the schools. These committees found that they needed to formulate definitions and objectives, a task that soon brought to

---

[13] Kardatzke, "The Origin and Development of the Public High School System in Kentucky."

[14] "A Program of Curriculum Study in Kentucky," *Commonwealth of Kentucky Educational Bulletin*, II, No. 8 (October, 1934).

light many views and concepts. The general goals were believed by the committee to be knowledges and understandings, attitudes, automatic responses, and appreciations. The procedure of the general committee was democratic in that topics were sent to teachers' meetings all over the state to encourage discussion and in the hope that much material in the form of opinions would come back to the managing committee. After considerable work, a preliminary report was prepared and sent to the Department of Education at Frankfort, where it remained in manuscript form. The teachers and administrative officers had learned a good deal, but the move to change the school curriculum by direct attack had failed.

A different approach to the problems involved in the arrangement of the curriculum was tried by John W. Brooker, Superintendent of Public Instruction, when he called a teachers' educational conference at the Eastern State Teachers College, September 4-13, 1940. The effort in 1934 was largely one that dealt with the pupil's needs and his relation to the community, whereas the conference held in 1940 emphasized teacher education, pre-service and in-service, and the teacher's experience and knowledge of educational procedures and needs.[15] Following the initial conference, regional meetings were scheduled in eleven cities during the month of November, 1940. Attendance at these meetings was highly satisfactory to the State Department of Education. In some respects the findings of the regional conferences were decidedly realistic. The aims and purposes of the school were well stated under the heads of objectives, functions, administration, leadership, and the program of school activities. Compared with the curriculum of fifty years ago, a marked difference is to be noted in the emphasis placed upon the scope of the school program. The members of the conferences evidently valued training for vocations, physical education, moral education, citizenship, and the relation of the

---

[15] *Commonwealth of Kentucky Educational Bulletin*, VIII, No. 10 (December, 1940).

school to the community as the high purposes of public education.[16] In the report there appears to be a new emphasis on national defense and the teaching of the democratic way of life. All of this is to the good, but there runs through much of the discussions a confusion between the direct purpose of a school and the by-products that come out of the operation of the school as a going concern. Such confusion as may exist is a natural result of the stress on community relations as opposed to pupil education, training, and discipline. War on a global scale brought out weaknesses in the education of the youth who had not thoroughly acquired work habits and a knowledge of fundamental skills. It is evident that more and better teachers are needed who by their own habits and ideals can instill honor, good citizenship, democracy, unselfishness, and the values of right living in the pupil. Instruction in the schools should be thoroughgoing, so that skills may be acquired.

By skills two things are implied: one, vocational training; and the other, facility in the three R's as well as in the higher forms of composition, language, and mathematics. Under the Smith-Hughes Act and other Federal legislation such as the George-Dean Law, the high schools in several areas received considerable sums to support instruction in home economics, agriculture, trades, and industry. In the independent districts, there is not much support from Federal funds going to the schools for vocational purposes. As a result, the curriculum holds to the liberal traditions with some training in automobile mechanics, home economics, and wood and iron work. The fact is that until recently schools in towns of some size had found no outlets for pupils who were given instruction in crafts, with the result that the courses followed the older trends.

The city of Louisville established the duPont Manual High School in 1892 and there provided fundamental instruc-

---

[16] *Ibid.*, VIII, No. 12 (February, 1941).

tion in mathematics and the sciences as a foundation for technical training in various industrial fields. When the courses were completed, the graduates who went to engineering colleges were admitted with advanced standing. Those who did not go on with college work received valuable training, but they were not craftsmen. To fill the gap which was left open by the absence of instruction in the crafts and trades, Theodore Ahrens established and financed the Ahrens Trade School in Louisville in 1924. This school had its beginnings in a prevocational school, started in 1913 when the principles and purpose of the school required the fundamentals of an academic education, instructions in trades and occupations, and the choosing of a vocation through guidance. The generosity of Ahrens was shown not only in his original gift but later in providing for the housing and equipment of a highly useful school. Nowhere in the state may the young craftsman find so much in the way of instruction in the crafts and trades; for the list includes printing, electrical appliances, plumbing, machinery, sheet-metal work, cabinetmaking, carpentry, masonry, bookkeeping, stenography, sewing, and millinery. In 1927 additional gifts from Ahrens were used to include a cafeteria and a gymnasium. Upon his death the school received a considerable sum which financed a large addition to the plant. Throughout the long history of the school, Miss Ethel Lovell has been its principal.[17]

Here and there in the state, other schools have attempted to do some work in craft and trade instructions, but speaking broadly, outside of Louisville the instruction in that field is not extensive. Since this is a mechanical age, the schools will be forced to find means to give training in the mechanical trades. Kentucky as an agricultural state has naturally emphasized agriculture and home economics, and much has been done in those subjects; but the opportunity in the crafts and industries will be knocking oftener and louder

---

[17] Roman T. Brom, "History of the Public Secondary Schools in Louisville" (M.A. thesis, University of Kentucky, 1935), 76-81.

on the doors of the board rooms where school authorities gather to pass upon educational policies and management.

The report of the Superintendent of Public Instruction contains some interesting figures on attendance in the schools maintained in the independent districts and the cost of operation during the year 1940-1941. One of the tables shows that in the independent districts there were enrolled 181,143 white and colored pupils, 30 per cent of the total enrollment in the public schools of the state. In the independent districts, there were 50,147 children in the city high schools and 44,021 in the county high schools, or more than half of the high school enrollment in the state. It is also worth while to observe that the report of the state department shows a reduction in the number attending all grades of the county schools of 7,186 under the year 1939-1940, and 968 in the independent districts in the same period. The report tells the inquirer that the schools had an income of $29,714,845 including reserve receipts and nonreserve receipts. Of this sum, the independent districts spent $12,643,257 and the county schools $16,477,999. When placed on an enrollment basis, the independent districts distributed for each pupil in school almost exactly seventy dollars, whereas the county school districts had to get along on forty dollars per pupil. One more comparison with the national per capita expenditure of eighty dollars leaves the independent districts with ten dollars less and the county districts with forty dollars less than the national figure. Kentucky has increased her gross expenditures on public education markedly in the last twenty-five years, but the lag behind the national per capita expenditures for education places the state much too far down on the scale of educational progress.

CHAPTER XVII

THE CRISES OF TODAY AND THE CHALLENGE OF TOMORROW

ALTHOUGH the depression of the 1930's laid heavy burdens upon public and private enterprises, Kentucky made some gains in her educational system due to the help that came from the Federal government. Many new buildings replaced old and inadequate schoolhouses; luncheon programs helped to build up the children's health; and teachers, not yet tempted by the monetary rewards in industry and government employment that were to be opened to them in the 1940's, continued in service. The state was able to pay its per capita quotas to the counties for education. When the attack on Pearl Harbor struck the nation, there followed a series of events, new methods, and actions which changed materially the educational picture in Kentucky, as well as in other states.

In a period of two years, 1942-1944, emigration from Kentucky cost the state 11 per cent of its population. The loss in men who were called to serve in the armed forces of the nation was greatly increased by the migration of thousands of men and women to the factories and offices of other states. More than a quarter of a million people were lured to near and distant parts of the country by the high wages and salaries offered under the impetus of the war effort. Public education in particular suffered by the withdrawal of large numbers of the best teachers to new occupations which gave them greater rewards for their services. Here and there, schools were closed, and those remaining carried on with reduced and less efficient staffs.

The seriousness of the situation in the schools of the state was well presented by John Fred Williams, State Superintendent of Public Instruction, in a memorandum issued in February, 1946. He declared: "The teacher shortage in Kentucky is tragic, for we do not have sufficient teachers for our pre-war class room demands for 18,180 positions." The decline was not only in numbers, but in the quality and experience of the teaching profession of the state. In 1945-1946 five thousand emergency certificates were granted to teachers. Of these teachers 1,400 had no college training, 1,600 had less than one year of such training, and 800 had less than two years of college work. This devastation, for it really amounted to that, is further shown in the fact that since 1941 more than 9,180 qualified teachers have left the profession, probably permanently. The turnover of 35,000 teachers during the war was harassing to the supervising officers. Today, a sparse 60 per cent of the teachers have the qualifications required by the law. In addition, overcrowded classrooms resulted in combination classes, the elimination of some subjects, and even the discontinuance of departments, particularly those of art and music. The number of one- and two-teacher schools staffed by emergency teachers has been increased. The hope for better conditions and for the return of former teachers to their profession at the close of the war has failed to materialize because the rise in the cost of living has not been met by any substantial increase in teachers' salaries. What seemed to be merely a temporary situation created by war conditions now appears as a problem of present and future proportions calling for real statesmanship and a larger financial support of the schools.

These and other conditions in public education brought the Committee for Kentucky face to face with a crisis.[1] To know how much money was needed, it was necessary for this committee to learn several things. Among these were the

[1] Maurice F. Seay, *A Report on Education* (Committee for Kentucky, 1945). The statistical information given in the following pages may be found in this *Report*.

number of children in the state from five to seventeen years of age; how many attend school; what kind of education they receive; the adequacy of teacher training and experience; how much a school costs and how much must be expended to assure a good school. When these questions are looked at seriously and carefully, those concerned about public education join the committee in asking: Does Kentucky recognize the size of the task?

To begin with, the entire number of school-aged children in proportion to total population is larger in Kentucky than the national average; and in the southern group of states, only four have fewer children than Kentucky per thousand of population. Here at the outset of any inquiry, the student and citizen are faced with a stupendous fact, for there are 267 children of school age in Kentucky for each 1,000 of the population. But of that number only 78 per cent are enrolled, which means that more than 130,000 children of the 704,190 school-aged children reported by the census are not in school; and the per capita school fund is distributed on the basis of school children in a district and not on their attendance. In the field of secondary schools there is a great variation in attendance. There are 775 pupils in Kenton County to 1,000 children of high school age, while there are only 124 in Casey County. The proportion of children going to high school in the state is distressingly low. One reason for the low attendance is the number of small schools that are poorly located. Not hundreds of children, but literally thousands of high school age find it impossible to get to the schools as they are now located. It is also distressing to note in the committee's report that only 2.5 per cent of those enrolled in the twelve grades actually finish high school each year, as against 4.5 per cent throughout the nation. On the economic side, a great number of boys and girls who do graduate from high school and stand in the upper half scholastically cannot find the means to finance a college education. Such were the conditions existing just before the close of the war, but the situation has been aggravated by the inflation of prices and by the opportunities teachers have found in other callings.

To bring these facts into a statistical statement having to do with schoolkeeping and teacher preparation is essential if the whole picture is to be presented. The average length of the school term in the state is 159 days, but the average number of days in which the child actually goes to school is but 129. The extremes are to be found in the figures for Leslie County of 84 days school attendance and in Campbell County of 146 days. In another place, comment has been made about the certification of schoolteachers and their qualifications to do satisfactory work. Not in twenty-five years have there been in the schools of the state so many teachers who did not meet the certification requirements. Such a condition is not only pathetic, it is dangerous, because the effects of inadequate education are extended for a generation at least, a situation which leaves the state to struggle with problems complicated by lack of understanding among its citizens. Education when such conditions exist is held in low esteem.

In Kentucky those who are classified as functional illiterates constitute 20 per cent of the population over twenty-five years of age. The census shows that in Kentucky men and women over twenty-five years of age have completed on the average 7.7 years of schooling, whereas the figure for the nation is 8.4. To go on with these interesting and necessary comparisons, it is found that 16 per cent of the population in Kentucky of twenty-five years of age or over have had four years of high school, while the figure for the nation is 24 per cent. On the college level, Kentucky has a 3 per cent proportion; for the nation the figure is 5 per cent. In the professions which require graduate work before the individual can practice his calling, 2.6 per cent of the colored population are professional men and women, while 3.6 per cent of the white population are so designated. The figures set forth in this paragraph are not new in the sense that the situation is one that has suddenly come upon the state, but rather what has been said is a statement of conditions of long standing. Kentucky has gone along for many decades slowly improving its educational procedures and support of the schools, but the state has not done enough to keep up with the advance of education in the nation. It is sad to say, but Kentucky has lost ground relatively in the last thirty years because it has not been really alive to what is happening. Too little and too late may well describe the failure to maintain the modern program of education. In reality, high prices for equipment, building maintenance, supplies, salaries, and bus operation have laid a burden upon the conduct of the schools that cannot yet be seen in their full consequences at this time, 1948. In actual fact, the people are faced with a grave responsibility which if not met means still further decline in standards of education throughout the state.

The trends and forces set loose by the war have affected the colleges and universities located in Kentucky. A questionnaire sent to these institutions brought replies from three-fourths of them to the queries about enrollment, faculties, income, and housing problems. The attendance of male students by 1943 had fallen to about 75 per cent of the number attending in the year 1940-1941, while the number of women students continued approximately at the figures for the pre-war year. The faculties of the private colleges were not so much affected by the drafting of their staffs or by the employment of large numbers in war activities, but the public institutions were called upon to give up a considerable number of teachers to serve in camps, government departments, and research projects. In nearly every college, the income went down due to the decline in enrollment, until, in most public institutions of higher education, the fall in income from tuition was made up by the payment for drafted men who were sent to these colleges and universities for special instruction.

The student military training program inaugurated by the War and Navy departments resulted in special classes for servicemen, while the regular college program of studies continued, though greatly reduced as compared to that maintained in the prewar years. In the engineering colleges, practically the whole effort of the two located in Kentucky was given over to the instruction of drafted men sent to those institutions for special training. Such increase of numbers on the campuses crowded every dormitory and private accommodation in the towns where the colleges were located. In some instances, temporary structures were built to house these students. When the war was over, the influx of students to the colleges was further increased owing to the desire of the soldiers and sailors to avail themselves of the benefits of the G. I. Bill of Rights, which gives allowances for educational fees and support while in college. The attendance during the war was suddenly augmented by as much as 100 per cent when the men and women in the armed forces returned to civilian life. The burden of teaching and of providing houses and staffs to give the instruction was a very heavy one. Such happenings threw the colleges off their usual procedures and made administration and teaching at high standards hard to maintain.

In the questionnaire replies, no evidence appears that the military program of studies has affected the general college curriculum except in the language courses. In this respect, the methods inaugurated in the training camps to give a matter-of-fact speaking and reading knowledge of foreign languages produced considerable results which were recognized by language teachers as valuable. In another way, the war brought a wider appreciation of world problems, the importance of national ideologies, and the compactness of the world as a whole. Thus in the field of the political sciences a new searching for values placed added importance on the complexities of government and the need to understand the obligations of citizenship. Instruction in the sciences suffered from reduction in staffs to a larger degree than in any other field on account of the demand for trained men in the government and industrial laboratories and as fieldmen to supervise the use of new appliances. This call for scientific men reduced the staffs in many departments, particularly in chemistry, physics, biology, and mathematics. Graduate student registration was cut to less than 10 per cent of the prewar enrollment, and the teaching staffs were reduced by the loss of many of the younger men. This wholesale raiding of faculties in the science fields and the reduction of the number of graduate students have left institutions with inadequate staffs and with no backlog from which to fill the places vacated by the many changes in personnel produced by the war. Our government did not place too high a value upon the supply of trained men and women who would be needed when the war should end. Thus the lag in supply of teachers, technicians, and research experts cannot be made up for many years. What this means to the state and national economies is not well understood by the great majority of people, since the result of such a policy cannot be measured.

The effect of the war on teacher supply has been discussed in another place, yet little has been written about its effect upon the preparation of teachers in the colleges of the state. In 1939-1940 there were 715 persons in the public institutions of higher education preparing for elementary teacher certificates; five years later the number had declined to 137. On the secondary level, 667 students were preparing to teach in 1939-1940; five years later there were only 241 such students. The decrease in terms of percentages was 80.8 in the first group and 64 in the second; combined, the decline was 72.6 per cent. The total number of students preparing for teaching had dropped in the five years from 1,383 to 378. In the private colleges, the percentage of trainees was lower than that of the public institutions by 8 per cent. Not only was the number of teachers in the school system declining markedly, but the number of prospective teachers in training fell far below that of 1939-1940. In order to check the exodus and to encourage newcomers to enlist in the teaching staff of the state, the legislature was urged to appropriate money for salary increases; and at the 1944 session a million dollars was provided for that purpose. In addition, the per capita school fund was increased by five million dollars. By these means, the average salary was raised to $1,094, a gain of $372. For the time being the exodus was checked, yet the teacher shortage problem was not solved, and the Department of Education was obliged to issue five thousand emergency certificates.

The growing cost of living during the years since 1944 has found many teachers hard pressed to maintain a decent standard. Appeals to boards of education by teachers have been answered by the statement that the funds for salary increases are not available. In a number of cities of the nation, the teachers have organized, and sometimes as members of local units of labor unions they have refused to continue in the classroom until their demands were met. The deadlock thus created has been broken now and then by compromises. In Louisville the teachers organized as a local union and engaged in discussions with the board of education which resulted in promises but no increase in salary. A somewhat different turn in the wage situation was reported in Robertson County in the neighboring state of Tennessee when the teachers in the county system resigned after their request of an increase of twenty dollars a month had been denied them by the Quarterly Court. The teachers made no threats and indicated that they were not opposed to being replaced.

A number of problems were raised by the difficulties over the salary question: one, the ability of the state, county, and independent districts to provide the funds to meet the additional costs of instruction; another, the methods used by teacher groups to bring pressure on boards of education. The Kentucky Education Association through the Board of Directors declared "that if chaos and catastrophe are to be avoided, drastic action must be taken immediately." The directors called for a minimum salary of $2,400 for teachers holding a teacher's certificate based on an A.B. degree. The board pointed out the surplus in the state treasury and the ability of the legislature to find the means to pay the bill.[2] Since the legislature was not to meet until 1948, Governor Simeon Willis was asked to call a special session to provide funds to relieve the teacher situation.

In Kentucky, with one or two exceptions, the teachers have not resorted to pressure tactics, but the protests against not only salary matters but conditions of work and cost of living facilities may yet result in demands that will bring about their organization into labor unions. **Attempts have been made to organize teachers in Kentucky, but so far they have not been successful.**[3] The unionizing of teachers will bring demands for rules on hours of work and other restrictions which will place a heavy hand upon the main essentials of good teaching. The unionization of the teachers in the nation's schools would certainly offer opportunities for propaganda in addition to emphasizing a class consciousness not in accord with the democratic spirit which should prevail in the public schools. Probably some gains might be made in salary and conditions of work, but those gains would be bought at the expense of independence and by placing a premium upon mediocrity. Overemphasis is sometimes given to the importance of the missionary spirit in education, yet it is an essential element in the attitude of any good teacher. That the child is the center of the whole process of education must be accepted if teaching is to be really effective in any place, at any time. If this important attitude is ignored and the teacher becomes a mere puppet in a powerful organization, something happens to education that reduces it to a kind of mass production carried on along an assembly line. First, a clear understanding of the incentives, opportunities, and rewards of teaching must be accepted by the teacher. Again, the state must have a philosophy of education that is sound and fundamental; and the people must base their faith

---

[2] Lexington *Herald,* January 7, 1947.
[3] Associated Press Report, December 31, 1946.

in an educational program and a real understanding of the part it plays in the life of the child and in the growth and progress of the nation.

All through the history of education in Kentucky it is quite apparent that the people of the state have not had much interest in education, but have left it largely to the teachers and the administrative officers. Certainly the State Department of Education has stressed the need for a stronger backing by the public. This requirement has been stressed by presidents of colleges, by teachers, by citizens, and often by the press; but in the main, the people have been indifferent to the demands of the school leaders that something be done. The figures on illiteracy may explain this attitude toward education so apparent in the history of Kentucky. And as a result, it is to be noted that many graduates of Kentucky high schools and colleges have gone to other states to follow their careers.

In his emphatic recommendations to the people of the state on the educational situation, Dr. John W. Brooker, former Superintendent of Public Instruction, listed, after suggesting methods of publicity, a number of pertinent steps to be taken to stimulate action. He stressed the necessity for promoting compulsory school attendance of all children from seven to seventeen years of age, inclusive. Dr. Brooker advocated the following important steps, among others, which the state would be well advised to accept and to act upon:

"Promote compulsory school attendance for all children 7 to 17 years of age, inclusive.

"Encourage the development of an enriched school curriculum with expanded opportunities in vocational education.

"Stimulate and encourage the establishment and proper maintenance of county and municipal libraries.

"Work for the elimination of small, inefficient and expensive school districts.

"Urge a constitutional change which will provide for the professional selection of the State Superintendent of Schools.

"Inaugurate a teacher recruitment campaign in each local organization to encourage outstanding youth to enter the teaching profession.

"Establish Scholarship Loan Funds to enable capable but needy young people to enter college.

"Advocate more adequate appropriations for state institutions of higher learning.

"Promote a program of parent education, greater utilization of school buildings, playgrounds and facilities for recreational purposes and full co-operation with all agencies combatting juvenile delinquency and engaged in the education, protection and care of youth.

"Promote the development of a school program which will guarantee the following educational services for all the children of Kentucky:

"(a) A minimum school term of nine months.

"(b) A well trained and qualified teacher earning a minimum monthly salary of $150.

"(c) Safe and comfortable transportation for those not living within reasonable walking distance of school.

"(d) Modern textbooks and instructional materials suited to local needs.

"(e) Safe and sanitary school buildings and more adequate playground and recreational facilities.

"(f) A health program providing for periodic physical examinations for all children with a follow-up to correct all remedial defects."[4]

It requires no seer or crystal ball to learn what the main difficulty is in developing public education in Kentucky. As in the case of many another public enterprise, the availability of funds limits what can be done. According to the statistics,

[4] Dr. John W. Brooker, "A Plan of Action," in Seay, *A Report on Education*, 27-28.

a great variance exists in the ability to maintain schools by local taxation. For example, the average family income in Knott County is placed at $554, whereas the figure in Fayette County is $4,828. The cost of education in Kentucky for the elementary and secondary public schools is $9.11 per capita of the population. The nation's figure is $17.77. Another test of ability to support education is the amount of assessed valuation for each child of school age in a state or county. The valuation in the state as a whole is $2,087; in Clinton County, $478; in Woodford County, $8,264. The state has collected taxes for school purposes under the provisions of the school fund acts; but in proportion to the total revenue of the state, Kentucky paid 62 per cent in 1905 and 48 per cent in 1945. Under the provisions of an amendment to the constitution ratified in 1944, the legislature of 1946 provided for a distribution of 10 per cent of the school fund on the basis of need. Still the schools are lagging behind in the national count due to changing conditions that have developed in the war and postwar years.

The situation is well stated in the Hughes and Lancelot book, *Education, America's Magic:*

"The annual income of Kentucky is $1,105 for each child. Its rank in ability to support schools is 43, which places it in the lowest eighth of the states as to this criterion. The state also faces the necessity of maintaining separate school systems.

"It places a relatively low value upon education, devoting but 3.54 per cent of its income to the support of its school system and ranking thirty-seventh with respect to effort. This is counterbalanced by well above average efficiency in the use of school funds, its rank as to this criterion being 17. Thus the state presents the familiar picture of effort and efficiency working against each other. The result is that its rank as to accomplishment is precisely the same as that in ability, 43.

As to the degree in which its accomplishment measures up to its ability, its rank is 33.

"Kentucky occupies the thirty-eighth place with respect to all-around educational performance. On the whole, its record can be regarded as no better than fair. In particular, its rank as to effort is low. While its low income forbids an exceptionally high rank as to effort, it is true that the two states which rank next below Kentucky as to ability, North and South Carolina, hold ranks of 10 and 14 respectively as to effort; and Mississippi, which ranks forty-eighth as to ability, still ranks eleventh with respect to effort. Considerable gains are doubtless possible as to both effort and efficiency. Yet if these are made, it is apparent that Kentucky would be unable without federal help to provide for its children education comparable with that which is available to most other children of the nation."[5]

Although Kentucky is given a place of thirty-eighth in the educational rank of the states, the authors quoted above were certain the state cannot reach a payment of $70 per child for the support of public education. The figures show clearly that this conclusion is true. If Kentucky raised 3.5 per cent of its income for education, a figure set as a fair test of ability to pay, it would be necessary to rely upon the Federal treasury for $23,700,000 to give the state $70 per annum to maintain the national standard of expenditures for education. Thus a real issue is raised of vast importance to a balanced and equalized national growth. Meantime, it is the duty of Kentucky to try with all of its ability and strength to advance its educational facilities. The state can do more in raising money, and it can improve the administration of the public schools. To stand back and await the coming of Federal funds is to invite a continued decline in the educational program. Kentucky is inhabited by a proud people who, once thoroughly aroused, could better materially the education of their children.

[5] Hughes and Lancelot, *Education, America's Magic*, 22.

There are other factors involved in the educational history of the state which are not financial but have to do with the laws on the statute books which determine matters of administration. Every four years the people select by ballot a new head of the state public schools. This is done under a constitutional provision which also states that no Superintendent of Public Instruction can succeed himself. As a result, plans and policies are interrupted, dropped, or modified by the new superintendents who come into office at four-year intervals. Each new man requires two years of study and of inquiry to learn what the department has done and where it stands. So, by fits and starts, the administration of public education jerks along. The wonder is that so much has been accomplished. Under a well-trained and experienced administrator, unhampered by elections and short terms, Kentucky's educational effort would be much more effective than it is. The only way by which the situation can be strengthened is by amending the constitution in this regard.

In the legislative session of 1934, an act was passed to reorganize the government of the state. By this act the governor had the power to remove members of boards without stating cause or bringing charges. Under this law Governor Chandler called for the resignation of all members of boards of public educational institutions. Again, in 1946, the members of the Board of Trustees of Morehead State Teachers College were changed by Governor Willis. The new board refused to reappoint President Vaughn and elected William Jesse Baird as president of the college. This action of the board brought protests which finally reached the Commission of the Southern Association of Colleges and Secondary Schools and resulted in a review of the situation at the Morehead school. At the meeting of the Association in Memphis, December, 1946, the Morehead Teachers College was dropped from the approved list, which gave great embarrassment to the new president and seriously handicapped the college. Two years later, after study of the situation at Morehead, a committee appointed by the Association recommended that the college be restored to the approved list. Reinstatement was approved in December, 1948, by the Association. What happened in the case of Morehead might have happened in any of the other public institutions of higher education, including the university, under the provisions of the Reorganization Act of 1934. Protection of the state's colleges and the university from political interference clearly required a change in the law to avoid possible future calamity. Happily the legislature meeting in 1948 changed the law giving the governor power to remove members of state college boards without cause. The new law offers protection of board members against removal for political reasons.

The unprecedented demands made upon the medical profession during World War II modified the ideas previously prevailing concerning the ability of existing medical schools to furnish the trained men and women for health and medical services. According to the authorities, there is a shortage of physicians in the country amounting to at least thirty thousand and possibly to forty thousand doctors. To meet this demand it is apparent that new medical schools must be established. At legislative sessions in Kentucky for the past ten years, representatives of the University of Kentucky have been asked when the university will establish a medical school. The answer to this important question is that such a school cannot be established unless a large sum of money is provided not only for the construction of a plant in which to house the school and hospital, but additional funds to support them as going concerns. So the question has remained unanswered for a decade.

These inquiries from members of the legislative sessions before the war have grown in number and insistence since the state's need for medical service has been greatly augmented by events during the war. In Kentucky there is one medical school, located in Louisville as a part of the University of Louisville. This institution has had a history of a hundred years, in which time many difficulties and obstacles have been overcome until it has attained rating as an A school. The demands in the last fifteen years made upon this school as well as the other colleges of the University of Louisville have strained the financial support of the institution until the medical school is hard pressed to maintain its standing. Such a situation has raised the question whether or not the state should in its own university establish a medical school which the original charter of the State University has already authorized.

The wisdom of creating in Kentucky just another run-of-the-mine medical school is certainly to be questioned. In the words of Dr. John S. Chambers, "If the new school should be conceived, planned and founded as a superior school, a great school, the wisdom of its establishment would be accepted by all." To bring a great medical school into being would require not only large annual appropriations, but a considerable sum of money with which to build and equip the college and hospital. Certainly private funds would be required not only for the building of the plant, but also for its endowment. To think of this great enterprise in small terms would be of no avail, "but with funds from both state and private sources, the conception, the planning, the founding of a superior school might be undertaken."[6] Thus another problem and a great enterprise rest upon the will to persevere. It is the same situation that has faced Kentucky in the past, not once but many times. With vision and purpose behind the movement, a great medical school as a part of the University of Kentucky is more than a possibility within a decade.

What are the problems in the field of education facing the people of Kentucky at the middle of the twentieth century, the solution of which may well produce a new era and place the state in the higher bracket of the nation's educational

---

[6] Dr. J. S. Chambers, "Medical School at the University of Kentucky," typed memorandum.

systems? Such an accomplishment would bring to the people of Kentucky a new respect and confidence in themselves.

A better organization is needed, which requires a revision of the constitution so that the educational efforts of the state may have a continual and trained leadership, a permanent Superintendent of Public Instruction.

The law as stated in the constitution must be changed if a more effective system of support is to apply where it is most needed. The per capita distribution of the school funds as now carried out is quite incapable of meeting the needs of education in rural areas.

All school instruction must be raised to a nine-months term if the great inequalities in the education of the boys and girls of the state are to be removed.

The teacher personnel must be required to meet at least those standards prevailing before the war. The specific means of doing this is by increasing the salaries of teachers. With a larger payment for services, the state can well insist upon a better trained teacher in every school.

Better co-operation of the state institutions of higher education and co-ordination of the public schools in districts and counties must be effected. Since 1934, when the State Council on Public Higher Education was established, very little has been accomplished along such lines owing to the personal and local interests centered in these institutions. There is lacking here a state-wide concept of education necessary to an effective growth and development of the public system of education in Kentucky.

A brief summary of the opposing forces at work against the advancement of education in the state for more than a century includes legal difficulties, sectarian attitudes, political interference, unstable enthusiasms, and economic conditions. The first two constitutions barely referred to education; the third, in 1850, contained a good many restrictions and the authorization of a meager financial support of education; the fourth, 1891, further enlarged the state ideas of education but could hardly be said to have developed a long view of its requirements. For at least three-quarters of a century, sectarian influences interfered with the growth of Transylvania University; and in the 1870's similar influences disrupted the Kentucky University concept of John B. Bowman. Public education, especially on the higher level, was frowned upon by many of the religious bodies in the state, a situation now happily passed. Politicians and political parties were slow to encourage the local organization of schools and opposed the levying of taxes by state authority. The story of the school fund, particularly in 1837 and 1870, is evidence of the willingness to divert school money to other purposes. Today, a marked betterment in political attitudes is to be noted, especially in the increase of the per capita school fund for use in the public schools. Several times there have been great awakenings among the people concerning education. Speeches, rallies, much advertising have aroused them for a brief time to the needs of their schools. Particularly effective were the campaigns in 1907 and in 1933; though the interest declined, the schools did attain a somewhat higher level. Economic conditions have varied greatly in the state as they have elsewhere; and in every depression the schools have suffered seriously. Still, progress has been made through the century and a half of state history. The future will surely bring advancement even though Kentucky may have to rely upon her own efforts to maintain and develop her public system of education. The time is now here when the state must have the purpose, the enthusiasm, and the vision to throw open the gates to the youth of Kentucky so that they may have a chance to meet the obligation and the opportunity of the immediate future.

APPENDIXES

APPENDIX A

STATE SUPERINTENDENTS OF PUBLIC INSTRUCTION, 1836-1948

Joseph James Bullock, 1838-1839
Hubbard H. Kavanaugh, 1839-1840
Benjamin Bosworth Smith, 1840-1842
George W. Brush, 1842-1843
Ryland Thompson Dillard, 1843-1847
Robert Jefferson Breckinridge, 1847-1853
John D. Mathews, 1853-1859
Robert Richardson, 1859-1863
Daniel Stevenson, 1863-1867
Zachary F. Smith, 1867-1871
H. A. M. Henderson, 1871-1879
Joseph Desha Pickett, 1879-1887
Ed. Porter Thompson, 1887-1895
William Jefferson Davidson, 1895-1899
H. V. McChesney, 1899-1903
James H. Fuqua, 1903-1907
John Grant Crabbe, 1907-1910 (resigned April 2, 1910)
Ellsworth Regenstein, 1910-1912
Barksdale Hamlett, 1912-1916
Virgil O. Gilbert, 1916-1920
George Colvin, 1920-1924
McHenry Rhoads, 1924-1928
W. C. Bell, 1928-1932
James H. Richmond, 1932-1936
Harry W. Peters, 1936-1940
John W. Brooker, 1940-1944
John Fred Williams, 1944-1948
Boswell B. Hodgkin, 1948-

APPENDIX B

COLLEGES IN KENTUCKY ACCREDITED BY THE SOUTHERN ASSOCIATION OF COLLEGES AND SECONDARY SCHOOLS

SENIOR COLLEGES

Asbury College, Wilmore. Z. T. Johnson, president
Berea College, Berea. Francis S. Hutchins, president
Centre College, Danville. Walter A. Groves, president
Eastern Kentucky State College, Richmond. W. F. O'Donnell, president
Georgetown College, Georgetown. Samuel S. Hill, president
Morehead State College, Morehead. William Jesse Baird, president
Murray State College, Murray. Ralph H. Woods, president
Nazareth College, Louisville. Sister M. Anastasis Coady, president
Transylvania College, Lexington. Raymond F. McLain, president
Union College, Barbourville. Conway Boatman, president
University of Kentucky, Lexington. Herman L. Donovan, president
University of Louisville, Louisville. John W. Taylor, president
Western Kentucky State College, Bowling Green. Paul L. Garrett, president
Kentucky State College for Negroes, Frankfort. R. B. Atwood, president
Municipal College for Negroes, Louisville. Bertram W. Doyle, dean (Organized as part of the University of Louisville and as such fully accredited)

JUNIOR COLLEGES

Cumberland College, Williamsburg. James M. Boswell, president
Mt. St. Joseph Junior College, Maple Mount. Mother M. Laurine Sheeran, president
Nazareth Junior College, Nazareth. Sister Ann Sebastian Sullivan, president
Pikeville College, Pikeville. A. A. Page, president
Sue Bennett College, London. Oscie Sanders, president

APPENDIX

3. **SENIOR COLLEGES ON NON-MEMBER LIST OF SOUTHERN ASSOCIATION**
   Kentucky Wesleyan College, Winchester. Paul S. Powell, president
   Ursuline College, Louisville. Mother M. Rosalin Schaeffer, president

4. **COLLEGES WHICH ARE MEMBERS OF THE KENTUCKY ASSOCIATION OF COLLEGES AND SECONDARY SCHOOLS AND ACCREDITED BY THE UNIVERSITY OF KENTUCKY**

   Senior Colleges

   Bowling Green College of Commerce, Bowling Green. Murray Hill, president
   Villa Madonna, Covington. Thomas A. McCarthy, dean.

   Junior Colleges

   Ashland Junior College, Ashland. L. C. Cauldwell, dean
   Bethel Woman's College, Hopkinsville. Powhatan Wright James, president
   Campbellsville College, Campbellsville. W. M. Caudill, president
   Caney Junior College, Pippapass. Alice S. Loyd, president
   Lee's Junior College, Jackson. R. G. Lanbolt, president
   Lindsey Wilson Junior College, Columbia. V. P. Henry, president
   Loretto Junior College, Loretto. Sister M. Francisca, president
   Paducah Junior College, Paducah. R. G. Matheson, Jr., dean
   St. Catherine Junior College, St. Catherine. Mother Margaret Elizabeth, president

APPENDIX C

THE EVOLUTION CONTROVERSY

I

Released for publication Sunday, February 12, 1922

The following explanatory statement has been sent to the press by the President of the University of Kentucky:

TO THE PEOPLE OF KENTUCKY:

In view of the many statements, the confusion and misunderstandings that have arisen relative to the bills introduced in the Legislature providing for the prohibiting of the teaching of evolution in the public schools and institutions of higher learning supported by taxation, it seems desirable that some direct comment should be made.

I have an abiding faith in the good sense and fairness of the people of this State. When they understand what the situation means and when they come to comprehend the motives underlying this attack upon the public schools of the State they will hold the University and the school system in greater respect than ever before. While it is true that the proposed legislation prohibits the teaching of evolution in the public schools and educational institutions maintained by the State, the attack is narrowing itself more and more to one upon the University.

As President of the University, I desire to say as emphatically as possible that the charge that there is teaching in the University of atheism, agnosticism, and Darwinism (in the sense that a man is descended from baboons and gorillas) is absolutely false. No such teaching is carried on in the University. Moreover no member of the staff of the University attempts, directly or indirectly, to modify, alter, or shape the religious beliefs of students.

The University, however, does teach evolution. It is, in fact, bound to do so since all the natural sciences are based upon it and failure to teach evolution would mean elimination of courses and textbooks relating to astronomy, botany, bacteriology, biology, geology, and zoology. The students in the University, as well as in the normal schools and high schools, would have to go elsewhere to get instruction in modern sciences. It does not seem to be generally appreciated what this means, but it means that the State would be shutting itself off from all contact with the modern world as a consequence of such an attitude on the part of the Commonwealth.

APPENDIX

Most of this discussion is due to lack of understanding and lack of knowledge of what has happened in the world of science.

What is evolution? Evolution is development; it is change; and every man knows that development and change are going on all the time. Evolution is a great general principle of growth. It is that idea that development goes on during long ages under varying influences of climate, surroundings, food supply, and changing conditions. It is the belief that the earth was formed ages ago and has evolved gradually and slowly. It is known today that man has lived on the earth a long time; that he has evolved from lower conditions to the one he occupies now. Science has brought to our knowledge some conception of the greatness of the universe. It has made clearer than ever before that God works through law and that men are to use their God-given minds in order that they may learn more of the power and glory of God as manifested in His works in the universe.

It is necessary to know that there are many theories of evolution and the man who attempts to put in one phrase all the views regarding the development of the universe and state that evolution is comprehended in the phrase "man is descended from a monkey" is simply betraying his ignorance and his lack of an analytic mind.

There is a scientific theory of evolution; there is the theistic theory; there is the materialistic theory, and there is the so-called Darwinian theory.

The scientific theory of evolution seeks to determine the historical succession of various species of plants and animals on earth. It tries to arrange them according to natural series of descent. "This theory is in perfect agreement with the Christian conception of the universe, for the Scriptures do not tell us in what form the present species of plants and of animals were originally created by God."

The theistic theory of evolution regards the entire history of the world as a harmonious development, brought about by natural law. This conception is in agreement with the Christian theory of the universe. God is the Creator of heaven and earth and if God produced the universe by a single creative act of His will, then its natural development by law implanted in it by the Creator is to the greater glory of His divine power and wisdom.

The atheistic theory of evolution maintains that the cause of the world's development was material and that through the process of law the development of the universe has proceeded to its present form, but such a theory accepts neither Creator nor Law Giver.

The theory of Darwin placed special emphasis upon the survival of the fittest, of sex selection, of hereditary influences in forms of life that appear today. The men of science have found that Darwin's theory does not explain the new facts that are being discovered from time to time, but the important thing is that Darwinism frequently stands in popular usage for all these theories of evolution. This use of the word rests upon a confusion of ideas.

The foremost thinkers everywhere, religious and scientific, have accepted the idea of evolution. The testimony of many men throughout the world is given again and again that there is no conflict between the theory of evolution and the Christian view.

If this be true, it follows that legislation of this character is unnecessary, particularly when the principle of it is already safeguarded in the public school laws, found in Section 4368 of the Kentucky Statutes. But more than this, such legislation is exceedingly dangerous in that it places limitations on the right of thought and freedom of belief. If the history of America has stood for anything it has stood for freedom of belief, freedom of speech, and tolerance in religious matters. The Constitution of the State of Kentucky found in Section 5 of the Bill of Rights reads as follows:

> No preference shall ever be given by law to any religious sect, society or denomination; nor to any particular creed, mode of worship or system of ecclesiastical policy; nor shall any person be compelled to attend any place of worship, to contribute to the erection or maintenance of any such place, or to the salary or support of any minister of religion; nor shall any man be compelled to send his child to any school to which he may be conscientiously opposed; and the civil rights, privileges and capacities of no person shall be taken away, or in any wise diminished or enlarged, on account of his belief or disbelief of any religious tenet, dogma or teaching. No human authority shall, in any case whatever, control or interfere with the rights of conscience.

Adherence to the Bill of Rights means that such legislation as is proposed at the present time is unwise and unconstitutional.

The weakness of the position of those who are backing these bills is shown in the fact that the first bill provided for prohibition of the teaching of atheism, agnosticism, Darwinism, and evolution and attached fines of from $50 to $5,000, a prison sentence of from 10 days to one year, and revocation of charter of the institution. The second bill eliminated prison sentence and reduction of fines from $10 to $1,000. The third bill is merely a declaration against the teaching of anything that will weaken or undermine religious faith of pupils in any school or college or institution of learning maintained in whole or in part in this State by funds produced by taxation. It provides no penalty but that of dismissal of teachers giving such instruction. Such provisions already exist on the Statute books of Kentucky as indicated above and are entirely unnecessary.

In closing, I may say that the University has an unusually fine body of students. The morals, ideals, and spiritual attitudes of the students cannot be excelled anywhere. Last year two hundred men, during the winter, studied the life of Christ in classes that met in various fraternity and boarding houses near the University. These classes were conducted by members of the faculty. This year the same thing is being done and the membership is now three hundred. The Y.M.C.A., the Y.W.C.A., and other religious organizations are active and well supported. There is absolutely no reason for this attack upon the University and when analyzed it will be seen that it is really an attack on the public education that is maintained and carried on by the State.

(Signed) FRANK L. McVEY
President, University of Kentucky

II

DR. McVEY'S STATEMENT

By President E. Y. Mullins

Louisville Post, *February 4, 1922*

EDITOR EVENING POST:

Will you permit me to say a few words about the published statement of President McVey, of the State University, in connection with the teaching of evolution in that institution. In my judgment, Dr. McVey's conciliatory and reasonable statement supplies a needed element in this whole discussion.

Dr. McVey makes four statements which are pertinent to the situation: First, the evolution or Darwinism in the sense that man is descended from apes and baboons is not taught; second, that evolution in the general sense of the term as assumed in science is taught; third, that atheism, agnosticism, and other irreligious views are not taught; and fourth, that no effort is made by any teacher, directly or indirectly, to undermine or destroy the religious beliefs of students.

Now, in my opinion, the attitude of the university, as expressed in this statement from President McVey, meets every requirement that any reasonable person can make of the university. It recognizes the freedom of teaching and indicates the folly of laws prescribing what is and what is not science. It also recognizes the religious rights of students in that they are not compelled to sit in classes where religion is attacked.

The statement is also calculated to reassure and allay the fears of religious people who have been alarmed over alleged teaching of anti-religious and irreligious views in State schools. The statement respects our American principle of a "free church in a free State." That principle recognizes freedom of teaching for teachers and freedom of religion for religious people.

Neutrality in religious matters is all that can be required of teachers in State schools. This is all that was contained in the substitute bill which I was willing to accept and which seems to have been discarded in Frankfort. I do not accept the measure now pending, which provides that "the teaching of any theory that will weaken or undermine the religious belief of the pupil in any school or college maintained by taxation shall be abolished." The phrase "any theory" seems to be just a thin disguise thrown over the very objectionable anti-Darwin bill itself and offered as a substitute. I make this correction because my name is being connected with a pending substitute bill containing the above clause. I am against such a bill.

There has been needed just such a statement as Dr. McVey has issued from the side of the State schools; something to explain, clarify, and guide the popular mind and to remove misunderstandings. It is very poor policy and anything but good judgment to denounce and stigmatize and ridicule in situations such as the present. Some of the vehement antagonists of the anti-Darwin bill have asserted that the proponents of the bill have never read Darwin, and do not understand evolution. Some of the proponents have been equally illogical and unwise. The truth probably is that many of both the pros and antis have not read "The Origin of the Species," and know little of evolution. But that is aside from the main point. The main point is that there are two distinct American rights involved; one is the religious rights of the pupils, and the other the right of freedom in teaching. Dr. McVey shows in his statement that he appreciates both. Unfortunately, this cannot be said of some others who have taken part in the recent discussion.

May I add a word on the inspiring opportunity of the teacher of modern science in guiding young minds. He takes those minds at a great crisis, when the walls of ignorance begin to crumble and at the dawn of a new day of knowledge. He draws aside the curtain and discloses the glories of a wonder-crowded universe, illimitable in its sweep and fascinating in its mysteries. If such a teacher is reverent and scientific in his attitude, he will guide the young mind with an ever-deepening sense of responsibility. He will not teach religious dogma nor anti-religious dogma. He will rather inculcate loyalty to truth and fact in every sphere. The greatest sin against science and the greatest sin against religion is disloyalty to truth. This is the common standing ground of true religion and true science; loyalty to all facts in all spheres of knowledge. It is the basis of the harmonious operation of our great American principle of a free church in a free State.

E. Y. MULLINS

APPENDIX D

STATE AID FOR NEGROES

I

6. STATE AID FOR NEGROES

Sec. 4527-81. *State to pay tuition and fees for students in institutions outside state, when.*—That pending the full development of the educational institutions of the Commonwealth of Kentucky, all bona fide residents of this State at the time of making written application for the benefits provided in this Act and have been such residents continuously for five (5) years next preceding the time of filing said application, and who are duly qualified for matriculation in courses of study offered at the University of Kentucky, but who because of Section one hundred eighty-seven (187) of the Constitution of Kentucky cannot pursue such courses at the University of Kentucky or other State institutions at which such courses are offered, or who have otherwise qualified to pursue such courses therein, and who are now pursuing or may hereafter pursue such courses in educational institutions outside of the State whereof no courses of study are provided for such persons within this State, shall have their tuition and fees paid at such institutions by the Commonwealth of Kentucky. (1936, c. 43, sec. 1. Eff. February 25, 1936.)

Sec. 4527-82. *Payments, how made.*—That such tuition and fees be ascertained by the State Superintendent of Public Instruction and paid upon requisition of him out of funds not otherwise appropriated. (1936, c. 43, sec. 2. Eff. Feb. 25, 1936.)

Sec. 4527-83. *State board to make rules; funds prorated; maximum allowance.*—That the State Board of Education shall prescribe the rules and regulations governing the granting of State aid under this Act. In event the funds appropriated for the purpose of carrying out the provisions of this Act are insufficient for the purpose in any year, said Board of Education shall have the right to prorate the same among such persons whose applications are approved therefor pursuant to the provisions of this Act; and provided further, that not more than one hundred and seventy-five ($175.00) dollars shall be allowed to any such person for the purposes and under the provisions of this Act during any one school year of nine (9) months. (1936, c. 43, sec. 3. Eff. Feb. 25, 1936.)

Sec. 4527-84. *Appropriations.*—That for the purpose of carrying out the provisions of this Act and for no other purpose, there is hereby appropriated for the State Board of Education of Kentucky, out of funds in the State Treasury not otherwise appropriated the following sums: Five thousand ($5,000.00) dollars for the fiscal year ending June thirtieth (30th) one thousand nine hundred thirty-seven, and five thousand ($5,000.00) dollars for the fiscal year ending June thirtieth (30th), one thousand nine hundred thirty-eight. (1936, c. 43, sec. 4. Eff. Feb. 25, 1936.)

Carroll's (Eighth Edition) *Kentucky Statutes,* Annotated
Baldwin's 1936 Revision, Containing all Laws to October, 1936
William Edward Baldwin, D. C. L., Editor-in-Chief
Richard Priest Dietzman, A. B., LL. B., Annotator
Banks-Baldwin Company, Cleveland. 1936
Page 2445

II

The Anderson-Myer State Aid Act
(For Negroes)

An Act to provide State aid for education in certain courses of study of State students pursuing certain courses of study at educational institutions outside of the State for whom no such courses are provided in the educational institutions of the State, and prescribing the conditions under which such State aid may be granted and authorizing and directing the State Board of Education of Kentucky to administer provisions of this Act, making an appropriation therefor and declaring an emergency. This Act to be known as the "Anderson-Myer State Aid Act."

Be it enacted by the General Assembly of the Commonwealth of Kentucky: *Section One.* That pending the full development of the educational institutions of the Commonwealth of Kentucky, all bona fide residents of this State at the time of making written application for the benefits provided in this Act and have been such residents continuously for five (5) years next preceding the time of filing said application, and who are duly qualified for matriculation in courses of study offered at the University of Kentucky, but who, because of Section one hundred eighty-seven (187) of the Constitution of Kentucky cannot pursue such courses at the University of Kentucky or other State institutions at which such courses are offered, or who have otherwise qualified to pursue such courses therein, and who are now pursuing or may hereafter pursue such courses in educational institutions outside of the State whereof no courses of study are provided for such persons within this State, shall have their tuition and fees paid at such institutions by the Commonwealth of Kentucky.

Section Two. That such tuition and fees be ascertained by the State Superintendent of Public Instruction and paid upon requisition of him out of funds not otherwise appropriated.

Section Three. That the State Board of Education shall prescribe the rules and regulations governing the granting of State aid under this Act. In event the funds appropriated for the purpose of carrying out the provisions of this Act are insufficient for the purpose in any year, said Board of Education shall have the right to prorate the same among such persons whose applications are approved therefor pursuant to the provisions of this Act; and provided, further, that not more than one hundred and seventy-five .($175.00) dollars shall be allowed to any such person for the purposes and under the provisions of this Act during any one school year of nine (9) months.

Section Four. That for the purpose of carrying out the provisions of this Act and for no other purpose, there is hereby appropriated for the State Board of Education of Kentucky, out of funds in the State Treasury not otherwise appropriated the following sums: Five thousand ($5,000.00) dollars for the fiscal year ending June thirtieth (30th) one thousand nine hundred thirty-seven, and five thousand ($5,000.00) dollars for the fiscal year ending June thirtieth (30th), one thousand nine hundred thirty-eight.

Section Five. That if any part of this Act shall be held unconstitutional, such holding shall not invalidate any other portion thereof.

Section Six. It being immediately necessary for educational opportunities to certain persons of this Commonwealth, and for the preservation of the public peace, health and safety, an emergency is hereby declared to exist, by reason whereof this Act shall take effect and be in full force from and after passage and approval. (Approved February 25, 1936.)

Acts of The General Assembly of the Commonwealth of Kentucky, 1936
The State Journal Printing Company
Frankfort, Kentucky. 1936
Pages: 110-112. Chapter 43

APPENDIX E

SUPPLEMENTARY EDUCATION IN KENTUCKY

Education is too often thought of as confined to schools, but it is more than that, for it extends into every phase of life. In this book, much has been written about the efforts of men to provide schools for their children; but education is carried on through the home, church, press, radio, and many other agencies. For instance, various associations, the Scout movement, libraries, museums, concerts, and programs contribute to the education of a people. The service clubs and chambers of commerce add to knowledge and understanding in certain fields of men's activities. It is apparently worth while to ask how much has been done in Kentucky by these "extracurricular activities," as the school man calls them. To answer this query is the purpose of this appendix.

Progress and change have ways of modifying or even destroying customs and methods of living. A third or more of a century ago, the theater flourished in the smaller cities of the nation, but not now. The old nickelodeon has developed until, housed in a great palace of entertainment, it now provides lavish moving picture productions which have absorbed the theaters where plays formerly were given by good road companies. As long ago as 1801, the *Kentucky Gazette* mentioned a play to be presented in the town of Lexington. The Usher and the Drake families became interested in theaters as early as 1815 and maintained playhouses in the larger towns around Louisville and Lexington.[1] For many years, the Macauley Theater in Louisville won much praise and prestige for the character of the entertainment offered. This glamorous house was built in 1872 and continued until 1925, when it was razed to provide land for the Starks office building. In Lexington, the Ada Meade Theater has had a long history. Its patronage was divided with the Opera House on Broadway where stock companies held sway for many years. Those days are now passed, for with one exception there is no legitimate theater in the whole state where good actors and good road companies can find facilities for the presentation of plays and musicals. In Louisville, the Memorial Auditorium, used for many purposes, can be equipped to present plays and musical shows to large audiences. It is the only adequate place in Kentucky where the legitimate theater can find even temporary quarters.

There are, however, a considerable number of "little theaters" in the

---

[1] *Kentucky: A Guide to the Bluegrass State* (New York, 1939), 110-14.

various towns of the state in which the light of the drama is kept burning. Most of these may be found in college towns where the local colleges provide a stage and an auditorium for aspiring students who, under adequate and professional leadership, furnish entertainment for student groups and interested citizens living in the communities. The plays presented by the little theaters have been well done on the whole; and, as a consequence, they have added much to the pleasure and intellectual opportunities of the people. Wholly spontaneous in its development, the little theater in Kentucky has grown rapidly with astonishing vigor and has often attained professional standards.[2]

Interest in painting and sculpture has been confined in the main by Kentucky collectors to portraits, busts, and statues. The only art museum in the state is housed in the fine Speed Museum on the campus of the University of Louisville. Here a considerable collection has been brought together through gifts and occasional purchases. There is no other art gallery in Kentucky under a professional director. Now and then exhibits are shown at the University of Kentucky, Berea, and other colleges. The citizen who wishes to see the great pictures must travel beyond the borders of his state. There are in private hands a good many excellent portraits, much silverware, and antique furniture treasured by the owners.

In the early days, Lexington was a center for portrait painters. Matthew Jouett practiced this profession from 1787 to 1827 in the city. He painted many portraits of distinguished men and women which adorn the walls in homes, the Speed Museum, the Historical Society at Frankfort, Transylvania College, and the University of Kentucky. Other painters who attained some distinction are John James Audubon, Chester Harding, Joseph H. Bush, Oliver Frazer, James Reid Lambdin, Frank Duveneck, Charles Sneed Williams, and Paul Sawyier. Throughout the state, notably in Louisville, Lexington, and Harrodsburg, public monuments may be found, many of which are well done. The section entitled "The Arts" in the American Guide Series volume on Kentucky has the interesting statement: "Of major interest is the current revival of mural painting."[3] Under the auspices of the Federal Art Project, various artists were encouraged to work during the years 1936-1939. The results of their work are to be seen in the Marine Hospital and the Federal building in Louisville. At the University of Kentucky are two murals by Frank Long and a fresco by Anne Rice depicting pioneer activities. There are murals to be found also in St. Peter's Church in Louisville, the state capitol at Frankfort, and in the Seelbach Hotel, Louisville. While many interesting art objects are located in the public squares and buildings, as well as in the homes of the people, no attempt has been

[2] *Ibid.*, 115-16.
[3] *Ibid.*, 120.

made, with the exception of the Speed Museum, to establish art centers where the people may see and enjoy the work of painters and sculptors.

For a half century, the Federation of Women's Clubs has been an important factor in Kentucky life and interest. Organized at Ashland in 1892, with a small number of local clubs, sixteen in fact, the Federation now includes 221 clubs with a membership of 13,000 women. During the history of the federation these clubs have maintained well-planned programs; and as a federation, they have influenced legislation having to do with education, health, morals, care of dependents, and the betterment of conditions for the inmates of state penal and charitable institutions. The federation has also established a student loan fund and a graduate fellowship for young women seeking professional training. Organized into departments, through its annual conventions and local meetings it has sponsored notable discussions of importance to the state. Without doubt the Federation of Women's Clubs is an active educational agency in Kentucky.

For many years there has been a growing purpose to extend library services throughout rural areas. In some states the movement has had notable success, and in all of the forty-eight states, some plan of subsidizing county libraries is now on the statute books. In Kentucky, the State Library Commission has created what is called the Kentucky Library Division.[*] In addition, the legislature has increased the tax rate that may be levied for the support of libraries both in urban and rural communities. The report of the committee for 1943-1944 says that there were in that year seventy-five public libraries in the state with seventy-one of the number actually open and functioning; but only 35 per cent of the population was served by these libraries. The report further shows that sixty-four counties had libraries of some kind, with the remaining fifty-six counties without such service. The total expense of these libraries was $411,952, or fourteen cents per capita. For some years Berea College has operated a book wagon covering a considerable area around Berea. The stories told by the attendants who accompany the wagon, as well as by the users of the books, show how greatly this service is appreciated, not only by borrowers but by the people who learned in turn from the readers of the books. In the western end of the state, a regional library with headquarters at Murray State College has been organized with the aid of funds provided by the college and the Tennessee Valley Authority. The work is carried on throughout the Purchase Area and requires a staff of sixty-five persons for its accomplishment.

According to recent figures issued by the United States Office of Education, the libraries of the eleven colleges included in the list and located in Kentucky possess 890,000 volumes. Three colleges have 100,000 or more volumes: Berea, 100,000, University of Kentucky, 367,000, and the

[*] *Annual Report of Kentucky Library Division* (1943-44).

University of Louisville, 127,000. If the other colleges of junior level were added to the total, the volumes owned by educational institutions in the state would reach a figure of 1,300,000 volumes.

When educational extension is approached in a broad attitude of mind, the movement may be traced back to the itinerant universities of the early Middle Ages when groups of teachers, often chosen by students, moved from one city to another seeking satisfactory conditions for the lodging of students and the housing of classes. In modern times, extension groups were organized in Britain by interested persons from the laboring population and with the assistance of Oxford and Cambridge universities. The workmen wanted courses in history, economics, and literature for self-culture and not for vocational training. The idea was brought to the United States by persons who saw in it possibilities for a wider and more effective education of adults. The system of university extension begun in England in 1866 was taken up by the institutions in this country where it received sufficient attention to bring about the organization of the American Society for the Extension of University Teaching. Some of the universities, notably the University of Chicago, have expanded instruction by providing opportunities for adults who could, if they wished, secure college credit for work done in extension courses. In other institutions of higher education, extension classes were conducted at first by the voluntary service of teachers who met classes organized by local groups. Now, what is called a Department of University Extension provides instruction by correspondence courses, lectures, and institutes. In Kentucky, after the establishment of higher requirements for teachers' certificates, the extension work both by correspondence and organized classes at a distance from the colleges reached a boom stage and continued for some years with large enrollments. However, most of that type of instruction has passed, leaving extension in general fields of learning to interested persons and clubs. Berea College was one of the earliest entries into the field of extension. In 1893, President Frost and Franklin Hays made a tour through the mountain area of eastern Kentucky which convinced them that there was need for this work among the people. Thus began an interesting and effective program for Berea. "The extension outfit included two wagons and a stereopticon. Later, the book wagons made regular visits to outlying districts to deliver books and periodicals for the use of families along the route followed by the wagons." "It was a picturesque and helpful service."[5]

Prior to 1900 the agricultural colleges had carried extension work into various other fields. As early as 1861 the Michigan legislature had voted

---

[5] William G. Frost, *For the Mountains: An Autobiography* (New York, 1937), Chap. XV.

that professors of the state college might give lectures to farmers away from the college. Cornell University and Pennsylvania State College, in 1894 and 1897, extended instruction in agriculture beyond the campus. The work suffered, however, because the burden thus placed upon college teachers was greater than they could bear. Yet the service was continued. Several bills were introduced in Congress to provide funds for the expansion of instruction in agriculture, but Congress was not ready to act until 1914, when it passed the Smith-Lever Co-operative Extension Act. The fund provided in the bill was $600,000 in 1915, but was increased for seven years until the annual expenditure reached $4,100,000.* Three years later, the Smith-Hughes Vocational Educational Act was passed, February 23, 1917; the act provided for the training of teachers of agriculture. Other legislation has been enacted since then and has materially increased the Federal funds to be used for instruction in the rural high schools of the state. By the co-operation of the Federal government, the state, and the counties, much is now done in the field of agricultural extension. The Extension Division of the Experiment Station of the University of Kentucky conducts great programs of education throughout the state which require an expenditure of a million dollars annually to maintain. For the past half dozen years the Experiment Station has had an agent in every county and seventy-eight home demonstration agents at work in rural Kentucky.

"The county agents have two methods of program building: one is the community program organized with the farm families of each community. At these community-building meetings, the local people are asked to name their farm interests and to tell how they meet their problems. A solution is suggested for these problems. One of their members is selected for each project undertaken in that community. A goal of accomplishment is set, and it is a problem for the leader and the county agent to devise and bring about methods to accomplish the goal.

"The other system of program building is to build county commodity programs. By this method there is a greater unity of interest but less idealism than is found in the community program. The community program is planned to welcome and include all interests and levels of the community membership. The commodity program appeals strongly to the active members dealing with a specific subject but excludes those who cannot or will not become producers of that commodity. The number of community programs for the state ranges from 900 to 1,200 and the county commodity programs vary in number from 200 to 300 each year. The number of local leaders or committeemen actively engaged in forwarding the extension program is 23,000 or 208 adult and 424 Four-H Club leaders per county. One

---

*Alfred C. True, *A History of Agricultural Education in the United States, 1785-1925* (Washington, 1929), 288-93.

of the principal methods used by county agents is that of demonstration. From 4,000 to 6,000 demonstration meetings are held by county agents each year, and about 15,000 general meetings are held per year at which demonstrations are frequently used.

"The Kentucky county agents have made about 100,000 farm visits per year, to about 50,000 different farms."[7]

In addition to the eighty counties served by home demonstration agents, there are fourteen counties in which six Negro agents work within counties where there is a large colored population. The programs which these agents direct and assist are centered around five main phases of home building, such as the production, care, and preparation of foods, clothing, and millinery; home furnishing and home management; child development and family relations; civic activities; and other interests including landscaping, gardening, poultry, and dairying.[8] The home demonstration agents are assisted by many volunteer local leaders and by a staff of supervisors and specialists from the University of Kentucky.

The organization of farmers to better their place in the national economy through political power, co-operative enterprises, and the dissemination of information has had a long history in this country. The Kentucky Farm Bureau, formed in 1940, is an example of the value of well-planned projects and their use of educational programs to instruct and inform members. In 1938 there was a membership of 12,416 in the local organizations; now combined in a state federation, the membership is 47,427. As the organization has grown, more funds have become available for financing additional activities. Without question, the Farm Bureau is a useful and helpful association for advancing the interests of the rural people.

A highly important experiment in the instruction of grade children was started in 1939 when the Alfred P. Sloan Foundation gave a grant-in-aid to the University of Kentucky for the purpose of conducting an experiment in applied economics. The purpose of the study was to improve the dietary practices in selected communities through the education of children. The foundation sought to inform pupils about diet, housing, and other living factors through readers, arithmetic problems, and texts prepared for this purpose. The results of the experiment show real progress in rural communities where it has been set up.

Fairs have been for centuries an important factor in the trades; they have also been conspicuous in their influence on groups through their recreation and amusement features. The county fair, which was a considerable institution up to half century ago, has been replaced by regional and state

[7] Letter from R. S. Mahan, State Agent, February 21, 1947.
[8] Letter from Miss Myrtle Weldon, February 25, 1947.

fairs, increased greatly since the coming of the automobile and the wider interests of patrons. In 1902 the state fair was established in Louisville after considerable protest and opposition from the Bluegrass section. The fortieth annual exposition was held in 1941; following that year, the property owned by the state fair was used for war purposes. In 1947 the fair returned to its grounds after a stay of two years at Churchill Downs. Premiums, prizes, and stakes have been offered in considerable amounts by the management; manufacturers bring exhibits, and horse owners enter their animals in the races. Attendance upon the Kentucky fair seldom goes over one hundred thousand for the week's session. A steady improvement in the program has been seen in recent years, but the fair has been retarded by lack of money and by political domination. The managers are political appointees and seldom hold office beyond the control of the party in power. A fair has great possibilities as an educational institution, but that is a view not fully recognized in Kentucky as yet.

During the depression years of the 1930's, many efforts were made to provide relief for boys and girls and men and women who were unable to keep on in school or to find work. President Franklin D. Roosevelt, early in his first term of office, said, "I have determined to do something for the nation's unemployed youth because we can ill afford to lose the skill and energy of these young men and women." On June 27, 1935, the National Youth Administration was created by the President's executive order with a sum of $50,000,000 allocated for a general relief appropriation. This sum was divided, one portion to be used for a student aid program, and another portion for unemployed out-of-school youths. The student aid in high schools, colleges, and graduate schools was allotted $577,347 for the year ending March 31, 1936. During that year, 10,000 students participated in the school aid, and 2,852 in the college program for needy students, in addition to which 47 persons were engaged in graduate work—a total of 12,899. The second group coming under the head of work projects was created to provide work experience and training and to develop vocational interests for young people from needy families.[9] The report for the year states that there were 215 work projects in 112 of the 120 counties of the commonwealth. The original work projects covered the age period of sixteen to twenty-five years; then the required age was raised to eighteen years in 1936. That the National Youth Administration was an important agency during a distressing time is quite apparent to those who saw it at work, because the analysis of what the organization had done showed improved standards of living, plus improved schooling, in thousands of instances. In

---

[9] Smith G. Ross, "Review of Activities of the National Youth Administration in Kentucky, 1935-1943" (mimeographed; n.p., n.d.).

other places and in many a family, there was a rehabilitation, improved social viewpoint, a betterment of skills and attitudes, and, what is most important of all, a strong determination to be self-supporting. It can be said if there were a "lost generation," then the National Youth Administration contributed significantly in meeting its problems.

Another Federal agency, known as the CCC, Civilian Conservation Corps, was established in the states to employ young men in conservation work; and at the time, these young men were receiving pay for training in crafts and trades so that they might find employment when better times returned and the nation's economy was restored to normal conditions.

There are four outstanding movements affecting 200,000 teen-age youngsters in the state. The Four-H Clubs, the Future Farmers of America, and the Boy and Girl Scout troops have been going for two or more decades, during which time much has been accomplished by these organizations. The Four-H Club movement is supported by Federal and state funds under the co-operative extension work in agriculture and home economics. In the year 1946 the report of the state leader showed 73,008 members enrolled. The greater number of the clubs are in schools, but a smaller number are organized separately. The programs followed by the clubs are broad and general, with considerable emphasis placed upon projects such as beef growing, poultry exhibits, and corn contests. Through these projects and other enterprises, the members learn to use the most up-to-date methods in farming and homemaking. The main emphasis is upon the development of leadership, co-operation, and responsibility. The organization in various parts of the state sponsors camps, fair shows, and judging and demonstration teams.

In 1930 the Future Farmers of America was organized in Kentucky as an independent society which would stand or fall on its own efforts without Federal or state support. In 1947 there were 211 chapters enrolling 6,800 members. The creed of the organization emphasizes faith in the farm life of the nation and declares that it believes in less dependence upon begging and more power through bargaining. Farmers are urged to safeguard their rights against practices that are unfair. The Future Farmers of America place considerable emphasis upon contests such as that of the America Farmer degree and of public speaking. These contests are held in districts; and at the annual meeting in August, awards are made by individuals and industrial concerns. The organization emphasizes recreation, scholarship, and community service and encourages the chapters to buy shares of stock in the Kentucky Future Farmers of America Cooperative, Inc.

The Scout movement in America has grown to huge proportions. In a history of nearly fifty years, emphasizing character building and citizenship training, the Boy Scouts of America has extended its program to every part of the country until it reports a membership of 2,630,347 in 61,026 troops.

In Kentucky, there are ten councils with a total membership of 20,638 Scouts; 6,680 adult members are associated with the membership in 1,025 troops and packs. In most instances, the groups are financed by the "chest" campaigns or by local solicitation of funds. The organization has done notable work, but finds its greatest difficulty in securing trained and adequate adult leadership for the local troops and packs. The National Council is alert to this problem and is now giving much attention to the recruitment of leaders for Scout groups.

In recent years, the idea of organizing and leading teen-age youth in programs of interest to young people of towns and rural areas has been widened to include girls of grade and high school age. With this in mind, forward-looking women have organized on a national basis the Girl Scouts of America. The program set up by the National Council is wider than that of the boys' movement, in that it includes home duties, chorus groups, and music training as well as citizenship and character building. The report for the activities in Kentucky in 1946 indicates that there were then twenty-seven councils and forty-seven separate troops. There were 4,498 girl members in the state with 2,158 adults assisting as leaders and as members of supervisory councils. It is important to bring into the local groups interested women anxious to give the girls opportunities for recreation, leadership, and instruction. When well conducted, these groups are of great assistance to the public schools and supplement home training.

The Christian Associations known as the Y.M.C.A. and Y.W.C.A. have had a long history, as time is counted in the United States; and they have made great contributions to the welfare, recreation, and education of boys and girls and young men and women. Student religious societies existed before Sir George Williams organized a group among his fellow draper clerks in London in 1844. He is the real founder of the association. Seven years later, in 1851, a similar club was established in Boston. The idea appealed to a group in Lexington, Kentucky, who thought so well of it that a Y.M.C.A. was established there in 1853.[19] In London, young women interested Lady Mary Jane Kinnaird, who, after becoming familiar with the conditions under which they worked, organized a Young Women's Christian Association in 1855. A Y.W.C.A. was established in Boston in 1860. The different urban groups were brought together in 1906.

The Y.M.C.A. and the Y.W.C.A. have a common purpose in the building of a better society and of interpreting Christianity in terms of life today. These organizations began as urban societies. They conducted extensive programs of recreation, education, and Bible study; and both emphasized and recognized the oneness of the world by extending their services to foreign lands.

---

[19] Sherwood Eddy, *A Century with Youth* (New York, 1944), Chap. II.

APPENDIX 309

In Kentucky, the Y.M.C.A. has railroad and community associations at Ashland, Corbin, and Russell; and there are other associations in Covington, Frankfort, Henderson, Lexington, Louisville, Owensboro, and Paris. The membership in these urban associations, including the High-Y activities, a high school service, is approximately 15,000. Both the Y.M.C.A. and Y.W.C.A. are to be found in the state colleges where some emphasis is placed by the associations upon religious instruction. Social activities and employment service make up a considerable part of the program. Among the outstanding contributions of these associations have been the courses of studies offered to young men and young women outside of college, and the furnishing of club and living quarters at reasonable rates. In addition, both associations have state organizations that supervise the work of Bible instruction in the colleges and high schools, and conduct summer camps for boys and girls where camping technique, use of boats, and craft work are taught.

It was in May, 1929, that Professor J. C. Jones called a meeting at the University of Kentucky to discuss the organization of the municipalities of Kentucky. The cities and towns of the state were in need of help, especially in view of the increasing problems confronting the administrators of urban places. At this meeting there were a dozen towns represented, enough to encourage those present to organize a Kentucky Municipal League. In the constitution adopted by the league, the emphasis was placed upon the ideas of a mutual agency to co-operate in and to study civic affairs, to promote the best methods of administration, to gather and to circulate information and experience, and to secure legislation for the benefit of the municipalities. Today, the league has a membership of 141 city and town members which support the work it does by the payment of fees based on population. In addition, *Kentucky City* is published quarterly by the league. The organization has sponsored by grants and aided by supervision a number of important surveys. A study of the finances of cities and towns was published in 1947, giving citizens in urban areas a clear and carefully considered report on the taxing, founding, and expending programs of the towns and cities of the state. This report was the most recent of the many studies made by the league in co-operation with various state and Federal agencies. Now nearly twenty years old, the Kentucky Municipal League has proved the wisdom of its founders in the resultant benefits accruing to the municipalities of Kentucky.

The title, "service clubs," has been used as a general term to identify the considerable number of luncheon clubs in the state that meet weekly throughout the year. In this group are organizations known as Cooperative, Kiwanis, Lions, Optimist, Exchange, and Rotary. All of these clubs are organized nationally, and some of them have extended their membership to people living in foreign countries. An example of how extensive this movement has become is the fact that there are 5,674 Lions Clubs throughout the world, of which 117 are located within this state. In Kentucky there are eighty-four Rotary chapters with 3,587 members. The other clubs have increased in numbers until their total membership in Kentucky is close to 25,000. The purpose of these clubs, speaking generally, is much the same, though the different activities vary according to the community in which the clubs are located and the needs which exist. However, their projects fall into a general policy of assistance to worthy charitable and public enterprises. Among these are to be found the Eye Glass Fund, Playground Equipment, Boys' and Girls' Camps, Baby Milk Supply, Crippled Children, Young Men's and Young Women's Christian Associations. Often the clubs take on some particular project such as sight conservation, vocational training, and various youth programs. In addition, the weekly meetings are used to present a speaker on a topic selected by the program committee. Rotary emphasizes international topics that are important in peacetime conversion. Many of these talks have an educational value which from week to week and year to year must amount to something important in community education.

It is almost a folkway in America to call a meeting, get together, organize, appoint a committee, and then wait for the committee to hatch out something to do. At other times, a community may call a meeting of citizens to take some action about a problem that confronts the dwellers in a given area. These meetings often result in a permanent body that becomes a useful agency and continues to work for years. In Kentucky there are many such organizations; in fact, hardly any group that has a common interest fails to build up some kind of an association. Some of these associations have wide public appeal; others are created to foster propaganda and to advance their own interests. The chambers of commerce are supported, in the main, by the business people of the town or county and have a well-informed and trained secretary. In the state there are 42 chambers of commerce with 22 full-time secretaries and 21 part-time officers. The interest of these chambers of commerce is to bring new business to the community, to work for local improvements, and to help generally in making the town a better place. In consequence, these bodies issue reports, discuss problems, and inform their members about state and national legislation. Undoubtedly, citizen members come into a larger knowledge of public matters as a result of these activities. Other similar organizations seek to inform their members about their mutual interests and advance their special causes of retail and wholesale trade, banking, labor, medicine, law, teaching, nursing, engineering, and even undertaking. From these groups come a considerable body of reports, comments, and articles about their purposes and interests. Such work as they do and the material that these organizations print can be called educational for the most part.

APPENDIX 311

The first radio station in Kentucky was WHAS, sponsored and owned by the Louisville *Courier-Journal* and *Times* with a power of 5,000 watts. Later, this was increased to 50,000 watts, giving the station a wide coverage over the Midwest. In 1947 there were twenty-four stations in Kentucky varying from the large one, WHAS, to the 250-watt stations; of these there were fifteen; one was powered to 5,000 watts in WAVE at Louisville, two, at 1,000 watts; and two others, operated as F. M. (frequency modulation) stations at Louisville and the University of Kentucky, had asked for radio licenses. Applications were pending before the Federal Communications Commission from Hazard, Pikeville, Murray, Campbellsville, and Somerset.

In granting licenses to operate stations, the commission has established certain rules and requirements which must be met by the operators of the local radios. The book issued by the commission gives six definitions of programs. These are listed as sustaining, recorded, wire, local line, non-commercial spot announcements, and spot announcements. Throughout its history as a regulatory body, the commission has been impressed by the variance between promises and performance; and in consequence it has constantly endeavored to lift the character of the programs.[11] On applying for a license, the applicant must make representation as to the type of service he proposes; and when he does so, certain time must be made available for civic, educational, agricultural, and other public services. A good deal of leeway has been permitted in the past; but more recently the commission has been comparing promises with performance. The smaller stations have resorted to the use of recorded music, and music produced by a local pianist or singer is not always to the satisfaction of the listener. To fill the air with mediocre performances or recorded popular music hardly meets the desired civic and educational purposes, while advertising is broadcast through the air to ears of bored owners of radio sets. The larger stations endeavor to maintain a fair amount of required programs necessary to keep the suspicious ears of the commission from spotting an unbalanced program with too many advertisements injected in the day's schedule. The prosperous stations can use the sustaining programs provided by the great networks and thus bring variety into the offerings throughout the day. The time of operation extends from about six hours used by smaller stations to the twenty-hour coverage of the larger broadcasting organizations.

Radio programs are in the main devoted to entertainment sponsored by national advertisers, news coverage offered half a dozen times a day, and announcements of weather and time nearly every hour. Looking at the offerings with a tolerant mind, it can be said that educational programs do

---

[11] Federal Communications Commission, *Federal Responsibility of Broadcast Licensees* (March 7, 1946).

not fill any considerable time over the radio. On Sunday, WHAS in Louisville and WLAP in Lexington have broadcast forums and college hours provided by Indiana University, the University of Louisville, and the University of Kentucky. These programs are transcribed and sent over the large radio station at fairly convenient hours, but no institution in the state has any large coverage through the operation of its own station. No doubt the day will come, and soon, when every county superintendent will have the facilities by which he can reach every schoolhouse in his county; in the meantime, the Federal Communications Commission may be able to better materially the programs now going to the people over the air.

In 1929 the University of Kentucky began broadcasting by remote control through WHAS. A poll taken of the listeners to these broadcasts showed that the "folks east of the Blue Grass were conspicuous by their absence." The radio census of 1930 indicated that one mountain county was the possessor of eight radios and another of eleven. Since then the radio sets in the mountain area have been multiplied by the hundreds. The belief in the radio as a means of education has resulted in a plan to establish "Listening Centers where people of a community could come together and hear what they wished, and then talk over what they heard, providing the program was that provocative." Under considerable difficulties, the first listening center was installed at Cow Creek, in Owsley County. At present, there are eighty such centers operated in eleven counties in the state. In some places, radio service has been located in community centers such as Carcassonne, Morris Fork, Pippapass, and Wooton. Other sets were placed in general stores, postoffices, schoolhouses, and private homes. The establishment of these centers has brought people together not only to hear but to discuss what they hear. Attempts have been made to provide supervisors who, after spending a week at such centers, would be able to increase the value of the broadcasts by organizing the listening groups. The University of Kentucky has augmented the broadcasts to the listening centers by building a new frequency modulation station, known as WBKY, which has given to Kentucky its first regular F. M. program service. Over this station, noncommercial broadcasts of a high class are sent at regular intervals. The purpose in operating such a station is to train students in the technics of radio and to experiment with noncommercial programs.

Far from the least valuable agency of education in the state and nation is the rich resource of newspapers and periodicals. John Bradford, born in Virginia, imported an antiquated printing outfit from Pennsylvania to Lexington in 1787. He and his brother, Fielding Bradford, in 1787 began publication of the tiny paper called the *Kentucke Gazette*. A second Lexington newspaper appeared in 1793, the *Kentucky Herald*. Other papers were published for a short time, only to expire. William Worsley and Samuel

APPENDIX 313

Overton established the *Reporter* in 1807, which twenty-five years later was united with the *Observer*. The Lexington *Press* entered the field in 1870, but was soon consolidated with the *Transcript* under the name of the *Herald*. The Lexington *Leader* was founded in 1883 as a Republican organ.

The first successful paper to be established in Louisville was the *Advertiser*, which started publication in 1818; it became a daily in 1826. The *Journal* appeared on the scene in 1830, under the editorship of George D. Prentice, a staunch champion of the Whig party, who was followed as editor by Henry W. Watterson in 1868. A newspaper called the *Democrat* began in 1843 and the *Courier* in 1844. These, with the *Journal*, were united as the *Courier-Journal* in 1868. The *Times* was first published in 1884. In 1918 Robert W. Bingham bought the *Courier-Journal* and the *Times*.

The record shows that there were 188 newspapers published in Kentucky in 1946. Of this number, 32 were dailies and 155 were weeklies. Most of the papers were published from county seats, and all but forty-five had their headquarters in towns. The present total circulation of all papers in the state is approximately 750,000. Fifty-two periodicals are printed in the state, one-half of them appearing monthly.[12]

In earlier days the newspapers were personal organs reflecting the opinions of their editors. Today the newspaper is a concern engaged in the dissemination of news without bias. As such it is an educational agency of great importance.

On a wide scale, the National Congress of Parents and Teachers provides effective co-operation between homes and the American community by emphasizing the need of a close-working relationship. The congress, therefore, endeavors to assist effective training and the improvement of the schools, child welfare in home and community, better parenthood, and higher standards of home life through the utilization of community forces in the interest of the child. The organization, created in 1897, has learned much in its fifty years of history and knows that the only thorough way of getting results is co-operative partnership with boards of education, teachers, and parents. Today, there are 25,000 chapters in the country, with a membership of 3,054,950. Kentucky, organized in eleven district councils, has a membership in 525 units of 80,000. The program of the congress is extensive, directed through thirty-three committees. Each state group, however, may emphasize special projects and use its strength and influence to forward them. Beginning in a limited way, the state organization has moved steadily forward in better co-operation with the school authorities and in the advancement of the interests of the school child.[13]

---

[12] *Kentucky: A Guide to the Bluegrass State*, 102-106.
[13] National Congress of Parents and Teachers, *The Parent-Teacher Organization, Its Origins and Development* (Chicago, 1944).

Kentucky was one of the first states to provide care and instruction for the blind and the deaf. The School for the Blind at Louisville was founded a hundred years ago; today this institution has 293 children enrolled in the elementary and high schools for children from six to eighteen years of age. The legislature appropriated $110,000 for the support of this institute. The School for the Deaf, at Danville, was established in 1823, and at that time was the fourth school for the deaf in the nation. The enrollment is now about 350 pupils, from six to twenty-two years of age. The teaching staff numbers forty. The value of the property of the school is $400,000, and the cost of maintaining each pupil is $378.82.

Educational programs in the prisons of the state have been meager and unsatisfactory. Certainly it has been demonstrated in the field of penology that education has great value in helping prisoners to a better attitude by laying a foundation for citizenship when they return to their communities. Progress has been quite marked in the housing and care of prisoners, but not much has been done in the educational field. In his report of 1946, the warden of the Kentucky state penitentiary said: "Enrollment in educational activities during the past year showed unusual interest and enthusiasm. The academic work included subjects through the elementary grades; a course in welding was the only industrial training provided."[14] This statement can be used to estimate as well what is being done in the reformatory, the women's prison, and the schools of reform. This record shows a backward condition which should be rectified. In some places teachers are employed part-time; and in other instances, the chaplain of the prison undertakes some educational work. The program in all these institutions is too limited; the libraries are small and inadequate; and vocational education is hardly more than a name. Some progress has been made in all these institutions, but not enough. More money, trained teachers, and shops must be provided so that something real can be accomplished for the education of the unfortunate men and women, boys and girls in the custody of the state.

What has been recounted in this appended chapter confirms the fact that education in its various forms and ways reaches the people through many different organizations and mediums influencing their thought and action.

[14] *Report of Department of Public Welfare of the Commonwealth of Kentucky* (1946), 37-52.

INDEX

Academies, land-grant, 12, 33-46; failure of, 33
Adair, Governor John, message, 83
Adams, John, reply to legislature, 160
Agents, home demonstration, 305
"Agricola," letter on Filson's school, 22-24
Agricultural Society, plans for school, 108-109
Ahrens, Theodore, vocational school, 269
Ambrose, Lester M., on county academy system, 38, 40, 42
Asbury College, 95
Association, Kentucky Education, 191-205; co-operation with educational agencies, 199; presidents and secretaries of, 202
Attendance, hours per day in public schools, 258; report of Superintendent of Public Instruction (1941), 270, 274
Atwood, Rufus B., 153

Bacon College, 95
Baird, William Jesse, 190
Bank of Kentucky, and Literary Fund, 161
Bank of the Commonwealth, and Literary Fund, 161, 162
Baptists, and education, 49, 58, 93
Barker, Henry S., 120
Beckham, Governor J. C. W., and school fund, 171
Berea College, origin, 97; extension work, 94
Bible, College of, 187; use of in school, 73
Blind, School for, 314
Boards, trustees and membership of, 284
Bond issue, campaign for, 210, 211
Books, family, used in schools, 67; texts, 63-78
Boonesborough, early settlement of, 5
Boulter, Archbishop Hugh, on Irish migration, 5
Bowman, John B., plans for University, 96; regent of Kentucky University, 107, 108, 113
Breckinridge, Desha, editorial on evolution controversy, 234

Breckinridge, Robert J., 195; champions better curricula, 73; declares school fund perpetual debt, 166; fights for school fund, 58, 59; opposes uniformity of textbooks, 74, 75; recommends school for teachers, 180; report on school fund (1857), 169
Brooker, John W., study of curricula (1940), 267; Superintendent and recommendations, 280, 281
Bryan, William Jennings, and Scopes trial, 221; death of, 236; letter to Dr. J. W. Porter, 227; speech on evolution, 225.
Bullock, Rev. Joseph J., Superintendent of Public Instruction report, 56, 179
Burke, Edmund, on European settlement in America, 4
Butler, Mann, agent of public schools, Louisville, 257
Butler, Noble, on college for teachers, 194
Button, Frank C., founds school at Morehead, 184, 190

Cammack, James W., Jr., Secretary of Survey Commission (1933), 218
Carnegie Foundation for the Advancement of Teaching, 207; report on medical education, 133
Carr, John W., first president of Murray State College, 189
Catholic Church, and education, 98-105
Central University, 89, 90
Centre College, and Presbyterian Church, 81, 86; growth of, 88; split by slavery question, 88; unites with Central University, 90
Chambers, John S., on establishment of a medical school, 286
Chambers of Commerce, 310
Chandler, Governor A. B., on demands for increased school funds, 173-174
Cherry, Henry H., and State Normal School, 187
Church of the Disciples, and Kentucky University, 110
Civilian Conservation Corps, 307

INDEX

Civil War, effect on public schools, 256

Class antagonisms, 9

Coates, T. J., president of Richmond State College, 188

Colleges, church-affiliated, association of, 205; cost in dollars, 80; dentistry and University of Louisville, 134; in Kentucky, accredited by Southern Association of Colleges and Secondary Schools, 290-291; state teachers, 175

Collins, Lewis, on colleges in 1847, 79; history of education, 72

Colvin, George, president of University of Louisville, 137

Common schools, report of committee (1821), 51, 52

Constitution of Kentucky, and education, 12; of 1850, provides for education, 167

Cooper, Thomas Poe, appointed director of Experiment Station, 118; acting president of University of Kentucky, 122

Counties, distributions of grants for academies to, 38; school systems, 255

County agents, 304

County Board of Education, 77

County Superintendents, controversy over, 241

Court decisions, on schools for Negroes, 149, 158-159

Covington, beginning of school system, 263

Crawford, A. B., history of state educational association, 205

Crittenden, Governor John J., issues bonds to State Board of Education, 167

Cumberland College, 92

Curricula, 63-78; criticism of, 265; of Cynthiana High School (1873), 266; public school, additions to, 74; study of state system, 266

Danville Theological Seminary, 87

Darwinism, penalties for teaching, 221

Day Law, 153, 158-159

Deaf, school for, 314

Desha, Governor Joseph, comment on Literary Fund, 162; message to legislature, 83

Donovan, H. L., 187; appointed president of University of Kentucky (1941), 122; begins work as president, 124

Drama, and the theater in Kentucky, 300

DuPont Manual High School, 268

Eastern State College, 175

Education, beginning of, 16; campaigns and surveys, 206-209, 214-220; color line in, 141-159; curricula and textbooks, 149; equalization of opportunities in, 252; first high school for Negro boys in Louisville (1882), 150; friends of, 192, 194; inequalities of, 173; Journal of, beginnings and developments, 201; low expenditures for Negro school buildings, teachers, and equipment, 142-143; obligation to support, 174; pre-school and handicapped, 253; public indifference to, 48; public, message of Governor Metcalfe on, 53-54; sectarian, a century of, 79-105; State Conference on, University of Kentucky, 205; summary of development, 287; United States Office of, 207; whirlwind campaigns, 187, 207, 208, 209

Educational Association, charter (1858), 196; Civil War, 196; controlled by State Board of Education, 197; extension, development, and growth, 303

Enrollment, children's (1941), 240

Evolution, action of state legislatures, 235; action in Tennessee, 234; change in viewpoint, 222; controversy over, 221-236; defeat of bill in House and Senate, 233-234; discussion of bills before legislature, 231; letter of President F. L. McVey to people of Kentucky, 292-295; letter of President E. Y. Mullins, 295-296; opponents of its teaching, 225; organizations opposed to teaching, 229; replies of educators, ministers, and journalists, 230.

Expenditures, for schools on per capita basis, 270

Experiment Station, growth and development, 118; substation, gift of E. O. Robinson and F. W. Mowbry, 118

Extension, agricultural, 304

INDEX 317

Fairs, county and state, 305, 306
Farm Bureau, 305
Federal funds, W.P.A. and P.W.A., 210; distribution of surplus, 164; surplus of (1837), 47; government aid to school building projects, 243; use of, 165
Federation of Women's Clubs, contributions to Illiteracy Commission, 213
Fee, John G., founder of Berea College, 97
Filson, John, early map and history of Kentucky, 17; proposal for school, 21-24
Fleischman, Charles L., advocates instruction in agriculture (1838), 109
Flexner, Abraham, report on medical school at Louisville, 133
Flint, Timothy, comments on Lexington and Louisville, 128-129
Ford, A. Y., first salaried president of University of Louisville, 136; death of, 137
Ford, Judge H. C., opinion on educational equality, 158
Fortune, A. W., 95
Fosdick, Harry Emerson, comment on Bryan's evolution position, 227-228
Four-H Clubs, 304, 307
Franklin, Benjamin, idea of a free library, 67-68
Free textbooks, 78
Friends of Education, and curricula of schools, 73
Frontier, T. P. Abernethy on, 8; Frederick J. Turner on significance of, 7-8; and revivalism, 223
Frost, William G., president of Berea College, 97
Frost, William J., and library extension, 303
Fuqua, James H., Superintendent of Public Instruction, campaign for education, 85
Future Farmers of America, 307

Gaines, Lloyd, Negro, applies for admission to University of Missouri, 155
Garrett, Paul, president of Western State College, 188
General Education Board, 207; division of Negro Education, 152; grant to College of Education, 183; Survey of 1921, 214

Georgetown College, history of, 91-92
Goodrich, S. T., author of textbooks, 69

Hardin, Ben, opposition to public schools, 60-61
Harrod's Town, 5
Hatch Act, 117
Helm, Governor John L., message on School Fund, 168
Higher education, promise of, in Kentucky, 105; State Council on, 287
Holley, Horace, president of Transylvania University, 13, 82, 83; speech at funeral of James Morrison, 87
Hughes, Raymond M., on rank of Kentucky in education, 282-283
Hutchins, Francis S., president of Berea College, 98
Hutchins, William J., president of Berea College, 98

Illiteracy, Commission on, 207; functional, 274; in 1850, 64; reduction in, 213; report of United States Census Bureau, 212; Cora Wilson Stewart and State Commission on, 211
Internal improvements, and School Fund, 165

Jackson, Andrew, signs bill to distribute surplus, 164
Jaggers, J. E., supervisor of certification, 250, 251
Jeanes Fund, assists teachers in Negro schools, 152
Jefferson Seminary, 129
Johnson, Lyman T., Negro, applies for admission to University of Kentucky, 158

Kavanaugh, H. H., Superintendent of Public Instruction, 57; report on teacher training, 180
Kennedy, M. F., quoted, 63
Kent, Raymond A., president of University of Louisville, 137-138; death of, 140
Kentucky, ability to support education, 282-283; admission to Union, 11; battleground of evolution, 224; beginnings of, 3; Committee for, report,

Kentucky—Continued
272-273; Common School Society (1834), 193; effect of depression on, 271; first constitution, 6; population, 4, 7; reduction of population, 271; requirements for better school system, 286-287; supplementary education in, 300-314

Kentucky Education Association, constitution (1829), 192-193; standards of salary, 278

Kentucky University, 81; created (1865), 85; dissatisfaction with management of agricultural college, 111; enrollment and endowment, 110; legislative committee (1872), 111

Lancasterian system, used in Louisville, 257

Land, conflict of claims, 41; titles, 5, 10, 11

Land grants, academies and trustees, 45; and endowments, 161; failure to endow academies, 43; inadequacy of, 44

Lawyers, and clients, 6

Lee's Collegiate Institute, Jackson, Kentucky, 91

Legislature, appropriates money for normal school at Transylvania, 181; bill against evolution, 224; bill to penalize teaching of evolution, 231; Educational (1908), 209

Lewis, J. O., history of Kentucky Educational Association, 192

Lexington, comments on by Timothy Flint, 128-129; development of high schools in, 262; effect of cholera on schools, 261; gifts to Transylvania University, 82; organization of Board of Education, 261-262; public schools, 261

Libraries, public and college, 303

Lincoln Institute, 154

Lindsey, William, attacks State College support, 115

Literary Fund, 15, 39, 51; act to establish, 160, 161

Louisville, beginning of public schools in, 257; Female High School, 258; founding of, 126-127; independent district, 184; maintenance of schools (1870),

Louisville—Continued
259; Male High School, 130; Presbyterian Theological Seminary, 87; and river trade, 127; School Board, 260; and teacher training school, 184

Louisville, University of, 125-140; departments of law and medicine, 130, 131; Medical School, 284; origin, 126

Louisville and Nashville Railroad, 128

McGuffey, William H., eclectic readers, 69

McLain, Raymond F., president of Transylvania College, 86

McVey, Frank L., appointed president of University of Kentucky, 122; letter on teaching of evolution, 292-295

May, A. N., supervisor of trades and industry, 250

Medical education, in Kentucky, 285; memorandum by Dr. John S. Chambers on, 286; at University of Louisville, 131-132

Meece, L. E., report on Negro education in Kentucky, 143

Mentelle, Madame V. C. LeC., school of, 28

Methodist Church, and slavery controversy, 94; and Transylvania University, 84; education, 49, 58, 79

Migration, into Kentucky, 3

Miller, Arthur M., on teaching of evolution, 226

Moonlight schools, 212

Morehead State College, 175, 189; office of president, 285

Morrill Act, and Kentucky University, 81, 85; and Governor J. F. Robinson, 110; and State College, 117

Morrison, Col. James, gifts of, 82

Mt. Zion Association, 92

Municipal College, Louisville, for Negroes, 154, 155

Municipal League, Kentucky, 309

Murray State Teachers College, 189; library extension, 302

National Youth Administration, employment and instruction, 248; report on work done, 306

INDEX 319

Negroes, Anderson-Myer Act, state aid, 298-299; education, report of advisory committee (1940), 156-157; Education Association, 203-204; decisions of courts on segregation, 155, 158; dual system of schools, 148; inadequacy of education for, 148; Kentucky State College for, 185; law relating to state aid for education of, 297; Municipal College and University of Louisville, 138; quality of education, 158-159; school in Covington, 263

Newspapers and periodicals, 312-313

O'Donnell, W. F., president of Eastern State College, 188

Paducah, meeting of Education Association (1892), 198; vocational school for Negroes, 248

Painting and sculpture, in Kentucky, 301

Parent-Teachers, National Congress of, 313

Patterson, James K., defends State College, 115; long service as president of Kentucky University and State College, 108; opposes President Barker, 120; pledges savings, 114; resigns as president of State University, 120

Patterson, John L., president of University of Louisville, 135

Peers, Robert O., plan for teacher training, 84, 178; report on education, 54-55

Peter, Robert, professor of chemistry at Experiment Station, 117

Pickett, Joseph Desha, second president of Kentucky University, 108; Report (1879-1887), 76

Pikeville Junior College, 90

Population, proportion of Negroes, 141; shifting of Negro groups, 142

Portrait painters, early, 301

Powell, Governor Lazarus, declares obligation of state accepted, 169

Presbyterian Church, school at Danville, 34; education, 49, 57, 87

Public Education, Report of Commission on (1921), 16

Public Instruction, permanent superintendent, 216; state superintendent appointed by governor, 237; state super-

Public Instruction—Continued
intendents of, 1836-1948, 289; zeal and loyalty of superintendents of, 237

Public schools, transportation, 244, 245, 246; rely on support of State Fund, 238

P. W. A. See Federal funds.

Radio, stations and programs, 311-312

Religion, and the frontier, 223; revival, 48; Robert Davidson on the decline of, 34

Rhodes, McHenry, reports on schools for Negro children, 151

Rice, Rev. David, 34

Richmond, James H., Superintendent of Public Instruction, and president of Murray State College, 190

Roark, R. N., president of Eastern Normal School, 188

Roman Catholic Church, and education, 98-105

Rosenwald Fund, buildings and equipment for Negro schools, 152

School code (1933), 242

School Fund, apportionment, 173; attack upon, 56; Robert J. Breckinridge reports on (1857), 169; condition of, 171; constitution provides, 167; distribution of under Constitution (1891), 172; distribution, 170; failure of first, 163; made a debt of the state, 171; report of Superintendent R. T. Dillard on, 168

Schools, attendance and cost, 56; beginnings of public, 47; condition of, 1820-1836, 64; community responsibility, 73; consolidation of, 243-244; county system, 255; early programs, 21; high, attendance and growth, 264, 267; in forts, 18; independent districts, 255, 270; pioneer teachers, 19-20; public, move forward, 237-254; pupils of school age in, 273; rules in pioneer times, 30-32; and schoolteachers, 17; support, local, 282; teacher shortage in, 272; tuition and free education, 260; for young ladies, 26-28

Scopes, John T., trial of, 236

Scouts, Boy and Girl, 307-308

Seminaries, land endowments of, 36-37
Service clubs, 309-310
Simmons University, Louisville, for Negroes, 154
Slater Fund, support of high schools for Negroes, 152
Slaughter, Governor Gabriel, on education, 15, 38, 50
Slaves, in Kentucky, 141; condition of (1865), 147; limited instruction of, 143-146
Sloan, Alfred P., Foundation, experiment in applied economics, 305
Smith, B. B., Superintendent of Public Instruction, expounds teacher training, 180
Smith, Zachary F., report on condition of schools (1867), 61-62
Smith-Hughes Act, 74, 247
Smith-Lever Act, assistance to Experiment Station, 119
Sonne, N. H., quoted, 49
Southern Baptist Theological Seminary, 93
State Board of Education, change and composition (1904), 71, 76; rules and regulations (1878), 70
State College, beginnings of, 114; constitutionality of support affirmed (1890), 116; cornerstone laid, 114; creates normal department, 182; development and growth, 116; hostility to, declines, 117; separation from Kentucky University (1878), 112
State College for Negroes, establishment and support, 153
State Library Commission, 302
State Normal School, for Negroes, 152
State Prisons, instruction in, 314
State scholarships, declared unconstitutional (1917), 113
State University, beginnings of, 106, 107. *See also* University of Kentucky
Stevenson, Nathaniel, and Union College, 79
Sue Bennett College, 95
Sullivan Bill (1908), 209; establishes county school unit, 239
Superintendent of Public Instruction. *See names of Superintendents*

Surplus Revenue, United States, 163. *See also* School Fund *and* Federal funds
Survey Commission of 1933, report of, 216-220
Surveys, educational, 206-207, 214-220; members of, 214
Surveyors and explorers, 5

Taxation, 11; attack on State College support, 115; obligatory, 48; for local schools, a failure, 238; for schools, 47; for school support (1908), 239
Taylor, J. D., 167
Taylor, John W., president of University of Louisville, 140
Taylor, L. N., 151
Teachers, advertisements for, 29; certification of, 249-250; effect of World War II on supply of, 251; Institutes, 182; salaries, 278; unions, 279
Teacher training, 79, 175-190; beginnings, 176-177; established at three state institutions, 186-187; in private institutions, 183; report of commission on new state teachers colleges, 188-189; at Richmond and Bowling Green, 185
Tennessee, and evolution controversy, 234-236
Textbooks, 63-78; advance in uniformity, 75; character of, 65; commission (1930), 77; early, 20; free, Court of Appeals ruling (1934), 78; improvement in, 68; limitations on use, 70; publication of, 66; selection, comment of Educational Commission (1930), 77
Todd, Mary, education of, 28
Townsend, William H., quoted, 28
Transportation, of pupils, 253
Transylvania Seminary, 25, 34
Transylvania University, 13, 15, 81; becomes a state normal school, 84; effect of Civil War upon, 85; message of Governor Desha, 52; offers building and services for normal school, 180-181; support of, 82; teacher training, 177

Universities, attempt to establish, 80
University of Kentucky, becomes the State University, 119; establishes a Depart-

INDEX

University of Kentucky—Continued
 ment of Education, 183; growth (1907-1945), 123; letter to people on teaching evolution, 230; support of, 123; survey (1917), 121

University of Louisville, 81; and Collegiate Institute, 129; Court of Appeals determines status, 138-139; gifts to, 134-135

Vanderbilt University, freed from church control, 94

Vocational education, 246-247; Ahrens Trade School, 268; Mayo State School, 248

Wallace, Caleb, on University system, 13

Watterson, Henry, address at State College, 115

Wells, Rainey T., president of Murray State College, 189

Wesleyan College, 93

Western Kentucky Vocational Training School, for Negroes, 153

Western State College, 175; foundation, 184

Wickliffe, Governor Charles A., opposes common school system, 61

Wilderness Road, 6

Williams, John A., president of Kentucky University, 108

Williams, John Fred, report of State Superintendent (1946), 272

Women's Clubs, Federation of, 302

Woods, Rev. Alva, president of Transylvania University, 192

World War I, and University of Kentucky, 122; effect on education, 74

World War II, and University of Kentucky, 124; effect on Kentucky colleges, 275-276; effect on teacher supply, 277

W. P. A. *See* Federal funds

Y. M. C. A., 308

Y. W. C. A., 308

www.ingramcontent.com/pod-product-compliance
Lightning Source LLC
Chambersburg PA
CBHW020637230426
43665CB00008B/212